Evangelion

Evangelion

A Chronological Harmony

of the Four Gospels

Evangelical Heritage Version ®

Compiled by

James Daniel Gieschen

The Gieschen Foundation ®
Honolulu, Hawaii

"Evangelical Heritage Version" and "EHV" are registered trademarks of Wartburg Project, Inc. Used by permission.

Scripture quotations are from the Holy Bible, Evangelical Heritage Version® (EHV®) © 2020 Wartburg Project, Inc. All rights reserved. Used by permission.

All rights reserved. This publication may not be copied, photocopied, reproduced, translated, or converted to any electronic or machine-readable form in whole or in part, except for brief quotations, without prior written approval from the publisher.

The Gieschen Foundation
Honolulu, HI
www.thegieschenfoundation.com
Copyright © 2020 by The Gieschen Foundation
Published 2020
Printed in the United States of America
Library of Congress Control Number: 2020924130
ISBN 978-1-7362563-0-5
ISBN 978-1-7362563-1-2 (e-book)

Table of Contents

Introduction by St. Luke 1

Chapter I: In the Beginning
Pre-Incarnation through Youth 1

    Jesus before Incarnation 1
    The Genealogy of Jesus via Joseph's Line 2
    The Genealogy of Jesus via Mary's Line 3
    The Angel Gabriel Appears to Zechariah 3
    The Angel Gabriel Appears to the Virgin Mary 4
    Mary Visits Elizabeth 4
    An Angel Appears to Joseph 5
    John the Baptist Is Born 6
    Jesus is Born 7
    The Presentation in the Temple 7
    The Visit of the Magi 8
    Flight to Egypt 9
    Herod Kills the Boys 9
    Jesus Grows up in Nazareth 10
    The Boy Jesus in the Temple Courts 10

Chapter II: Look! The Lamb of God!
Public Ministry Begins in Judea 11

    John the Baptist Prepares the Way 11
    John Baptizes Jesus 12
    Satan Tempts Jesus 12
    The Testimony of John the Baptist 13

    The Lamb of God 14

    The First Disciples 14

    Jesus Changes Water into Wine 15

CHAPTER III: HE MUST INCREASE; I MUST DECREASE.
In Judea for Passover 17

    Jesus Clears out the Temple 17

    Jesus Teaches Nicodemus 17

    Jesus and John the Baptist 18

    John the Baptist Imprisoned 19

CHAPTER IV: COME, FOLLOW ME.
Preaching and Healing in Galilee 21

    The Samaritan Woman 21

    Jesus Begins the Galilean Ministry 22

    Jesus Heals the Official's Son 23

    A Prophet in His Hometown 23

    Jesus Moves to Capernaum 24

    "Come, Follow Me" 24

    Jesus Drives Out a Demon 25

    Jesus Heals Many 25

    Jesus Preaches in Galilee 25

    The First Miraculous Catch 26

    The Sermon on the Mount 26

    Jesus Heals a Leper 32

    Jesus Forgives Sins 33

    The Calling of Matthew (Levi) 33

    A Question about Fasting 34

    The Daughter of Jairus 34

    Two Blind Men 35

    Jesus Heals a Mute Man 35

    A Prophet without Honor 35

CHAPTER V: SON OF MAN AND SON OF GOD
In Judea for a Festival 37

    Healing at the Pool 37

God's Son 38

Lord of the Sabbath 39

Jesus Heals a Man with a Withered Hand 39

CHAPTER VI: I WILL GIVE YOU REST.
Preaching and Healing in Galilee 41

"Here Is My Servant" 41

Pray for Workers 41

Jesus Heals Many 41

Jesus Appoints the Twelve Apostles 42

The Sermon on the Plain 42

A Believing Centurion 44

Jesus Raises a Widow's Son 45

John the Baptist and Christ 45

Jesus Is Anointed by a Sinful Woman 46

Preaching the Gospel 47

The Lord's Prayer 47

Keep Praying 47

Woe to Unrepentant Cities 48

"Come to Me" and "I Will Give You Rest" 48

Jesus Has Power to Drive Out Demons 48

The Sign of Jonah 49

A Lamp and a Lampstand 50

Jesus' Mother and Brothers 50

Woes and Warnings 50

Warning Against Hypocrisy 51

Fear God, Not People 51

Confess Christ 51

The Rich Fool 52

Do Not Worry 52

Be Ready! 52

Division 53

Interpret the Time 53

- Repent 54
- Parable of the Fig Tree 54
- The Parable of the Sower 54
- Jesus Explains the Parable of the Sower 54
- A Lamp and a Lampstand 55
- Seed Sprouts and Grows 56
- The Parable of the Weeds 56
- Mustard Seed and Yeast 56
- Jesus Explains the Parable of the Weeds 57
- The Treasure, the Pearl, and the Net 57
- Follow Jesus 57
- Jesus Calms the Storm 58
- Two Demon-Possessed Men and a Herd of Pigs 58
- Jesus Sends Out the Twelve 59
- Recalling the Death of John the Baptist 61
- Jesus Feeds More Than Five Thousand 61
- Jesus Walks on Water 62
- Bread from Heaven 63
- Up to Jerusalem 65

CHAPTER VII: BEFORE ABRAHAM WAS BORN, I AM.
In Judea for the Feast of Shelters 67
- At the Feast of Shelters 67
- The Adulteress 69
- Jesus Is the Light of the World 69
- A Blind Man Sees 71
- The Good Shepherd 73
- Commandments and Traditions 73

CHAPTER VIII: YOUR FAITH IS GREAT!
In Tyre, Sidon, and the Decapolis 77
- The Faith of a Gentile Woman 77
- "Ephphatha! Be opened!" 78
- Jesus Feeds More Than Four Thousand 78

CHAPTER IX: YOU ARE THE CHRIST.
From Bethsaida to Caesarea Philippi 79

    Watch Out for the Teaching of the Pharisees and Sadducees 79

    Jesus Heals a Blind Man 79

    Jesus Is the Christ 80

    Jesus Predicts His Death and Resurrection 80

    Take Up the Cross 80

    The Transfiguration 81

    Jesus Heals a Boy with a Demon 82

    Jesus Predicts His Death and Resurrection Again 83

CHAPTER X: THE DAYS WILL COME.
From Galilee through Samaria to Judea and Perea 85

    A Coin in a Fish's Mouth 85

    Who Is the Greatest? 85

    Whoever Is Not Against Us Is for Us 86

    Do Not Cause Little Believers to Fall into Sin 86

    Increase Our Faith 87

    The Lost Sheep 87

    The Lost Coin 87

    The Lost Son 87

    The Shrewd Manager 88

    The Rich Man and Poor Lazarus 89

    Show Your Brother His Sin 90

    The Unmerciful Servant 90

    Ten Lepers Healed—One Thanks God 91

    The Kingdom of God Is Within You 91

    Jesus Will Return 92

    The Parable of the Persistent Widow 92

    The Pharisee and the Tax Collector 92

    Jesus Is Determined to Go to Jerusalem 93

    Follow Jesus 93

    Jesus Appoints Seventy-Two 93

- The Good Samaritan 94
- Mary and Martha 95
- "I and the Father Are One" 95
- Jesus Heals a Crippled Woman 96
- Mustard Seed and Yeast 96
- The Narrow Door 97
- Jesus Warns Jerusalem 97
- Jesus in a Pharisee's Home 97
- The Parable of the Great Banquet 98
- The Cost 99
- Marriage and Divorce 99
- Jesus Loves Little Children 100

CHAPTER XI: I AM THE RESURRECTION AND THE LIFE.
Withdrawal to Ephraim after Raising Lazarus 101

- The Rich Young Ruler 101
- The Workers in the Vineyard 102
- Jesus Raises Lazarus 102
- The Plot 104

CHAPTER XII: THE SON OF MAN HANDED OVER
To Jerusalem for the Final Passover 105

- The Final Passover Is Near 105
- Again Jesus Predicts His Death and Resurrection 105
- Jesus Heals Two Blind Men 106
- Zacchaeus 106
- Parable of the Ten Minas 107
- Mary Anoints Jesus 108
- The King Comes to Jerusalem 108
- Jesus Curses a Fig Tree 109
- Jesus Cleanses His Father's House 110
- The Withered Fig Tree 110
- Jesus' Authority Is Questioned 111
- Two Sons 111

The Parable of the Wicked Tenants	111
The Parable of the Wedding Banquet	112
Paying Taxes to Caesar	112
The God of the Living	113
Love God and Your Neighbor	114
David's Son and David's Lord	114
Do Not Do as They Do	114
Woes and Warnings	115
The Poor Widow's Offering	116
The Destruction of Jerusalem and the End of the World	116
Be Ready!	119
The Parable of the Ten Virgins	119
The Parable of the Talents	120
Jesus Will Judge the World	121
The Plot to Kill Jesus	121
Judas Plans to Betray Jesus	122
Death and Glory	122
Jesus Celebrates the Passover	124
No Greater Love—in Service	124
One Will Betray Jesus	125
The Lord's Supper	126
Who Is Greatest?	126
Jesus Predicts Peter's Denial	126
No Greater Love—in Peace	127
No Greater Love—in Good Fruit	128
No Greater Love—in Joy	129
Jesus' High Priestly Prayer	131
The Arrest	132
Peter Denies Jesus	134
Jesus before Annas	134
Jewish Court	135
The Guards Mock Jesus	135

Peter Denies Again 135

The End of Judas 136

Jesus' Trial in Pilate's Court 137

Pilate Sends Jesus to Herod 137

Barabbas or Jesus? 138

Soldiers Mock Jesus 139

"Behold the Man!" 139

The Crucifixion 140

Jesus' Compassion for His Mother 141

Jesus' Death 142

The Piercing of Jesus' Side 142

Jesus' Burial 143

The Guard 144

CHAPTER XIII: HE HAS RISEN! HE IS NOT HERE.
The Resurrection, Appearances, and Ascension 145

The Resurrection 145

Jesus Appears to Mary Magdalene 146

The Guards' Report 147

On the Way to Emmaus 147

Behind Locked Doors 148

Jesus Appears to the Disciples 148

Thomas Finally Believes 149

The Purpose of John's Gospel Account 149

Breakfast with the Lord Jesus 149

"Do You Love Me?" 150

"Go and Gather Disciples" 151

Jesus Ascends into Heaven 151

REFERENCES 153

Preface

"From infancy you have known the Holy Scriptures, which are able to make you wise for salvation through faith in Christ Jesus" (2 Timothy 3:15).

Gospel harmonies are certainly not a recent innovation. In fact, evidence of the first harmony emerged soon after the Apostle John was inspired by the Holy Spirit to pen his account of the gospel. At the latest, a harmony of the four Gospels was available by about 160 A.D., when Tatian compiled his famous *Diatessaron*. Since then, there has been no paucity of efforts to continue this endeavor.

Evangelion: A Chronological Harmony of the Four Gospels is a synthetic chronological harmony of the Gospels according to Matthew,[a] Mark,[b] Luke,[c] and John.[d] The following are some of the key features of this harmony:

- ***A single, continuous narrative*** in chronological order
- ***Precise sequencing*** based on internal and external evidence
- ***Comprehensive synthesis*** of content from all four Gospels
- ***The Evangelical Heritage Version® (EHV®)*** as source of text
- ***For all students of God's Word***, including pastors, teachers, and professors

Most Gospel harmonies are organized chronologically. Some organize the events in a more general order, while others attempt to identify the sequence of even the most minute event. Although this harmony tends strongly toward the latter, let the reader not presume that this chronological order is fully without error. The Word of God, however, *is*. (In other words, when in doubt, read the Bible.) Furthermore, chronological rearrangement of the text inevitably results in discontinuities (e.g.

---

[a] The apostle Matthew was the inspired writer of the Gospel according to Matthew. See Matthew 9:9-13 and 10:3 to read about Matthew (who is also called Levi in Mark 2:14-15 and Luke 5:27-29). The approximate date of writing may have been 50 AD.

[b] Mark was the inspired writer of the Gospel according to Mark. See Acts 12:12,25; 15:37,39; Colossians 4:10; 2 Timothy 4:11; Philemon 24; and 1 Peter 5:13 to read about Mark. The approximate date of writing may have been 63 AD.

[c] The inspired writer of the Gospel according to Luke was a physician by the name of Luke. Read Colossians 4:14; Philemon 24; and 2 Timothy 4:11 to learn about Luke. The approximate date of writing may have been 60 AD.

[d] The apostle John was the inspired writer of the Gospel according to John. See Matthew 4:21; 10:2; Acts 1:13; and Revelation 1:1 to read about John. The approximate date of writing may have been 90 AD.

antecedents and postcedents separated from their corresponding proforms). Accordingly, on rare occasion, a very few words are added in brackets.

Evangelion meticulously arranges the Gospels into a single, chronological narrative of the life and teachings of Jesus Christ. It is the product of strict exegesis combined with a deep respect for the conservative history and traditions of the Church. Sequencing such a monumental work requires a careful examination of internal and external evidence. Accordingly, a wide range of sources ancient to modern were consulted, including Tatian's *Diatessaron*, Toynard's *Evangeliorum Harmonia*, Broadus' and A.T. Robertson's *A Harmony of the Gospels*, and more.

The harmony is divided into chapters primarily according to the geographic location of events. Scriptural references for the text, as well as its comparable references from any of the other Gospel authors, are listed at the end of the book.

For the sake of exegetical accuracy and modern readability, the translation and footnotes used for this Gospel harmony are from the Evangelical Heritage Version® (EHV®).

Deo Gloria!

About the Cover

The cross on the cover incorporates most of the cross variants from the first millennium, as well as some other very important Christian symbols.

At the center, the octagon symbolizes baptism, the eight saved on the ark, and the eight days of Holy Week. The points protruding from the octagon form an octagram, which is the symbol of the Star of Bethlehem. The spirals represent the waters of baptism, as well as the spirit and Holy Spirit. The circle with crosses inside is a form of the Celtic cross, the cruciform halo, the *chi-rho* cross, and the very early, prevalent, and enduring IXTHYS wheel symbol.

Other crosses incorporated in the design include the Greek, Latin (Roman), and Byzantine crosses; the Crosses of Saints George, Cuthbert, Gilbert, James, Julian, Nino, Philip, John, and Andrew; the Cross of Jeremiah; the Cross of Lorraine; the Mariner's Cross; the forked cross; and the staurogram (*tau-rho* cross).

Finally, each finial point of the fully extended cross is a gothic fleur-de-lis, which recalls the East and West Syrian Orthodox crosses. Moreover, it represents the IXTHYS fish symbol, resurrection, life, Jesus, Joseph, Mary, and the Triune God.

Introduction by St. Luke

Many have undertaken to compile an account of the events that have been fulfilled among us, an account exactly like those handed down to us by those who were eyewitnesses and ministers of the word from the beginning. For this reason, it seemed good to me also, since I followed everything closely from the beginning, to write an orderly account to you, most excellent Theophilus, so that you may know the certainty of the things you were taught.[1]

Chapter I: In the Beginning
Pre-Incarnation through Youth

Jesus before Incarnation

The beginning of the gospel of Jesus Christ, the Son of God:[2] In the beginning was the Word, and the Word was with God, and the Word was God. He was with God in the beginning. Through him everything was made, and without him not one thing was made that has been made. In him was life, and the life was the light of mankind. The light is shining in the darkness, and the darkness has not overcome it.

There was a man, sent from God, whose name was John. He came as an eyewitness to testify about the light so that everyone would believe through him. He was not the light, but he came to testify about the light.

The real light that shines on everyone was coming into the world. He was in the world, and the world was made through him, yet the world did not recognize him. He came to what was his own, yet his own people did not accept him. But to all who did receive him, to those who believe in his name, he gave the right to become children of God. They were born, not of blood, or of the desire of the flesh, or of a husband's will, but born of God.

The Word became flesh and dwelled among us. We have seen his glory, the glory he has as the only-begotten from the Father, full of grace and truth.

John testified about him. He cried out, "This was the one I spoke about when I said, 'The one coming after me outranks me because he existed before me.'" For out of his fullness we have all received grace upon grace. For the law was given through Moses; grace and truth came through Jesus Christ. No one has ever seen God. The only-begotten Son, who is close to the Father's side, has made him known.[3]

The Genealogy of Jesus via Joseph's Line

A record of the genealogy of Jesus Christ, the son of David, the son of Abraham.

Abraham was the father of Isaac. Isaac was the father of Jacob. Jacob was the father of Judah and his brothers. Judah was the father of Perez and Zerah, whose mother was Tamar. Perez was the father of Hezron. Hezron was the father of Ram. Ram was the father of Amminadab. Amminadab was the father of Nahshon. Nahshon was the father of Salmon. Salmon was the father of Boaz, whose mother was Rahab. Boaz was the father of Obed, whose mother was Ruth. Obed was the father of Jesse. Jesse was the father of King David.

David was the father of Solomon, whose mother had been the wife of Uriah. Solomon was the father of Rehoboam. Rehoboam was the father of Abijah. Abijah was the father of Asa. Asa was the father of Jehoshaphat. Jehoshaphat was the father of Joram. Joram was the father of Uzziah. Uzziah was the father[a] of Jotham. Jotham was the father of Ahaz. Ahaz was the father of Hezekiah. Hezekiah was the father of Manasseh. Manasseh was the father of Amon. Amon was the father of Josiah. Josiah was the father of Jeconiah and his brothers, at the time of the Babylonian exile.

After the Babylonian exile, Jeconiah was the father of Shealtiel. Shealtiel was the father of Zerubbabel. Zerubbabel was the father of Abiud. Abiud was the father of Eliakim. Eliakim was the father of Azor. Azor was the father of Zadok. Zadok was the father of Achim. Achim was the father of Eliud. Eliud was the father of Eleazar. Eleazar was the father of Matthan. Matthan was the father of Jacob. Jacob was the father of Joseph, the husband of Mary, from whom Jesus was born (who is called Christ).

So altogether there were fourteen generations from Abraham to David, fourteen generations from David to the Babylonian exile, and fourteen generations from the Babylonian exile to Christ.[4]

---

[a] Matthew 1:8 The Greek word for father of does not always mean immediate ancestor, but can also mean grandfather or male ancestor. In this genealogy, some generations are deliberately skipped to arrive at three groups of fourteen generations (verse 17). Three names are omitted after Joram: Ahaziah (2 Kings 8:25; 2 Chronicles 22:1), Joash (2 Kings 11:21; 12:1 [Hebrew text]; 2 Chronicles 24:1), and Amaziah (2 Kings 14:1; 2 Chronicles 25:1).

The Genealogy of Jesus via Mary's Line

Jesus was the son (so it was thought) of Joseph, the son of Heli, the son of Matthat, the son of Levi, the son of Melchi, the son of Jannai, the son of Joseph, the son of Mattathias, the son of Amos, the son of Nahum, the son of Esli, the son of Naggai, the son of Maath, the son of Mattathias, the son of Semein, the son of Josech, the son of Joda, the son of Joanan, the son of Rhesa, the son of Zerubbabel, the son of Shealtiel, the son of Neri, the son of Melchi, the son of Addi, the son of Cosam, the son of Elmadam, the son of Er, the son of Joshua, the son of Eliezer, the son of Jorim, the son of Matthat, the son of Levi, the son of Simeon, the son of Judah, the son of Joseph, the son of Jonam, the son of Eliakim, the son of Melea, the son of Menna, the son of Mattatha, the son of Nathan, the son of David, the son of Jesse, the son of Obed, the son of Boaz, the son of Salmon, the son of Nahshon, the son of Amminadab, the son of Ram,[a] the son of Hezron, the son of Perez, the son of Judah, the son of Jacob, the son of Isaac, the son of Abraham, the son of Terah, the son of Nahor, the son of Serug, the son of Reu, the son of Peleg, the son of Eber, the son of Shelah, the son of Cainan,[b] the son of Arphaxad, the son of Shem, the son of Noah, the son of Lamech, the son of Methuselah, the son of Enoch, the son of Jared, the son of Malaleel, the son of Cainan, the son of Enos, the son of Seth, the son of Adam, the son of God.[5]

The Angel Gabriel Appears to Zechariah

In the days of Herod, king of Judea, there was a certain priest named Zechariah, who belonged to the priestly division of Abijah. His wife was from the daughters of Aaron, and her name was Elizabeth. They were both righteous before God, walking blamelessly in all the commandments and righteous decrees of the Lord. They did not have a child because Elizabeth was unable to bear children, and they were both well along in years. On one occasion, while Zechariah was serving as priest before God and his division was on duty, he was chosen by lot, according to the custom of the priesthood, to go into the temple of the Lord and burn incense. The whole crowd of people were praying outside the temple during the hour of the incense offering.

An angel of the Lord appeared to him, standing on the right side of the altar of incense. When Zechariah saw him, he was startled and overcome by fear. But the angel said to him, "Do not be afraid, Zechariah, because your prayer has been heard. Your wife Elizabeth will bear a son for you, and you are to name him John. You will have joy and gladness, and many will rejoice at his birth, because he will be great in the sight of the Lord. He is never to drink wine or beer. He will be filled with the Holy Spirit, even from his mother's womb. He will turn many of the sons of Israel back to the Lord their God. He will go before him in the spirit and power of Elijah, to turn the hearts of the fathers to the children, to turn the disobedient to the wisdom of the righteous, to prepare a people who are ready for the Lord."

---

[a] Some witnesses to the text read *Admin*; a few also add *Arni*.
[b] This name is not found in the Hebrew Old Testament, but it is in the Septuagint (Genesis 10:24; 11:12).

Zechariah said to the angel, "How can I be sure of this, because I am an old man, and my wife is well along in years?"

The angel answered him, "I am Gabriel. I stand in the presence of God and was sent to speak to you in order to tell you this good news. Now listen, you will be silent and unable to speak until the day when these things happen, because you did not believe my words, which will be fulfilled at the proper time."

Meanwhile, the people were waiting for Zechariah and wondering what was taking him so long in the temple. When he did come out, he was unable to speak to them. Then they realized that he had seen a vision in the temple. He kept making signs to them and remained unable to speak.

When the days of his priestly service were completed, he went back to his home.

After those days his wife Elizabeth conceived. She kept herself in seclusion for five months, saying, "The Lord has done this for me in the days when he looked with favor on me and took away my disgrace among the people."[6]

The Angel Gabriel Appears to the Virgin Mary

In the sixth month, the angel Gabriel was sent from God to a town of Galilee named Nazareth, to a virgin pledged in marriage to a man whose name was Joseph, of the house of David. The virgin's name was Mary. The angel went to her and said, "Greetings, you who are highly favored! The Lord is with you. Blessed are you among women."[a]

But she was greatly troubled by the statement and was wondering what kind of greeting this could be. The angel said to her, "Do not be afraid, Mary, because you have found favor with God. Listen, you will conceive and give birth to a son, and you are to name him Jesus. He will be great and will be called the Son of the Most High. The Lord God will give him the throne of his father David. He will reign over the house of Jacob forever, and his kingdom will never end."

Mary said to the angel, "How will this be, since I am a virgin?"

The angel answered her, "The Holy Spirit will come upon you, and the power of the Most High will overshadow you. So the holy one to be born will be called the Son of God. Listen, Elizabeth, your relative, has also conceived a son in her old age even though she was called barren, and this is her sixth month. For nothing will be impossible for God."

Then Mary said, "See, I am the Lord's servant. May it happen to me as you have said." Then the angel left her.[7]

Mary Visits Elizabeth

In those days Mary got up and hurried to the hill country, to a town of Judah. She entered the home of Zechariah and greeted Elizabeth. Just as Elizabeth heard Mary's greeting, the baby leaped in her womb, and Elizabeth was filled with the

---

[a] A few witnesses to the text omit this sentence. ("Witnesses to the text" mentioned in footnotes may include Greek manuscripts, lectionaries, translations, and quotations in the church fathers.)

Holy Spirit. She called out with a loud voice and said, "Blessed are you among women, and blessed is the fruit of your womb! But why am I so favored that the mother of my Lord should come to me? In fact, just now, as soon as the sound of your greeting reached my ears, the baby in my womb leaped for joy! Blessed is she who believed, because the promises spoken to her from the Lord will be fulfilled!"[8]

Then Mary said,

> My soul proclaims the greatness of the Lord,
>> and my spirit has rejoiced in God my Savior,
>> because he has looked with favor on the humble state of his servant.
> Surely, from now on all generations will call me blessed,
>> because the Mighty One has done great things for me, and holy is his name.
> His mercy is for those who fear him from generation to generation.
> He has shown strength with his arm.
> He has scattered those who were proud in the thoughts of their hearts.
> He has brought down rulers from their thrones.
> He has lifted up the lowly.
> He has filled the hungry with good things, but the rich he has sent away empty.
> He has come to the aid of his servant Israel, remembering his mercy,
>> as he spoke to our fathers, to Abraham and his offspring[a] forever.

Mary stayed with Elizabeth about three months and then returned to her home.[9]

An Angel Appears to Joseph

Mary was pledged in marriage[b] to Joseph. Before they came together, she was found to be with child by the Holy Spirit. Joseph, her husband, was a righteous man and did not want to disgrace her. So he decided to divorce her privately. But as he was considering these things, an angel of the Lord suddenly appeared to him in a dream and said, "Joseph, son of David, do not be afraid to take Mary home as your wife, because the child conceived in her is from the Holy Spirit. She will give birth to a son, and you are to give him the name Jesus,[c] because he will save his people from their sins."

All this happened to fulfill what was spoken by the Lord through the prophet: "Look, the virgin will be with child and will give birth to a son. And they will name him Immanuel,"[d] which means, "God with us."

---

[a] Or *seed*
[b] Or *betrothed*
[c] *Jesus* means *the Lord saves.*
[d] Isaiah 7:14

When Joseph woke up from his sleep, he did as the angel of the Lord had commanded him. He took Mary home as his wife, but he was not intimate with her until she gave birth to her firstborn son.[a] 10

John the Baptist Is Born

When the time came for Elizabeth to have her baby, she gave birth to a son. Her neighbors and relatives heard that the Lord had shown her great mercy, and they were rejoicing with her. On the eighth day they came to circumcise the child. They wanted to call him Zechariah after the name of the father. But his mother answered, "No. He will be called John."

They said to her, "There is no one among your relatives who is called by this name." They made signs to his father, to see what he wanted to name him.

He asked for a writing tablet and wrote, "His name is John." And they were all amazed.

Immediately Zechariah's mouth was opened, his tongue was loosed, and he began to speak, praising God. Fear came on all who lived around them. In the entire hill country of Judea people were talking about all these things. And everyone who heard this took it to heart, saying, "What then will this child be?" Clearly, the hand of the Lord was with him.11

His father Zechariah was filled with the Holy Spirit and prophesied:

> Blessed is the Lord, the God of Israel,
> > because he has visited us and prepared redemption for his people.
> He has raised up a horn of salvation for us in the house of his servant David,
> > just as he said long ago through the mouth of his holy prophets.
> He raised up salvation from our enemies and from the hand of all who hate us,
> > in order to show mercy to our fathers by remembering his holy covenant,
> > the oath which he swore to Abraham our father,
> > to grant deliverance to us from the hand of our enemies,
> > so that we are able to serve him without fear,
> > in holiness and righteousness before him all our days.
> And you, child, will be called a prophet of the Most High,
> > because you will go before the Lord to prepare his ways,
> > to give his people the knowledge of salvation by the forgiveness of their sins,
> > because of God's tender mercies,
> > by which the Rising Sun from on high will visit us,
> > to shine on those who sit in darkness and in the shadow of death,
> > to guide our feet into the way of peace.

---

[a] Some witnesses to the text omit *her firstborn* and simply read *she gave birth to a son*. ("Witnesses to the text" mentioned in footnotes may include Greek manuscripts, lectionaries, translations, and quotations in the church fathers.)

The child continued to grow and became strong in spirit. He lived in the wilderness until the day of his public appearance to Israel.[12]

Jesus is Born

This is how the birth of Jesus Christ took place.[13] In those days a decree went out from Caesar Augustus that all the world should be registered. This was the first census taken while Quirinius was governing Syria. And everyone went to register, each to his own town. And Joseph also went up from Galilee, out of the town of Nazareth, into Judea, to the town of David, which is called Bethlehem, because he was from the house and family line of David. He went to be registered with Mary, his wife,[a] who was pledged to him in marriage and was expecting a child.

And so it was that while they were there, the time came for her to give birth. And she gave birth to her firstborn son, wrapped him in swaddling cloths, and laid him in a manger, because there was no room for them in the inn.

There were in the same country shepherds staying out in the fields, keeping watch over their flock at night. An angel of the Lord appeared to them, and the glory of the Lord shone around them, and they were terrified! But the angel said to them, "Do not be afraid. For behold, I bring you good news of great joy, which will be for all people: Today in the town of David, a Savior was born for you. He is Christ[b] the Lord. And this will be a sign for you: You will find a baby wrapped in swaddling cloths and lying in a manger." Suddenly, there was with the angel a multitude from the heavenly army, praising God and saying, "Glory to God in the highest, and on earth peace, good will toward mankind."[c]

When the angels went away from them into heaven, the shepherds said to one another, "Now let's go to Bethlehem and see this thing that has happened, which the Lord has made known to us." So they hurried off and found Mary and Joseph, and the baby, who was lying in the manger. When they had seen him, they told others the message they had been told about this child. And all who heard it were amazed by what the shepherds said to them. But Mary treasured up all these things, pondering them in her heart. And the shepherds returned, glorifying and praising God for all the things that they had heard and seen, which were just as they had been told.[14]

The Presentation in the Temple

After eight days passed, when the child was circumcised, he was named Jesus[15], the name given by the angel before he was conceived in the womb.

When the time came for their purification according to the law of Moses, they brought him up to Jerusalem to present him to the Lord. (As it is written in the law

---

[a] Some witnesses to the text omit *his wife*.
[b] *Christ* is the Greek word for *Anointed One*. The Hebrew/Aramaic word is *Messiah*.
[c] A few witnesses to the text read *among people of his goodwill*.

of the Lord, "Every firstborn[a] male will be called holy to the Lord.")[b] And they came to offer a sacrifice according to what was said in the law of the Lord, "A pair of turtledoves or two young pigeons."[c]

Now there was a man in Jerusalem whose name was Simeon. This man was righteous and devout, waiting for the comfort of Israel, and the Holy Spirit was on him. It had been revealed to him by the Holy Spirit that he would not see death before he had seen the Lord's Christ. Moved by the Spirit he went into the temple courts. When the parents brought in the child Jesus to do for him what was customary according to the law, Simeon took him into his arms and praised God. He said,

> Lord, you now dismiss your servant in peace, according to your word,
>   because my eyes have seen your salvation,
>   which you have prepared before the face of all people,
>   a light for revelation to the Gentiles, and the glory of your people Israel.

Joseph[d] and the child's[e] mother were amazed at the things that were spoken about him. Then Simeon blessed them and said to Mary his mother, "Listen carefully, this child is appointed for the falling and rising of many in Israel and for a sign that is spoken against, so that the thoughts of many hearts may be revealed. And a sword will pierce your own soul too."

Anna, a prophetess, was there. She was a daughter of Phanuel, of the tribe of Asher. She was very old. She had lived with her husband for seven years after her marriage,[f] and then she was a widow of eighty-four years. She did not leave the temple complex, since she was worshipping with fasting and prayers night and day. Standing nearby at that very hour, she gave thanks to the Lord. She kept speaking about the child to all who were waiting for the redemption of Jerusalem.[g] 16

The Visit of the Magi

After Jesus was born in Bethlehem of Judea, when Herod was king, Wise Men from the east came to Jerusalem. They asked, "Where is he who has been born King of the Jews? We saw his star when it rose[h] and have come to worship him." When King Herod heard this, he was alarmed, and all Jerusalem with him. He gathered together all the people's chief priests and experts in the law. He asked them where the Christ was to be born. They said to him, "In Bethlehem of Judea, because this was written through the prophet:

---

[a] Literally *who opens the womb*
[b] Exodus 13:2,12,15
[c] Leviticus 12:8
[d] Some witnesses to the text read *His father*.
[e] Literally *his*
[f] Literally *after her virginity*
[g] Some witnesses to the text read *in Jerusalem*.
[h] Or *in the east*

You, Bethlehem, in the land of Judah, are certainly not least among the rulers of Judah: because out of you will come a ruler, who will shepherd my people, Israel."[a]

Then Herod secretly summoned the Wise Men and found out from them exactly when the star had appeared. He sent them to Bethlehem and said, "Go and search carefully for the child. When you find him, report to me, so that I may also go and worship him."

After listening to the king, they went on their way. Then the star they had seen when it rose[b] went ahead of them, until it stood still over the place where the child was. When they saw the star, they rejoiced with overwhelming joy. After they went into the house and saw the child with Mary, his mother, they bowed down and worshipped him. Then they opened their treasures and offered him gifts: gold, frankincense, and myrrh. Since they had been warned in a dream not to return to Herod, they went back to their own country by another route.[17]

Flight to Egypt

After the Wise Men were gone, an angel of the Lord suddenly appeared to Joseph in a dream. He said, "Get up, take the child and his mother, and flee to Egypt. Stay there until I tell you, because Herod will search for the child in order to kill him."

Joseph got up, took the child and his mother during the night, and left for Egypt. He stayed there until the death of Herod. This happened to fulfill what was spoken by the Lord through the prophet: "Out of Egypt I called my son."[c] [18]

Herod Kills the Boys

When Herod realized that he had been outwitted by the Wise Men, he was furious. He issued orders to kill all the boys in Bethlehem and in all the surrounding countryside, from two years old and under. This was in keeping with the exact time he had learned from the Wise Men. Then what was spoken through Jeremiah the prophet was fulfilled:

> A voice was heard in Ramah,
>> weeping and great mourning,
>
> Rachel weeping for her children,
>> and she refused to be comforted,
>> because they are no more.[d] [19]

---

[a] Micah 5:2
[b] Or *in the east*
[c] Hosea 11:1
[d] Jeremiah 31:15

Jesus Grows up in Nazareth

After Herod died, an angel of the Lord suddenly appeared in a dream to Joseph in Egypt. The angel said, "Get up, take the child and his mother, and go to the land of Israel, for those who were trying to kill the child are dead." 20

When they had accomplished everything according to the law of the Lord, they returned to Galilee, to their own town, Nazareth. 21

Joseph got up, took the child and his mother, and went to the land of Israel. But when he heard that Archelaus, Herod's son, had succeeded his father as ruler in Judea, he was afraid to go there. Since he had been warned in a dream, he went to the region of Galilee. When he arrived there, he settled in a city called Nazareth. So what was spoken through the prophets was fulfilled: "He will be called a Nazarene."[a] 22

The child grew and became strong.[b] He was filled with wisdom, and God's favor was on him. 23

The Boy Jesus in the Temple Courts

Every year his parents traveled to Jerusalem for the Passover Festival. When he was twelve years old, they went up according to the custom of the Festival. When the days had ended, as they were returning, the boy Jesus stayed behind in Jerusalem. His parents did not know it. Since they thought he was in their group, they went a day's journey. Then they began to look for him among their relatives and friends. When they did not find him, they returned to Jerusalem, searching for him.

After three days they found him in the temple courts, sitting among the teachers, listening to them and asking them questions. And all who heard him were amazed at his understanding and his answers. When his parents saw him, they were astonished. His mother said to him, "Son, why have you treated us this way? See, your father and I have been anxiously looking for you."

He said to them, "Why were you looking for me? Did you not know that I must be taking care of my Father's business?" They did not understand what he was telling them.

He went down with them and came to Nazareth. He was always obedient to them. And his mother treasured up all these things in her heart. Jesus grew in wisdom and stature, and in favor with God and with people. 24

---

[a] The text does not indicate that this is a direct quotation of the Old Testament, and it does not seem to be an exact quotation of any passage in the Old Testament Scriptures.

[b] Some witnesses to the text add *spiritually* or *in spirit*.

Chapter II: Look! The Lamb of God!
Public Ministry Begins in Judea

John the Baptist Prepares the Way

In the fifteenth year of the reign of Tiberius Caesar—while Pontius Pilate was governor of Judea, Herod was tetrarch of Galilee, his brother Philip was tetrarch of the region of Ituraea and Trachonitis, and Lysanias was tetrarch of Abilene—during the high priesthood of Annas and Caiaphas, the word of God came to John, the son of Zechariah, in the wilderness. He went into the whole region around the Jordan,[25] baptizing in the wilderness and preaching a baptism of repentance for the forgiveness of sins,[26] and saying "Repent, because the kingdom of heaven is near!" Yes, this is he of whom this was spoken[27] in the book of the words of Isaiah the prophet:[28]

> Look, I am sending my messenger ahead of you,
>   who will prepare the way for you.[29]
> A voice of one calling in the wilderness,
> "Prepare the way of the Lord! Make his paths straight.
> Every valley will be filled, and every mountain and hill will be made low.
> The crooked will become straight, and the rough ways smooth.
> And everyone[a] will see the salvation of God."[b] [30]

The whole Judean countryside and all the people of Jerusalem and all the region around the Jordan[31] were going out to him. They were baptized by him in the Jordan River as they confessed their sins. John was clothed in camel's hair, and he wore a leather belt around his waist. He ate locusts and wild honey.[32]

But when he saw many of the Pharisees and Sadducees coming for his baptism, he said to them, "You offspring of vipers, who warned you to flee from the coming wrath? Therefore produce fruit in keeping with repentance! Do not think of saying to yourselves, 'We have Abraham as our father.' For I tell you that God is able to raise up children for Abraham from these stones. Already the ax is ready to strike[c]

---

[a] Or *all flesh*
[b] Isaiah 40:3-5
[c] Literally *is placed against*

the root of the trees. So every tree that does not produce good fruit is cut down and thrown into the fire.³³

The crowds began to ask him, "What should we do then?"

He answered them, "Whoever has two shirts should share with the person who has none, and whoever has food should do the same."

Tax collectors also came to be baptized. They said, "Teacher, what should we do?"

To them he said, "Collect no more than what you were authorized to."

Soldiers were also asking him, "And what should we do?"

He told them, "Do not extort money from anyone by force or false accusation. Be satisfied with your wages."

The people were waiting expectantly and were all wondering in their hearts if John might be the Christ. John answered them all, "I baptize you with water. But someone mightier than I is coming. I am not worthy to untie the strap of his sandals. He will baptize you with the Holy Spirit and fire. His winnowing shovel is in his hand, and he will thoroughly clean out his threshing floor. He will gather the wheat into his barn, but he will burn up the chaff with unquenchable fire."³⁴

Then with many other words, he appealed to them and was preaching good news to the people.³⁵

John Baptizes Jesus

Then, when all the people were being baptized,³⁶ Jesus came from Nazareth of³⁷ Galilee to be baptized by John at the Jordan. But John tried to stop him, saying, "I need to be baptized by you, and yet you come to me?"³⁸

But Jesus answered him, "Let it be so now, because it is proper for us to fulfill all righteousness." Then John let him. After Jesus was baptized, he immediately went up out of the water. Suddenly, while he was praying,³⁹ the heavens were torn open⁴⁰ for him! He saw the Spirit of God, descending like a dove and landing on him,⁴¹ and a voice came from heaven: "You are my Son, whom I love. I am well pleased with you."⁴²

Jesus himself was about thirty years old when he began his ministry.⁴³

Satan Tempts Jesus

Jesus, full of the Holy Spirit, returned from the Jordan, and ⁴⁴ the Spirit immediately sent Jesus out into the wilderness. He was in the wilderness for forty days, being tempted by Satan. He was with the wild animals.⁴⁵

He did not eat anything during those days. When they came to an end, he was hungry. The Devil said to him, "If you are the Son of God, tell this stone to become bread."

Jesus answered him, "It is written:⁴⁶

> Man shall not live by bread alone,

but by every word that comes out of the mouth of God."ᵃ

Then,⁴⁷ the Devil led him to Jerusalem,⁴⁸ the holy city,⁴⁹ and had him stand on the pinnacle of the temple. "If you are the Son of God," he said, "throw yourself down from here, because it is written:

>He will command his angels concerning you, to protect you.

And,

>they will lift you up with their hands,
>so that you will not strike your foot against a stone."ᵇ

Jesus answered him, "It says: 'You shall not test the Lord your God.'"ᶜ ⁵⁰

Again the Devil took him to a very high mountain and showed him all the kingdoms of the world and their glory⁵¹ in a moment of time.⁵² The Devil told him, "I will give you all this⁵³ power and the glory of these kingdoms⁵⁴, if you will bow down and worship me.⁵⁵ It has been entrusted to me, and I can give it to anyone I want. So, if you worship me, it will all be yours."⁵⁶

Then Jesus said to him, "Go away, Satan! For it is written:

>Worship the Lord your God, and serve him only."ᵈ ⁵⁷

When the Devil had finished every temptation, he left him until an opportune time.⁵⁸

Just then angels came and served him.⁵⁹

The Testimony of John the Baptist

This is the testimony John gave when the Jews from Jerusalem sent priests and Levitesᵉ to ask him, "Who are you?"

He confessed and did not deny. He confessed, "I am not the Christ."

And they asked him, "Who are you then? Are you Elijah?"

He said, "I am not."

"Are you the Prophet?"

"No," he answered.

Then they asked him, "Who are you? Tell us so we can give an answer to those who sent us. What do you say about yourself?"

He said, "I am the voice of one crying out in the wilderness, 'Make straight the way of the Lord,'ᶠ just as Isaiah the prophet said."

They had been sent from the Pharisees. So they asked John, "Why then do you baptize, if you are not the Christ, or Elijah, or the Prophet?"

ᵃ Deuteronomy 8:3
ᵇ Psalm 91:11-12
ᶜ Deuteronomy 6:16
ᵈ Deuteronomy 6:13
ᵉ Some witnesses to the text add *to him.*
ᶠ Isaiah 40:3

"I baptize with water," John answered. "Among you stands one you do not know. He is the one coming after me,[a] whose sandal strap I am not worthy to untie."

These things happened in Bethany beyond the Jordan, where John was baptizing.[60]

The Lamb of God

The next day, John saw Jesus coming toward him and said, "Look! The Lamb of God, who takes away the sin of the world! This is the one I was talking about when I said, 'The one coming after me outranks me because he existed before me.' I myself did not know who he was, but I came baptizing with water so that he would be revealed to Israel."

John also testified, "I saw the Spirit descend like a dove from heaven and remain on him. I myself did not recognize him, but the one who sent me to baptize with water said to me, 'The one on whom you see the Spirit descend and remain, he is the one who will baptize with the Holy Spirit.' I saw this myself and have testified that this is the Son of God."[61]

The First Disciples

The next day, John was standing there again with two of his disciples. When John saw Jesus passing by, he said, "Look! The Lamb of God!" The two disciples heard him say this, and they followed Jesus.

When Jesus turned around and saw them following him, he asked, "What are you looking for?"

They said to him, "Rabbi" (which means "Teacher"), "where are you staying?"

He told them, "Come, and you will see." So they came and saw where he was staying. They stayed with him that day. It was about the tenth hour.[b]

Andrew, Simon Peter's brother, was one of the two who heard John and followed Jesus. The first thing Andrew did was to find his own brother Simon and say to him, "We have found the Messiah!" (which is translated "the Christ").[c] He brought him to Jesus.

Looking at him, Jesus said, "You are Simon, son of Jonah.[d] You will be called Cephas" (which means "Peter").[e]

---

[a] Some witnesses to the text add *who existed before me* (see 1:30 where this clause is definitely part of the text).

[b] 10 AM (Roman civil time) or 4 PM (Jewish time). John seems to use Roman civil time in 19:14 (compare Mark 15:25). John also seems to use Roman civil time in 20:19, because the evening is considered part of the *first day of the week*. Roman civil time began a new day at midnight. Jewish time regarded sunset as the beginning of a new day.

[c] *Messiah* is the Hebrew/Aramaic word for *Anointed One*. *Christ* is the Greek word for *Anointed One*.

[d] Some witnesses to the text have *John*.

[e] Both the Aramaic word *Cephas* and the Greek word *Peter* (*Petros*) are masculine nouns that mean *rock*.

The next day, Jesus wanted to leave for Galilee. He found Philip and said to him, "Follow me." Now Philip was from Bethsaida, the hometown of Andrew and Peter.

Philip found Nathanael and told him, "We have found the one Moses wrote about in the Law, and about whom the prophets also wrote—Jesus of Nazareth, the son of Joseph."

Nathanael said to him, "Nazareth! Can anything good come from there?"

"Come and see!" Philip told him.

Jesus saw Nathanael coming toward him and said about him, "Truly, here is an Israelite in whom there is no deceit."

Nathanael asked him, "How do you know me?"

Jesus answered, "Before Philip called you, while you were under the fig tree, I saw you."

Nathanael answered him, "Rabbi, you are the Son of God! You are the King of Israel!"

Jesus replied, "You believe because I told you that I saw you under the fig tree. You will see greater things than that!" Then he added, "Amen, Amen,[a] I tell you:[b] You will see heaven opened and the angels of God ascending and descending on the Son of Man."[62]

Jesus Changes Water into Wine

Three days later, there was a wedding in Cana of Galilee. Jesus' mother was there. Jesus and his disciples were also invited to the wedding.

When the wine was gone, Jesus' mother said to him, "They have no wine."

Jesus said to her, "Woman, what does that have to do with you and me? My time has not come yet."

His mother said to the servants, "Do whatever he tells you."

Six stone water jars, which the Jews used for ceremonial cleansing, were standing there, each holding twenty or thirty gallons.[c] Jesus told them, "Fill the jars with water." So they filled them to the brim. Then he said to them, "Now draw some out and take it to the master of the banquet." And they did.

When the master of the banquet tasted the water that had now become wine, he did not know where it came from (though the servants who had drawn the water knew). The master of the banquet called the bridegroom and said to him, "Everyone serves the good wine first, and when the guests have had plenty to drink, then the cheaper wine. You saved the good wine until now!"

---

[a] Usually people say *Amen* at the end of a prayer, but Jesus used this Hebrew word at the beginning of a statement, which was unique. The inspired writer simply transliterated the Hebrew word that Jesus spoke, instead of using a Greek term. This translation does the same in English. The basic meaning is *I solemnly tell you the truth*. Here it is emphasized by being used twice.

[b] Both uses of *you* in verse 51 are plural.

[c] Greek *two or three metretas*. One *metretes* held about ten gallons.

This, the beginning of his miraculous signs, Jesus performed in Cana of Galilee. He revealed his glory, and his disciples believed in him.

After this, he went down to Capernaum with his mother, brothers, and disciples, and they stayed there for a few days.[63]

Chapter III: He Must Increase; I Must Decrease.
In Judea for Passover

Jesus Clears out the Temple

The Jewish Passover was near, so Jesus went up to Jerusalem.

In the temple courts he found people selling cattle, sheep, and doves, and money changers sitting at tables. He made a whip of cords and drove everyone out of the temple courts, along with the sheep and oxen. He scattered the coins of the money changers and overturned their tables. To those selling doves he said, "Get these things out of here! Stop turning my Father's house into a place of business!"

His disciples remembered that it was written, "Zeal for your house will consume me."[a]

So the Jews responded, "What sign are you going to show us to prove you can do these things?"

Jesus answered them, "Destroy this temple, and in three days I will raise it up again."

The Jews said, "It took forty-six years to build this temple! And you are going to raise it in three days?" But Jesus was speaking about the temple of his body. When Jesus was raised from the dead, his disciples remembered that he had said this. Then they believed the Scripture and what Jesus had said.

While he was in Jerusalem for the Passover Festival, many believed in his name as they observed the miraculous signs he was doing. But Jesus, on his part, was not entrusting himself to them, because he knew them all. He did not need anyone to testify about man, because he himself knew what was in man.[64]

Jesus Teaches Nicodemus

There was a man of the Pharisees named Nicodemus, a member of the Jewish ruling council. He came to Jesus at night and said to him, "Rabbi, we know that you are a teacher who has come from God, for no one can do these miraculous signs you are doing unless God is with him."

---

[a] Psalm 69:9

Jesus replied, "Amen, Amen, I tell you: Unless someone is born from above,ᵃ he cannot see the kingdom of God."

Nicodemus said to him, "How can a man be born when he is old? He cannot enter a second time into his mother's womb and be born, can he?"

Jesus answered, "Amen, Amen, I tell you: Unless someone is born of water and the Spirit, he cannot enter the kingdom of God! Whatever is born of the flesh is flesh. Whatever is born of the Spirit is spirit. Do not be surprised when I tell you that you must be born from above.ᵇ The wind blows where it pleases. You hear its sound, but you do not know where it comes from or where it is going. So it is with everyone who is born of the Spirit."

"How can these things be?" asked Nicodemus.

"You are the teacher of Israel," Jesus answered, "and you do not know these things? Amen, Amen, I tell you: We speak what we know, and we testify about what we have seen. But you people do not accept our testimony. If I have told you earthly things and you do not believe, how will you believe if I tell you heavenly things? No one has ascended into heaven, except the one who descended from heaven, the Son of Man, who is in heaven.ᶜ

"Just as Moses lifted up the snake in the wilderness, so the Son of Man must be lifted up, so that everyone who believes in him shall not perish butᵈ have eternal life.

"For God so loved the world that he gave his only-begotten Son, that whoever believes in him shall not perish, but have eternal life. For God did not send his Son into the world to condemn the world, but to save the world through him. The one who believes in him is not condemned, but the one who does not believe is condemned already, because he has not believed in the name of the only-begotten Son of God. This is the basis for the judgment: The light has come into the world, yet people loved the darkness rather than the light, because their deeds were evil. In fact, everyone who practices wicked things hates the light and does not come toward the light, or else his deeds would be exposed. But the one who does what is true comes toward the light, in order that his deeds may be seen as having been done in connection with God."⁶⁵

Jesus and John the Baptist

After this, Jesus and his disciples went into the Judean countryside where he spent some time with them and was baptizing.

John also was baptizing in Aenon near Salim, because there was plenty of water there. People kept coming and were being baptized, for John had not been thrown into prison yet.

ᵃ Or *born again*

ᵇ Or *born again*

ᶜ A few witnesses to the text omit *who is in heaven*.

ᵈ A few witnesses to the text omit *not perish but*.

Chapter III: He Must Increase; I Must Decrease.

Then an argument broke out between John's disciples and a certain Jew[a] about purification. His disciples came to John and said to him, "Rabbi, the one who was with you across the Jordan, about whom you testified—look, he is baptizing, and everyone is going to him!"

John answered, "A man cannot receive a single thing, unless it has been given to him from heaven. You yourselves are witnesses that I said, 'I am not the Christ, but I have been sent ahead of him.' The one who has the bride is the bridegroom. But the friend of the bridegroom, who stands and listens for him, is overjoyed when he hears the bridegroom's voice. So this joy of mine is now complete. He must increase, but I must decrease."

The one who comes from above is superior to everyone. The one who is from the earth belongs to the earth and speaks in a way that belongs to the earth. The one who comes from heaven is superior to everyone. He testifies about what he has seen and heard, yet no one receives his testimony. The one who has received his testimony has certified that God is true. In fact, the one whom God has sent speaks God's words, for God[b] gives the Spirit without measure. The Father loves the Son and has put everything in his hands. The one who believes in the Son has eternal life, but the one who rejects the Son will not see life; instead, God's wrath remains on him.[66]

John the Baptist Imprisoned

After John rebuked Herod the tetrarch because of Herodias, his brother's wife, and because of all the evil things he had done—Herod added this to them all: He locked John in prison.[67]

---

[a] Some witnesses to the text read *and some Jews*.
[b] A few witnesses to the text read *he*.

CHAPTER IV: COME, FOLLOW ME.
Preaching and Healing in Galilee

The Samaritan Woman

When Jesus heard that John was put in prison,[68] [and when] Jesus[a] found out that the Pharisees had heard he was making and baptizing more disciples than John (though it was not Jesus himself who was baptizing but his disciples), he left Judea and went back again to Galilee.[69]

He had to go through Samaria. So he came to a town in Samaria called Sychar, near the piece of land Jacob gave to his son Joseph. Jacob's well was there. Then Jesus, being tired from the journey, sat down by the well. It was about the sixth hour.[b]

A woman from Samaria came to draw water. Jesus said to her, "Give me a drink." (His disciples had gone into town to buy food.)

The Samaritan woman said to him, "How is it that you, a Jew, ask for a drink from me, a Samaritan woman?" (For Jews do not associate with Samaritans.)

Jesus answered her, "If you knew the gift of God and who it is that is saying to you, 'Give me a drink,' you would have asked him, and he would have given you living water."

"Sir," she said, "you don't even have a bucket, and the well is deep. So where do you get this living water? You are not greater than our father Jacob, are you? He gave us this well and drank from it himself, as did his sons and his animals."

Jesus answered her, "Everyone who drinks this water will be thirsty again, but whoever drinks the water I will give him will never be thirsty ever again. Rather, the water I will give him will become in him a spring of water, bubbling up to eternal life."

"Sir, give me this water," the woman said to him, "so I won't get thirsty and have to keep coming here to draw water."

Jesus told her, "Go, call your husband, and come back here."

"I have no husband," the woman answered.

---

[a] Some witnesses to the text read *The Lord*.
[b] 6 PM (Roman civil time) or noon (Jewish time)

Jesus said to her, "You are right when you say, 'I have no husband.' In fact, you have had five husbands, and the man you have now is not your husband. What you have said is true."

"Sir," the woman replied, "I see that you are a prophet. Our fathers worshipped on this mountain, but you Jews insist that the place where we must worship is in Jerusalem."

Jesus said to her, "Believe me, woman, a time is coming when you will not worship the Father on this mountain or in Jerusalem. You Samaritans worship what you do not know. We worship what we do know, because salvation is from the Jews. But a time is coming and now is here when the real worshippers will worship the Father in spirit and in truth, for those are the kind of worshippers the Father seeks. God is spirit, and those who worship him must worship in spirit and in truth."

The woman said to him, "I know that Messiah is coming" (the one called Christ). "When he comes, he will explain everything to us."

Jesus said to her, "I, the one speaking to you, am he."

Just then his disciples returned and were surprised that he was talking to a woman. Yet no one asked, "What do you want?" or "Why are you talking to her?"

Then the woman left her water jar and went back into town. She said to the people, "Come, see the man who told me everything I ever did. Could this be the Christ?" They left the town and came to him.

Meanwhile, the disciples kept urging him, "Rabbi, eat."

But Jesus said to them, "I have food to eat that you do not know about."

Then the disciples said to each other, "Did anyone bring him something to eat?"

Jesus told them, "My food is to do the will of him who sent me and to finish his work. Do you not say, 'Four more months and the harvest will be here'? Pay attention to what I am telling you. Open your eyes and look at the fields, because they are already[a] ripe for harvest. The reaper is getting paid and is gathering grain for eternal life, so that the sower and the reaper may rejoice together. Indeed in this case the saying is true, 'One sows, and another reaps.' I sent you to reap a harvest for which you did no hard work. Others have done the hard work, and you have benefitted from their labor."

Many Samaritans from that town believed in him because of the woman's testimony: "He told me everything I ever did." So when the Samaritans came to him, they asked him to stay with them. And he stayed there two days. Many more believed because of his message. They told the woman, "We no longer believe because of what you said. Now we have heard for ourselves. And we know that this really is the Savior of the world."[70]

Jesus Begins the Galilean Ministry

After two days, Jesus left for Galilee. Now Jesus himself had testified that a prophet is not honored in his own country.[71]

---

[a] A few witnesses to the text place this word at the beginning of verse 36.

Jesus returned to Galilee in the power of the Spirit,[72] preaching the gospel of the kingdom[a] of God. "The time is fulfilled," he said. "The kingdom of God has come near! Repent, and believe in the gospel."[73] When he came to Galilee, the Galileans welcomed him. They had seen all the things he did at the Festival in Jerusalem, because they also had gone to the Festival,[74] and news about him spread through all the surrounding area. He was teaching in their synagogues and being honored by everyone.[75]

Jesus Heals the Official's Son

Jesus came again to Cana in Galilee, where he had turned the water into wine.

In Capernaum, there was a certain royal official whose son was sick. When this man heard that Jesus had come from Judea into Galilee, he went to him and begged him to come down and heal his son, because his son was about to die.

Jesus told him, "Unless you people see miraculous signs and wonders, you certainly will not believe."

The royal official said to him, "Lord, come down before my little boy dies."

"Go," Jesus told him, "your son is going to live."

The man believed this word that Jesus spoke to him and left.

Already as he was going down, his servants met him with the news that his boy was going to live. So he asked them what time his son got better. They told him, "Yesterday at the seventh hour[b] the fever left him." Then the father realized that was the exact time when Jesus had told him, "Your son is going to live." And he himself and his whole household believed.

This was the second miraculous sign Jesus did after he came from Judea into Galilee.[76]

A Prophet in His Hometown

He went to Nazareth, where he had been brought up. As was his custom, he went into the synagogue on the Sabbath day and stood up to read. The scroll of the prophet Isaiah was handed to him. He unrolled the scroll and found the place where it was written:

> The Spirit of the Lord is on me,
>   because he anointed me to preach good news to the poor.
> He has sent me to proclaim freedom to the captives
>   and recovery of sight to the blind,
>   to set free those who are oppressed,
>   and to proclaim the year of the Lord's favor.[c]

---

[a] A few witnesses to the text omit *of the kingdom*.
[b] 7 PM (Roman civil time) or 1 PM (Jewish time)
[c] Isaiah 61:1-2

He rolled up the scroll, gave it back to the attendant, and sat down. The eyes of everyone in the synagogue were fastened on him. He began to tell them, "Today, this Scripture is fulfilled in your hearing."

They all spoke well of him and were impressed by the words of grace that came from his mouth. And they kept saying, "Isn't this Joseph's son?"

He told them, "Certainly you will quote this proverb to me, 'Physician, heal yourself!' Do here in your hometown everything we heard you did in Capernaum." And he said, "Amen[a] I tell you: No prophet is accepted in his hometown. But truly I tell you: There were many widows in Israel in the days of Elijah, when the sky was shut for three years and six months, while a great famine came over all the land. Elijah was not sent to any of them, but to a widow of Zarephath, in Sidon. And there were many lepers in Israel in the time of Elisha the prophet, yet not one of them was healed except Naaman the Syrian."

All those who were in the synagogue were filled with rage when they heard these things. They got up and drove him out of the town. They led him to the brow of the hill on which their town was built, in order to throw him off the cliff. But he passed through the middle of them and went on his way.[77]

Jesus Moves to Capernaum

He left Nazareth and went to live[78] down[79] in Capernaum,[80] a town of Galilee,[81] which is by the sea, in the region of Zebulun and Naphtali. He did this to fulfill what was spoken through the prophet Isaiah:

> Land of Zebulun and land of Naphtali,
>> along the way of the sea, beyond the Jordan,
> Galilee of the Gentiles,
>> the people dwelling in darkness have seen a great light,
>> and on those dwelling in the region and the shadow of death a light has dawned.[b] [82]

"Come, Follow Me"

As Jesus was going along the Sea of Galilee, he saw Simon and his brother Andrew casting a net into the sea, since they were fishermen. Jesus said to them, "Come, follow me, and I will make you fishers of men." Immediately they left their nets and followed him. Going on a little farther, he saw James the son of Zebedee and his brother John. They were in a boat mending the nets. Immediately Jesus called them. They left their father Zebedee in the boat with the hired servants and followed him. Then they went into Capernaum.[83]

---

[a] Usually people say *Amen* at the end of a prayer, but Jesus used this Hebrew word at the beginning of a statement, which was unique. The inspired writer simply transliterated the Hebrew word that Jesus spoke, instead of using a Greek term. This translation does the same in English. The basic meaning is *I solemnly tell you the truth*.

[b] Isaiah 9:1-2

Chapter IV: Come, Follow Me.

Jesus Drives Out a Demon

On the next Sabbath day, Jesus went into the synagogue and began to teach. They were amazed at his teaching, because he was teaching them as one who has authority and not as the experts in the law. Just then there was a man with an unclean spirit in their synagogue. It cried out[84] with a loud voice, "Leave us alone![85] What do we have to do with you, Jesus of Nazareth? Have you come to destroy us? I know who you are—the Holy One of God!"

Jesus rebuked the spirit, saying, "Be quiet! Come out of him!"

The unclean spirit threw the man into convulsions, and after crying out with a loud voice, it came out of him[86] without harming him.[87] Everyone was so amazed that they began to discuss this with each other. They said, "What is this? A new teaching with authority[88] and power![89] He even commands the unclean spirits, and they obey him[90] and come out!"[91] News about him spread quickly[92] to every place in the surrounding area,[93] through all the region of Galilee.[94]

Jesus Heals Many

Jesus got up.[95] They left the synagogue and went with James and John to the home of Simon and Andrew.[96] Simon's mother-in-law was lying in bed, sick,[97] suffering from a high fever.[98] Without delay they told Jesus about her.[99] They asked him to help her.[100] When Jesus came into Peter's house, he saw Peter's mother-in-law sick in bed with a fever.[101] He went to her, took her by the hand, and raised her up.[102] He stood over her, rebuked the fever, and it left her. Immediately she got up and began to serve them.[103]

That evening,[104] as the sun was setting, they brought to him all who were sick with various diseases. He laid his hands on every one of them and healed them.[105] When the sun had set, the people kept bringing to him all who were sick and demon-possessed. The whole town gathered at the door. He healed many people.[106] Demons also came out of many people, crying out, "You are the Son of God!" He rebuked them and did not allow them to speak, because they knew that he was the Christ.[107] This was to fulfill what was spoken through Isaiah the prophet: "He took up our weaknesses and carried away our diseases."[a] [108]

Jesus Preaches in Galilee

Jesus got up early in the morning, while it was still dark, and went out. He withdrew to a solitary place and was praying there.[109] Simon and his companions searched for him, and, when they found him, they said to him, "Everyone is looking for you!"[110] The crowds were looking for him. They went up to him and were trying to prevent him from leaving them.[111]

He told them, "Let's go somewhere else, to the neighboring villages, so I can preach there too.[112] He told them, "I must preach the good news of the kingdom of

---

[a] Isaiah 53:4

God to the other towns too, because that is why I was sent.[113] In fact, that is why I have come."[114]

Jesus traveled throughout Galilee, teaching in their synagogues, preaching the gospel of the kingdom, and healing every disease and every sickness among the people.[115]

News about him spread throughout all Syria. People brought to him all who were ill with various diseases and suffering severe pains, the demon-possessed, those who experienced seizures, and the paralyzed. Then he healed them. Large crowds followed him from Galilee, the Decapolis, Jerusalem, Judea, and from beyond the Jordan.[116]

The First Miraculous Catch

One time, while the crowd was pressing in on Jesus and listening to the word of God, he was standing by the Lake of Gennesaret.[a] He saw two boats there along the lakeshore. The fishermen had left them and were washing their nets. Jesus got into one of the boats, which belonged to Simon, and asked him to put out a little from the shore. He sat down and began teaching the crowds from the boat. When he had finished speaking, he said to Simon, "Put out into the deep water, and let down your nets for a catch."

Simon answered him, "Master, we worked hard all through the night and caught nothing. But at your word I will let down the nets." When they had done this, they caught a great number of fish, and their nets were about to tear apart. They signaled their partners in the other boat to come and help them. They came and filled both boats, so that they began to sink. When Simon Peter saw this, he fell down at Jesus' knees, saying, "Go away from me, because I am a sinful man, Lord." For Peter and all those with him were amazed at the number of fish they had caught, and so were James and John, the sons of Zebedee, who were partners with Simon.

Jesus said to Simon, "Have no fear. From now on you will be catching people."

After they brought their boats to the shore, they left everything and followed him.[117]

The Sermon on the Mount

When Jesus saw the crowds, he went up onto a mountain. When he sat down, his disciples came to him. He opened his mouth and began to teach them. He said these things:

> "Blessed are the poor in spirit,
>   because theirs is the kingdom of heaven.
> Blessed are those who mourn,
>   because they will be comforted.
> Blessed are the gentle,
>   because they will inherit the earth.

---

[a] This is the Sea of Galilee.

> Blessed are those who hunger and thirst for righteousness,
>> because they will be filled.
> Blessed are the merciful,
>> because they will receive mercy.
> Blessed are the pure in heart,
>> because they will see God.
> Blessed are the peacemakers,
>> because they will be called sons of God.
> Blessed are those who are persecuted because of righteousness,
>> because theirs is the kingdom of heaven."

"Blessed are you when people insult you and persecute you and falsely say all kinds of evil against you because of me. Rejoice and be glad, because great is your reward in heaven. In fact, that is how they persecuted the prophets who were before you."[118]

Salt and Light

"You are the salt of the earth, but if salt has lost its flavor, how will it become salty again? Then it is no good for anything except to be thrown out and trampled on by people. You are the light of the world. A city located on a hill cannot be hidden. People do not light a lamp and put it under a basket. No, they put it on a stand, and it gives light to all who are in the house. In the same way let your light shine in people's presence, so that they may see your good works and glorify your Father who is in heaven."[119]

Jesus Fulfills the Old Testament

"Do not think that I came to destroy the Law or the Prophets. I did not come to destroy them but to fulfill them. Amen[a] I tell you: Until heaven and earth pass away, not even the smallest letter, or even part of a letter, will in any way pass away from the Law until everything is fulfilled. So whoever breaks one of the least of these commandments and teaches others to do the same will be called least in the kingdom of heaven. But whoever practices and teaches them will be called great in the kingdom of heaven. Indeed I tell you that unless your righteousness surpasses that of the Pharisees and experts in the law, you will never enter the kingdom of heaven."[120]

---

[a] Usually, people say *Amen* at the end of a prayer. But Jesus used this Hebrew word at the beginning of a statement, which was unique. The inspired writer simply transliterated the Hebrew word that Jesus spoke, instead of using a Greek term. This translation does the same in English. The basic meaning is *I solemnly tell you the truth.*

Sinful Anger

"You have heard that it was said to people long ago, 'You shall not murder,[a] and whoever murders will be subject to judgment.' But I tell you that everyone who is angry with his brother without a cause[b] will be subject to judgment, and whoever says to his brother, 'Raca,'[c] will have to answer to the Sanhedrin. But whoever says, 'You fool!' will be in danger of hell[d] fire."

"So if you are about to offer your gift at the altar, and there you remember that your brother has something against you, leave your gift there in front of the altar and go. First be reconciled to your brother. Then come and offer your gift."[121]

"If someone accuses you, reach an agreement with him quickly, while you are with him on the way. Otherwise your accuser may bring you to the judge, and the judge may hand you over to the officer, and you will be thrown into prison. Amen I tell you: You will never get out until you have paid the last penny."

Lust

"You have heard that it was said, 'You shall not commit adultery,'[e] but I tell you that everyone who looks at a woman with lust has already committed adultery with her in his heart. If your right eye causes you to fall into sin, pluck it out and throw it away from you. It is better for you to lose one part of your body than for your whole body to be thrown into hell. If your right hand causes you to fall into sin, cut it off and throw it away from you. It is better for you to lose one part of your body than for your whole body to be thrown into hell."[122]

Divorce

"It was also said, 'Whoever divorces his wife must give her a certificate of divorce.'[f] But I tell you that whoever divorces his wife, except for sexual immorality, causes her to be regarded as an adulteress. And whoever marries the divorced woman is regarded as an adulterer."[123]

Oaths

"Again you have heard that it was said to people long ago, 'Do not break your oaths, but fulfill your vows to the Lord.'[g] But I tell you, do not swear at all: not by heaven, because it is God's throne; and not by earth, because it is his footstool; and not by Jerusalem, because it is the city of the great King. And do not swear by your

---

[a] Exodus 20:13; Deuteronomy 5:17
[b] Some witnesses to the text omit *without a cause*.
[c] *Raca* was an insulting name in Aramaic which meant something like *numbskull* or *empty-head*.
[d] *Gehenna*
[e] Exodus 20:14; Deuteronomy 5:18
[f] Deuteronomy 24:1
[g] Leviticus 19:12; Numbers 30:2

own head, since you cannot make one hair white or black. Instead, let your statement be, 'Yes, yes,' or 'No, no.' Whatever goes beyond these is from the Evil One."[124]

Love Your Enemies

"You have heard that it was said, 'An eye for an eye, and a tooth for a tooth.'[a] But I tell you, do not resist an evildoer. If someone strikes you on your right cheek, turn to him the other also. If anyone wants to sue you to take away your shirt, give him your coat too. Whoever compels you to go one mile, go with him two. Give to the one who asks you, and do not turn away from the one who wants to borrow from you."

"You have heard that it was said, 'Love your neighbor[b] and hate your enemy.' But I tell you, love your enemies and pray for those who persecute you, so that you may be children of your Father who is in heaven. For he makes his sun to rise on the evil and the good and sends rain on the righteous and the unrighteous. Indeed if you love those who love you, what reward do you have? Even tax collectors do that, don't they? If you greet only your brothers, what are you doing more than others? Do not even the unbelievers do that? So then, be perfect, as your heavenly Father is perfect."[125]

Do Not Be Hypocrites

"Be careful that you do not do your righteous works[c] in front of people, so that they will notice. If you do, you have no reward from your Father who is in heaven. So whenever you perform acts of mercy, do not sound a trumpet for yourself, as the hypocrites do in the synagogues and on the streets to be praised by people. Amen I tell you: They have received their reward. Instead, when you perform acts of mercy, do not let your left hand know what your right hand is doing. Then your acts of mercy will be in secret, and your Father who sees what is done in secret will reward you."[d] [126]

"Whenever you pray, do not be like the hypocrites. They love to stand and pray in the synagogues and on the street corners so that they may be seen by people. Amen I tell you: They have received their reward. But whenever you pray, go into your private room, close your door, and pray to your Father who is unseen. And your Father, who sees what others cannot see, will reward you."[e]

---

[a] Exodus 21:24; Leviticus 24:20
[b] Leviticus 19:18
[c] Some witnesses to the text read *charitable giving*.
[d] Some witnesses to the text add *publicly*.
[e] Some witnesses to the text add *publicly*.

The Lord's Prayer

"And when you pray, do not babble like the heathen, since they think that they will be heard because of their many words. However do not be like them, because your Father knows what you need before you ask him. Therefore pray like this: 'Our Father in heaven, hallowed be your name. Your kingdom come. Your will be done on earth as it is in heaven. Give us today our daily bread. Forgive us our debts, as we also forgive our debtors. Lead us not into temptation, but deliver us from evil.'"[a]

"Indeed if you forgive people when they sin against you, your heavenly Father will also forgive you. But if you do not forgive people their sins, your Father will not forgive your sins."[127]

Fasting

"Whenever you fast, do not make yourself look sad like the hypocrites, for they disfigure their faces to show everyone that they are fasting. Amen I tell you: They have received their reward. But when you fast, anoint your head and wash your face, so that it is not apparent to people that you are fasting, but only to your Father who sees what is unseen. Then your Father, who sees what is done in secret, will reward you."[128]

Treasures

"Do not store up treasures for yourselves on earth, where moth and rust destroy, and where thieves break in and steal. But store up treasures for yourselves in heaven, where moth and rust do not destroy, and where thieves do not break in and steal. Because where your treasure is, there your heart will be also."

"The eye is the lamp of the body. So then if your eye is healthy, your whole body will be full of light. But if your eye is bad, your whole body will be full of darkness. So if the light that is in you is darkness, how great is the darkness!"

"No one can serve two masters. Either he will hate the one and love the other, or he will be devoted to the one and despise the other. You cannot serve both God and mammon."[b] [129]

Do Not Worry

"For this reason I tell you, do not worry about your life, what you will eat or drink, or about your body, what you will wear. Is not life more than food and the body more than clothing? Look at the birds of the air. They do not sow or reap or gather into barns, and yet your heavenly Father feeds them. Are you not worth much more than they?"

"Which of you can add a single moment to his lifespan by worrying? Why do you worry about clothing? Consider how the lilies of the field grow. They do not labor

---

[a] Or *the Evil One*. Some witnesses to the text add *For yours is the kingdom, and the power, and the glory forever. Amen.* See Daniel 7:14; 1 Chronicles 29:11.

[b] *Mammon* is an Aramaic term for worldly wealth and property.

or spin, but I tell you that not even Solomon in all his glory was dressed like one of these. If that is how God clothes the grass of the field, which is alive today and tomorrow is thrown into the furnace, will he not clothe you even more, you of little faith?"

"So do not worry, saying, 'What will we eat?' or 'What will we drink?' or 'What will we wear?' For the unbelievers[a] chase after all these things. Certainly your heavenly Father knows that you need all these things. But seek first the kingdom of God and his righteousness, and all these things will be given to you as well. So do not worry about tomorrow, for tomorrow will care for itself. Each day has enough trouble of its own."[130]

Consider the Beam in Your Own Eye

"Stop judging, so that you will not be judged. For with whatever standard you judge, you will be judged, and with whatever measure you measure, it will be measured to you. Why do you focus on[b] the speck that is in your brother's eye, but do not consider the beam that is in your own eye? How will you tell your brother, 'Let me remove the speck from your eye,' when, in fact, you have a beam in your own eye? Hypocrite! First remove the beam from your own eye, and then you will see clearly to remove the speck from your brother's eye."[131]

Do Not Throw Your Pearls to Pigs

"Do not give dogs what is holy, and do not throw your pearls to pigs. If you do, they will trample them under their feet and turn and tear you to pieces."[132]

Keep Praying

"Keep asking, and it will be given to you. Keep seeking, and you will find. Keep knocking, and it will be opened for you. For everyone who asks receives, and everyone who seeks finds, and to the one who knocks, it will be opened. Who among you, if his son asks him for bread, would give him a stone? Or who, if his son asks for a fish, would give him a snake? Then if you know how to give good gifts to your children, even though you are evil, how much more will your Father in heaven give good gifts to those who ask him!"[133]

The Golden Rule

"So do for others whatever you want people to do for you, because this is the Law and the Prophets."[134]

---

[a] Or *Gentiles*
[b] Or *look at*, or *notice*

The Narrow Gate

"Enter through the narrow gate, for wide is the gate and broad is the way that leads to destruction, and many are those who enter through it. How narrow is the gate, and how difficult is the way that leads to life, and there are few who find it."[135]

Watch Out for False Prophets

"Watch out for false prophets. They come to you in sheep's clothing, but inwardly they are ravenous wolves. By their fruit you will recognize them. You do not gather grapes from thorn bushes or figs from thistles, do you? So then, every good tree produces good fruit, but a bad tree produces bad fruit. A good tree cannot produce bad fruit, and a bad tree cannot produce good fruit. Every tree that does not produce good fruit is cut down and thrown into the fire. So then, by their fruit you will recognize them. Not everyone who says to me, 'Lord, Lord,' will enter the kingdom of heaven, but only the one who does the will of my Father in heaven. Many will say to me on that day, 'Lord, Lord, did we not prophesy in your name and drive out demons in your name and perform many miracles in your name?' Then I will tell them plainly, 'I never knew you. Depart from me, you evildoers.'"[136]

Wise and Foolish Builders

"Everyone who hears these words of mine and does them will be like a wise man who built his house on bedrock. The rain came down, the rivers rose, and the winds blew and beat against that house. But it did not fall, because it was founded on bedrock. Everyone who hears these words of mine but does not do them will be like a foolish man who built his house on sand. The rain came down, the rivers rose, and the winds blew and beat against that house, and it fell—it was completely destroyed."

When Jesus finished speaking these words, the crowds were amazed at his teaching, because he taught them as one who had authority, and not like their experts in the law.[137]

Jesus Heals a Leper

When Jesus came down from the mountain, large crowds followed him.[138] Jesus was in one of the towns, and there was a man full of leprosy.[139] Just then, [the] leper came to him.[140] He knelt[141] and bowed down to him.[142] He fell on his face and begged him, "Lord, if you are willing, you can make me clean."[143]

Moved with compassion, Jesus stretched out his hand and touched him. "I am willing," he told him. "Be clean." Immediately the leprosy left him, and he was healed. Then Jesus gave him a stern warning and immediately sent him away. He told him, "See that you do not say anything to anyone. Instead go, show yourself to the priest, and offer the sacrifices for your cleansing that Moses commanded, as a testimony to them."[144]

But after the man left, he began to proclaim it widely. He spread the word so much that Jesus was no longer able to enter a town openly.[145] The news about him spread even more, and large crowds gathered to listen and be healed of their sicknesses.[146] But Jesus often withdrew to deserted places and prayed.[147] Yet people kept coming to him from all directions.[148]

Jesus Forgives Sins

When Jesus again entered Capernaum some days later, people heard that he was home.[149]

On one of the days while Jesus was teaching, Pharisees and teachers of the law were sitting there who had come from every village of Galilee and Judea and from Jerusalem. The power of the Lord was with him to heal.[150] So many people were gathered together that there was no more room, not even by the door, and he was speaking the word to them.[151] Just then,[152] four[153] men who were carrying a paralyzed man on a stretcher tried to bring him in and lay him in front of Jesus. Since they did not find a way to bring him in because of the crowd, they went up on the roof,[154] dug through,[155] and lowered him down through the tiles on his stretcher into the middle of the crowd, right in front of Jesus.[156] When Jesus saw their faith, he said to the paralyzed man, "Take heart, son! Your sins are forgiven."[157]

But there were some experts in the law[158] and the Pharisees[159] sitting there and thinking in their hearts, "Why does this fellow speak like this? He is blaspheming![160] Who can forgive sins except God alone?"[161]

Jesus immediately knew in his spirit that they were thinking this way within themselves. He asked them, "Why are you thinking these[162] evil[163] things in your hearts? Which is easier: to tell the paralyzed man, 'Your sins are forgiven,' or to say, 'Get up, take your stretcher, and walk'? But, so that you may know that the Son of Man has authority on earth to forgive sins"—he said to the paralyzed man, "I tell you, get up, take your stretcher, and go home."[164]

Immediately, he stood up in front of them, picked up what he had been lying on, and went home glorifying God. They were all astonished and glorified God,[165] who had given such authority to men.[166] They were also filled with reverence and said, "We have seen wonderful things today."[167] They said, "We have never seen anything like this!"[168]

The Calling of Matthew (Levi)

Jesus went on from there,[169] out again along the sea.[170] The whole crowd went to him, and he taught them. As he was passing by, he saw Levi[171] (Matthew)[172] the son of Alphaeus sitting at the tax booth. "Follow me," Jesus told him.[173]

Levi left everything, got up, and followed Jesus.[174] Levi gave a great banquet for him in his house.[175]

Then when Jesus was reclining at a table in Levi's house, many tax collectors and sinners were reclining with Jesus and his disciples because many of them also were following him. When the experts in the law and the Pharisees saw that he was eating with the sinners and tax collectors, they said to his disciples, "Why is he eating and drinking with tax collectors and sinners?"[176]

When Jesus heard this, he said to them, "The healthy do not need a physician, but the sick do. Go and learn what this means: 'I desire mercy, and not sacrifice.'[a] In fact, I did not come to call the righteous, but sinners."[177]

A Question about Fasting

Then John's disciples came to him and said, "Why do we and the Pharisees fast often, but your disciples do not fast at all?"

Jesus said to them, "Can the attendants of the bridegroom mourn while the bridegroom is with them? But the days will come when the bridegroom will be taken away from them, and then they will fast. No one puts a piece of unshrunk cloth on an old garment, because the patch would tear away from the garment, and the hole would be made even worse. And people do not pour new wine into old wineskins. If they did, the skins would burst, the wine would be spilled, and the skins would be ruined. Instead they pour new wine into fresh wineskins. By doing that, both are preserved.[178] And no one wants new wine while drinking old wine, because he says, 'The old is fine.'"[179]

The Daughter of Jairus

As he was saying these things to them,[180] one of the synagogue rulers, named Jairus, came. When he saw Jesus, he fell at his feet[181] and begged him to come to his house, because he had an only daughter who was about twelve years old and she was dying.[182] The ruler who came, bowed down to him, and said, "My daughter has just died,"[183] and repeatedly pleaded with him, "My little daughter is near death. Please come and place your hands on her so that she may be healed and live."[184]

Jesus got up and followed him, as did his disciples,[185] and a large crowd was following him, pressing tightly against him. A certain woman who was there had a discharge of blood for twelve years. She had suffered much under the care of many physicians and had spent all that she had. Yet instead of getting better, she grew worse. When she heard what was being said about Jesus,[186] she approached Jesus from behind and touched the fringe of his garment.[187] For she had been saying to herself, "If I just touch his garment, I will be healed."[188] Immediately her flow of blood stopped, and she felt in her body that she was healed of her affliction.

At that moment, Jesus knew that power had gone out from him. He turned around in the crowd and asked, "Who touched my robe?"[189]

As everyone was denying it, Peter and those with him said, "Master, the crowds are pressing in and crowding you, yet you say, 'Who touched me?'"[190]

Nevertheless he kept looking around to see who had done this.[191] Jesus said, "Someone touched me, because I know that power has gone out from me." When the woman saw that she did not escape his notice, she came trembling and fell down before Jesus.[192] The woman was trembling with fear since she knew what had

---

[a] Hosea 6:6

happened to her.[193] In the presence of all the people she told him why she had touched him and how she was healed immediately.[194]

He said to her, "Daughter, your faith has made you well. Go in peace and be healed of your suffering."[195]

While he was still speaking, someone came from the synagogue ruler's house, saying, "Your daughter has died. Don't trouble the Teacher anymore."

But when Jesus heard it, he told Jairus, "Do not be afraid. Only believe, and she will be saved."

When he came to the house, he did not let anyone enter, except Peter, John, James, and the child's father and mother.[196]

They went into the house of the synagogue ruler, and Jesus saw a commotion with people weeping and wailing loudly. When he entered[197] and saw the flute players and the noisy crowd,[198] he said to them, "Why are you making a commotion and weeping?[199] Go away, for the girl is not dead but is sleeping."[200]

They laughed at him, knowing that she was dead.[201] But after he put everyone out, he took the father of the child, her mother, and those who were with him and went in where the child was. Grasping the hand of the child, he said to her, "*Talitha, koum!*" (When translated, that means, "Little girl, I say to you, arise!")[202] Her spirit returned, and she immediately got up.[203]

They were completely and utterly amazed. Then he gave them strict orders not to let anyone know about this, and he told them to give her something to eat.[204] News of this went out through the entire region.[205]

Two Blind Men

As Jesus left that place, two blind men followed him, calling out, "Have mercy on us, Son of David!"

When he entered the house, the blind men came to him. Jesus said to them, "Do you believe that I am able to do this?"

They told him, "Yes, Lord."

Then he touched their eyes and said, "According to your faith let it be done for you." And their eyes were opened. Then Jesus warned them emphatically, "See to it that no one learns about this." But they went out and spread the word about him throughout that entire region.[206]

Jesus Heals a Mute Man

Just as they were leaving, people brought to him a demon-possessed man who could not talk. After the demon was driven out, the mute man spoke. The crowds were amazed and said, "Nothing like this has ever been seen in Israel!"

But the Pharisees said, "He drives out demons by the ruler of demons."[207]

A Prophet without Honor

Jesus left there and went to his hometown. His disciples followed him. When the Sabbath came, he began to teach in the synagogue. Many who heard him were amazed. They asked, "Where did this man learn these things? What is this wisdom that has been given to this man? How is it that miracles such as these are performed by his hands? Isn't this the carpenter, the son of Mary and the brother of James, Joses[208] (Joseph)[209], Judas, and Simon? And aren't his sisters here with us?" And they took offense at him.

Jesus said to them, "A prophet is not without honor except in his hometown and among his own relatives and in his own house." He could not do any miracles there except to lay his hands on a few sick people and heal them. He was amazed at their unbelief. Then he went around the villages teaching.[210]

Jesus traveled through all the towns and villages, teaching in their synagogues, preaching the gospel of the kingdom, and healing every disease and every sickness.[211]

Chapter V: Son of Man and Son of God
In Judea for a Festival

Healing at the Pool

After this, there was a Jewish festival, and Jesus went up to Jerusalem. Near the Sheep Gate in Jerusalem there is a pool, called Bethesda[a] in Aramaic,[b] which has five colonnades. Within these lay a large number of sick people—blind, lame, or paralyzed—who were waiting for the movement of the water. For an angel would go down at certain times into the pool and stir up the water. Whoever stepped in first after the stirring of the water was healed of whatever disease he had.[c] One man was there who had been sick for thirty-eight years. When Jesus saw him lying there and knew he had already been sick a long time, he asked him, "Do you want to get well?"

"Sir," the sick man answered, "I have no one to put me into the pool when the water is stirred up. While I'm going, someone else goes down ahead of me."

Jesus said to him, "Get up! Pick up your mat and walk." Instantly the man was healed. He picked up his mat and walked.

That day was the Sabbath. So the Jews told the man who had been healed, "This is the Sabbath! You are not permitted to carry your mat."

He answered them, "The one who made me well told me, 'Pick up your mat and walk.'"

Then they asked him, "Who is the man who told you, 'Pick it up and walk'?" But the man who was healed did not know who it was, for Jesus had slipped away into the crowd that was there.

Later Jesus found him in the temple and said to him, "Look, you are well now. Do not sin anymore so that nothing worse happens to you."

The man went back and reported to the Jews that it was Jesus who made him well.[212]

---

[a] A few witnesses to the text have *Bethzatha*; a few others have *Bethsaida*.
[b] Or *Hebrew*
[c] Some witnesses to the text omit the text from verse 3b *who were waiting ...* to the end of verse 4.

God's Son

So the Jews began to persecute Jesus, because he was doing these things on the Sabbath. But Jesus answered them, "My Father is working right up to the present time, and I am working too."

This is why the Jews tried all the more to kill him, because he was not merely breaking the Sabbath, but was even calling God his own Father, making himself equal with God."

Jesus answered them directly, "Amen, Amen, I tell you: The Son can do nothing on his own, but only what he sees the Father doing. Indeed, the Son does exactly what the Father does. For the Father loves the Son and shows him everything he is doing. And he will show him even greater works than these so that you will be amazed. For just as the Father raises the dead and gives them life, so also the Son gives life to those he wishes."

"In fact, the Father judges no one, but has entrusted all judgment to the Son, so that all should honor the Son just as they honor the Father. Whoever does not honor the Son does not honor the Father who sent him. Amen, Amen, I tell you: Anyone who hears my word and believes him who sent me has eternal life. He is not going to come into judgment but has crossed over from death to life."

"Amen, Amen, I tell you: A time is coming and is here now when the dead will hear the voice of the Son of God, and those who listen will live. For just as the Father has life in himself, so also he has granted the Son to have life in himself. And he has given him authority to execute judgment, because he is the Son of Man."

"Do not be amazed at this, for a time is coming when all who are in their graves will hear his voice and will come out. Those who have done good will rise to live, but those who have practiced evil will rise to be condemned. I can do nothing at all on my own. I judge only as I hear. And my judgment is just, for I do not seek my own will, but the will of him who sent me."

"If I were to testify about myself, my testimony would not be valid. There is another who testifies about me, and I know that his testimony about me is valid. You sent to John, and he has testified to the truth. The testimony I receive is not from man, but I am saying these things so that you may be saved. John was a lamp that was shining brightly, and for a while you wanted to enjoy his light. But I have testimony greater than John's. For the works that the Father gave me to carry out, the very works that I am doing, these testify about me that the Father has sent me. The Father who sent me—he is the one who has testified about me. You have never heard his voice or seen his form. And you do not have his word remaining in you, because you do not believe the one he sent. You search the Scriptures because you think you have eternal life in them. They testify about me! And yet you do not want to come to me in order to have life."

"I do not accept honor from people. But I know you. I know that you do not have the love of God within you. I have come in my Father's name, yet you do not accept me. If someone else comes in his own name, you will accept him. How can you believe while you continue to accept glory from one another and you do not seek the glory that comes from the only God?"

"Do not think that I will accuse you to the Father. The one who accuses you is Moses, on whom you have set your hope. For if you believed Moses, you would believe me, because he wrote about me. But if you do not believe his writings, how will you believe what I say?"[213]

Lord of the Sabbath

At that time, Jesus went through the grain fields on the Sabbath. His disciples were hungry and began to pick heads of grain[214] as they walked along,[215] rubbing them in their hands, and eating them.[216] But when the Pharisees saw it, they said to him, "Look, what your disciples are doing is unlawful on the Sabbath."[217]

He replied to them, "Have you never read what David did when he was in need and hungry (he and his companions)? He entered the house of God in the time of Abiathar the high priest and ate the Bread of the Presence, which is not lawful for anyone to eat, except for the priests. He also gave some to his companions.[218] Or have you not read in the law that on the Sabbath days, the priests in the temple violate the Sabbath and yet are innocent? But I tell you that one greater than the temple is here. Yet if you had known what this means, 'I desire mercy, and not sacrifice,'[a] you would not have condemned the innocent."[219]

Then Jesus said to them, "The Sabbath was made for man, not man for the Sabbath. So the Son of Man is the Lord even of the Sabbath."[220]

Jesus Heals a Man with a Withered Hand

Going on from there,[221] on another Sabbath, he went into the synagogue and taught. A man was there whose right hand was withered. The experts in the law and the Pharisees were watching him closely, to see if he would heal on the Sabbath.[222] Looking for a way to accuse Jesus, they asked him, "Is it lawful to heal on Sabbath days?"[223]

But he always knew their thoughts. He said to the man with the withered hand, "Stand up and step forward."[b] He got up and stood there. Then Jesus said to them, "I will ask you something. Is it lawful on the Sabbath to do good or to do evil, to save life or to destroy it?"[224] But they were silent. Then he looked around at them with anger, deeply grieved at the hardness of their hearts.[225]

He said to them, "Who among you, if you have one sheep that falls into a pit on the Sabbath, will not take hold of it and lift it out? How much more valuable is a man than a sheep! So it is lawful to do good on the Sabbath."[226] Then he told the man, "Stretch out your hand." He stretched it out, and it was restored, as healthy as the other one.[227]

---

[a] Hosea 6:6
[b] Or *Get up and stand in the center*

The Pharisees,[228] filled with rage,[229] left and immediately began to conspire against Jesus with the Herodians, plotting how they might kill him.[230]

Chapter VI: I Will Give You Rest.
Preaching and Healing in Galilee

"Here Is My Servant"

Since Jesus was aware of this, he withdrew from that place. Large crowds followed him and he healed them all. He ordered them not to tell others about him. This happened to fulfill what was spoken through Isaiah the prophet:

> Here is my servant whom I have chosen,
> > the one I love, in whom I am[a] well pleased.
>
> I will put my Spirit on him,
> > and he will proclaim justice to the nations.[b]
>
> He will not quarrel or cry out,
> > and no one will hear his voice in the streets.
>
> A bruised reed he will not break.
> A smoldering wick he will not put out,
> > until he leads justice to victory.
>
> And in his name the nations[c] will hope.[d] 231

Pray for Workers

When he saw the crowds, he was moved with compassion for them, because they were troubled and downcast, like sheep without a shepherd. Then he said to his disciples, "The harvest is plentiful, but the workers are few. Therefore pray that the Lord of the harvest will send out workers into his harvest."232

Jesus Heals Many

Jesus withdrew to the sea with his disciples. A large crowd followed him from Galilee, Judea, Jerusalem, Idumaea, and beyond the Jordan, as well as from around Tyre and Sidon. A large crowd came to him when they heard all that he was doing. He told his disciples to have a boat ready for him because of the crowd, so that the

---

[a] Literally *my soul is*
[b] Or *Gentiles*
[c] Or *Gentiles*
[d] Isaiah 42:1-4

people would not crush him. Since he had healed many people, all those who had illnesses were pressing forward to touch him. Whenever the unclean spirits saw him, they fell down in front of him, crying out, "You are the Son of God!" But he warned them sternly that they should not tell who he was.[233]

Jesus Appoints the Twelve Apostles

It happened in those days that Jesus went up on the mountain to pray, and he spent all night in prayer to God. When it was day, he summoned his disciples,[234] and they came to him. He appointed twelve whom he designated apostles,[a] so that they would be with him and so that he could send them out to preach and to have authority to drive out demons[235] and to heal every disease and every sickness.[236] He appointed the Twelve: Simon, to whom he gave the name Peter,[237] and his brother Andrew; James the son of Zebedee and his brother John,[238] to whom he gave the nickname Boanerges, which means "Sons of Thunder";[239] Philip and Bartholomew; Thomas and Matthew the tax collector; James the son of Alphaeus,[240] also Simon, who was called the Zealot; Judas[241] (Thaddaeus)[242] of James, and Judas Iscariot,[243] who betrayed him.[244]

The Sermon on the Plain

He went down with them and stood on a level place with a large crowd of his disciples and a large number of people from all Judea and Jerusalem, as well as from the coastal area of Tyre and Sidon. These people came to listen to him and to be healed of their diseases. Those who were troubled by unclean spirits were also cured. The whole crowd kept trying to touch him, because power was going out from him and healing them all.[245]

Blessings and Woes

He lifted up his eyes to his disciples and said:

> Blessed are you who are poor,
>   because yours is the kingdom of God.
> Blessed are you who hunger now,
>   because you will be satisfied.
> Blessed are you who weep now,
>   because you will laugh.
> Blessed are you whenever people hate you,
>   and whenever they exclude and insult you
>   and reject your name as evil because of the Son of Man.

"Rejoice in that day and leap for joy because of this: Your reward is great in heaven! The fact is, their fathers constantly did the same things to the prophets."

> But woe to you who are rich,

---

[a] Some witnesses to the text omit *whom he designated apostles*.

because you are receiving your comfort now.
Woe to you who are well fed now,
    because you will be hungry.
Woe to you who laugh now,
    because you will be mourning and weeping.
Woe to you when all people speak well of you,
    because that is how their fathers constantly treated the false prophets.[246]

Love Your Enemies

"But I say to you who are listening: Love your enemies. Do good to those who hate you. Bless those who curse you. Pray for those who mistreat you. If someone strikes you on one cheek, offer the other too. If someone takes away your coat, do not withhold your shirt. Give to everyone who asks you, and if anyone takes away your things, do not demand them back."

"Treat others just as you would want them to treat you. If you love those who love you, what credit is that to you? To be sure, even the sinners love those who love them. And if you do good to those who do good to you, what credit is that to you? Even the sinners do the same thing. If you lend to those from whom you expect to be repaid, what credit is that to you? Even the sinners lend to sinners in order to be paid back in full. Instead, love your enemies, do good and lend, expecting nothing in return. Your reward will be great, and you will be sons of the Most High, because he is kind to the unthankful and the evil. Be merciful, just as your Father is merciful."[247]

Consider the Beam in Your Own Eye

"Do not judge, and you will not be judged. Do not condemn, and you will not be condemned. Forgive, and you will be forgiven. Give, and it will be given to you. A good measure pressed down, shaken together, and running over will be poured into your lap. In fact, the measure with which you measure will be measured back to you."

He also told them a parable: "A blind man cannot guide a blind man, can he? Won't they both fall into a pit? A disciple is not above his teacher, but everyone who is fully trained will be like his teacher. Why do you look at the speck in your brother's eye, but fail to notice the beam in your own eye? Or how can you tell your brother, 'Brother, let me remove the speck in your eye,' when you do not see the beam in your own eye? Hypocrite! First remove the beam from your own eye, and then you will see clearly to remove the speck in your brother's eye."[248]

Listen and Do

"Certainly a good tree does not produce bad fruit, and a bad tree does not produce good fruit. In fact, each tree is known by its own fruit. For people do not gather figs from thorn bushes, and they do not gather grapes from a bramble bush. The good person brings what is good out of the good stored in his heart, and the evil person brings what is evil out of the evil within.ᵃ To be sure, what his mouth speaks flows from the heart."

"Why do you call me, 'Lord, Lord,' and do not do what I say? Everyone who comes to me and listens to my words and does them—I will show you what he is like: He is like a man building a house who dug down deep and laid a foundation on bedrock. When a flood came, the river beat against that house but could not shake it, because it was founded on bedrock.ᵇ But the one who listened to my words and did not do them is like a man who built a house on the ground without a foundation. When the river broke against it, it fell immediately, and that house was completely destroyed."[249]

A Believing Centurion

After Jesus had finished saying all these things to the people who were listening, he went into Capernaum. A centurion's servant, who was valuable to him, was sick and about to die. When the centurion heard about Jesus, he sent some elders of the Jews to him, asking him to come and heal his servant.[250] [The] centurion came to him and pleaded with him, "Lord, my servant is lying at home paralyzed and suffering terribly."[251] They begged him earnestly, saying, "He is worthy of having you do this for him, because he loves our nation, and he built our synagogue for us."[252]

Jesus said to him, "I will come and heal him."[253] Jesus went with them. When he was not far from the house, the centurion sent friends to tell Jesus, "Lord, do not trouble yourself, because I do not deserve to have you come under my roof. That is why I did not consider myself worthy to come to you. But say the word, and my servant will be healed. For I am also a man placed under authority, having soldiers under me. I say to this one, 'Go!' and he goes; and to another one, 'Come!' and he comes; and to my servant, 'Do this,' and he does it."

When Jesus heard these things, he was amazed at him. He turned to the crowd that was following him and said, "I tell you, I have not found such great faith, not even in Israel.[254] I tell you that many will come from the east and the west and will recline at the table with Abraham, Isaac, and Jacob in the kingdom of heaven. But the children of the kingdom will be thrown out into the outer darkness, where there will be weeping and gnashing of teeth."

Jesus said to the centurion, "Go. Let it be done for you as you have believed."[255]

And when the men who had been sent returned to the house, they found the servant well,[256] healed at that very hour.[257]

ᵃ Some witnesses to the text read *out of the evil treasure of his heart*.
ᵇ A few witnesses to the text read *because it was well built*.

Jesus Raises a Widow's Son

Soon afterward[a] Jesus went on his way to a town called Nain, and[b] his disciples and a large crowd were traveling with him. As he was approaching the town gate, there was a dead man being carried out, the only son of his mother. She was a widow, and a considerable crowd from the town was with her. When the Lord saw her, he had compassion on her and said to her, "Do not cry." He went up to the open coffin, touched it, and the pallbearers stopped. He said, "Young man, I say to you, get up!" The dead man sat up and began to speak, and Jesus gave him to his mother.

Fear gripped all of them, and they glorified God, saying, "A great prophet has arisen among us" and "God has visited his people!" This was reported about him in all of Judea and in all the surrounding countryside.[258]

John the Baptist and Christ

While John was in prison,[259] John's disciples told him about all these things. Calling two of his disciples to him, he sent them to Jesus[c] to ask, "Are you the one who was to come or should we look for someone else?" When the men had arrived, they said to Jesus, "John the Baptist sent us to ask you, 'Are you the one who was to come or should we look for someone else?'"

At that time Jesus healed many people of their diseases, afflictions, and evil spirits. And he gave many blind people the ability to see. Jesus answered them, "Go, tell John what you have seen and heard: The blind receive their sight, the lame walk, the lepers are healed, the deaf hear, the dead are raised, and the good news is preached to the poor. Blessed is the one who does not fall away on account of me."

After John's messengers had left, Jesus began to talk to the crowds about John: "What did you go out into the wilderness to see? A reed shaken by the wind? No. Then what did you go out to see? A man dressed in soft clothing? Yet those who are dressed in splendid clothing and live in luxury are in royal palaces. But what did you go out to see? A prophet? Yes, I tell you, and much more than a prophet. This is the one about whom it is written: 'Look, I am sending my messenger ahead of you, who will prepare your way before you.'[d] [260]

Amen I tell you: Among those born of women there has not appeared anyone greater than John the Baptist. Yet whoever is least in the kingdom of heaven is greater than he.[261] From the days of John the Baptist until now, the kingdom of heaven has been advancing forcefully[e] and forceful people are seizing it. In fact, all the prophets and the law prophesied until John. If you are willing to receive it, he is the Elijah who was to come. Whoever has ears to hear,[f] let him hear.[262]

---

[a] Some witnesses to the text read *On the next day*.
[b] Some witnesses to the text add *many of*.
[c] Some witnesses to the text read *the Lord*.
[d] Malachi 3:1
[e] Or *has suffered violence*
[f] A few witnesses to the text omit *to hear*.

When all the people (including the tax collectors) heard this, they declared that God was just, since they were baptized with the baptism of John. But the Pharisees and the legal experts rejected God's purpose for themselves by not being baptized by him.[263]

"To what then will I compare the people of this generation? What are they like? They are like children sitting in the marketplace and calling to one another, 'We played the flute for you, and you did not dance. We sang a dirge, and you did not weep.' For John the Baptist has come without eating bread or drinking wine, and you say, 'He has a demon.' The Son of Man has come eating and drinking, and you say, 'Look, a man who is a glutton and a drunkard, a friend of tax collectors and sinners!' Yet wisdom is declared right by all her children."[264]

Jesus Is Anointed by a Sinful Woman

A certain one of the Pharisees asked Jesus to eat with him. Jesus entered the Pharisee's house and reclined at the table. Just then a sinful woman from that town learned that he was reclining in the Pharisee's house. She brought an alabaster jar of perfume, stood behind him near his feet weeping, and began to wet his feet with her tears. Then she began to wipe them with her hair while also kissing his feet and anointing them with the perfume. When the Pharisee who had invited him saw this, he said to himself, "If this man were a prophet, he would realize who is touching him and what kind of woman she is, because she is a sinner."

Jesus answered him, "Simon, I have something to tell you."

He said, "Teacher, say it."

"A certain moneylender had two debtors. The one owed five hundred denarii,[a] and the other fifty. When they could not pay, he forgave them both. So, which of them will love him more?"

Simon answered, "I suppose the one who had the larger debt forgiven."

Then he told him, "You have judged correctly." Turning toward the woman, he said to Simon, "Do you see this woman? I entered your house, but you did not give me water for my feet. Yet she has wet my feet with her tears and wiped them with her hair. You did not give me a kiss, but she, from the time I entered, has not stopped kissing my feet. You did not anoint my head with oil, but she has anointed my feet with perfume. Therefore I tell you, her many sins have been forgiven; that is why she loved so much. But the one who is forgiven little loves little." Then Jesus said to her, "Your sins have been forgiven."

Those reclining at the table with him began to say among themselves, "Who is this who even forgives sins?"

He said to the woman, "Your faith has saved you. Go in peace."[265]

---

[a] A *denarius* was worth about one day's wage.

Preaching the Gospel

Soon afterward Jesus was traveling from one town and village to another, preaching and proclaiming the good news of the kingdom of God. The Twelve were with him and also some women who had been healed of evil spirits and diseases: Mary, called Magdalene, from whom seven demons had gone out; Joanna, the wife of Cuza, Herod's household manager; Susanna; and many others who provided support for them[a] out of their own possessions.[266]

The Lord's Prayer

On another occasion, Jesus was praying in a certain place. When he finished, one of his disciples said to him, "Lord, teach us to pray, just as John also taught his disciples."

He said to them, "When you pray, say, 'Our Father in heaven,[b] hallowed be your name. Your kingdom come. Your will be done on earth as it is in heaven.[c] Give us each day our daily bread. Forgive us our sins, as we also forgive everyone who sins against us.[d] And lead us not into temptation, but deliver us from evil.'"[e] [267]

Keep Praying

He said to them, "Suppose one of you has a friend, and you go to him at midnight and tell him, 'Friend, lend me three loaves of bread, because a friend of mine who is on a journey has come to me, and I do not have anything to set before him.' And the one inside replies, 'Don't bother me. The door is already locked, and my children and I are in bed. I can't get up and give it to you.' I tell you, even if he will not get up and give him anything because he is his friend, yet because of his bold persistence, he will get up and give him as much as he needs.

"I tell you, keep asking, and it will be given to you. Keep seeking, and you will find. Keep knocking, and it will be opened to you. For everyone who asks receives. The one who seeks finds. And to the one who knocks, it will be opened.

"What father among you, if your son asks for bread, would give him a stone? Or if he asks for a fish, would give him a snake instead of a fish? Or if he asks for an egg, would give him a scorpion? If you then, though you are evil, know how to give good gifts to your children, how much more will your heavenly Father give the Holy Spirit to those who ask him?"[268]

---

[a] Some witnesses to the text read *him*.
[b] Some witnesses to the text omit *Our* and *in heaven*.
[c] Some witnesses to the text omit *Your will be done on earth as it is in heaven*.
[d] Literally *everyone who is indebted to us*
[e] A few witnesses to the text omit *but deliver us from evil*. See the footnote on Matthew 6:13 for the traditional ending of the Lord's Prayer.

Woe to Unrepentant Cities

Then Jesus began to denounce the towns in which most of his miracles were performed, because they did not repent. "Woe to you, Chorazin! Woe to you, Bethsaida! For if the miracles which were performed in you had been performed in Tyre and Sidon, they would have repented long ago in sackcloth and ashes. But I tell you, it will be more bearable for Tyre and Sidon on the day of judgment than for you. You, Capernaum, will you be lifted up to heaven? No, you will go down to hell.ᵃ For if the miracles performed in you had been performed in Sodom, it would have remained until this day. But I tell you that it will be more bearable for the land of Sodom on the day of judgment than for you."²⁶⁹

"Come to Me" and "I Will Give You Rest"

At that time, Jesus continued, "I praise you, Father, Lord of heaven and earth, that you have hidden these things from clever and learned people and have revealed them to little children. Yes, Father, because this was pleasing to you. Everything has been entrusted to me by my Father. No one knows the Son except the Father, and no one knows the Father except the Son and anyone to whom the Son wants to reveal him.

"Come to me all you who are weary and burdened, and I will give you rest. Take my yoke upon you and learn from me, because I am gentle and humble in heart, and you will find rest for your souls. For my yoke is easy and my burden is light."²⁷⁰

Jesus Has Power to Drive Out Demons

They wentᵇ into a house. A crowd gathered again so that they were not even able to eat a meal.²⁷¹ Then a demon-possessed man who was blind and unable to speak was brought to him. Jesus healed him so that he was able to speak and to see.²⁷² All the people were amazed and said, "Can this be the Son of David?"ᶜ ²⁷³ When his own peopleᵈ heard this, they went out to take control of him, because they were saying, "He is out of his mind." The experts in the law²⁷⁴ (the Pharisees)²⁷⁵ who came down from Jerusalem were saying, "He is possessed by Beelzebul,"²⁷⁶ They said, "It is only by Beelzebul, the ruler of the demons, that this fellow drives out demons."²⁷⁷

Knowing their thoughts, Jesus²⁷⁸ called them together and spoke to them in parables.²⁷⁹ Jesus said to them, "Every kingdom divided against itself is destroyed, and every town or household divided against itself will not stand. If Satan drives out Satan, he is divided against himself. How then can his kingdom stand?²⁸⁰ He cannot stand but is finished.²⁸¹ You say that I drive out demons by Beelzebul.²⁸² Now if I drive out demons by Beelzebul, by whom do your sons drive them out? Therefore they will be your judges. But if I drive out demons by the Spirit²⁸³ — the

---

ᵃ Greek *hades*
ᵇ A few witnesses to the text read *He went*.
ᶜ Or *Certainly this fellow is not the Son of David, is he?*
ᵈ Or *his family*

finger —²⁸⁴ of God, then the kingdom of God has come upon you.²⁸⁵ Or how can someone enter a strong man's house and take his goods, unless he first ties up the strong man? Only then can he plunder his house.²⁸⁶

"When a strong man, fully armed, guards his own house, his possessions are safe. But when someone stronger attacks him and defeats him, he takes away that man's full armor, in which he had trusted, and divides up his plunder."²⁸⁷

"Whoever is not with me is against me. And whoever does not gather with me scatters.²⁸⁸ Therefore I tell you, people will be forgiven every sin and blasphemy, but the blasphemy against the Spirit will not be forgiven. Whoever speaks a word against the Son of Man will be forgiven, but whoever speaks against the Holy Spirit will not be forgiven—either in this age or in the one to come.²⁸⁹ Jesus said this because they were saying, "He has an unclean spirit."²⁹⁰

"Either make a tree good and its fruit will be good, or make a tree bad and its fruit will be bad. Indeed, a tree is known by its fruit. You offspring of vipers! How can you say anything good, since you are evil? For what the mouth speaks flows from the heart. The good man brings good out of his good treasure, and the evil man brings evil out of his evil treasure. I tell you that on the day of judgment people will give account of every careless word they have spoken. In fact by your words you will be justified, and by your words you will be condemned."²⁹¹

While he was saying these things, a woman from the crowd raised her voice and said to him, "Blessed is the womb that carried you, and the breasts at which you nursed!"

But he said, "Even more blessed are those who hear the word of God and keep it."²⁹²

The Sign of Jonah

Then some of the experts in the law and Pharisees²⁹³ were testing him by demanding of him a sign from heaven.²⁹⁴ [They] replied, "Teacher, we want to see a sign from you."

But²⁹⁵ as the crowds were increasing,²⁹⁶ he answered them, "An evil and adulterous generation wishes for a sign, but no sign will be given it except the sign of Jonah²⁹⁷ the prophet.²⁹⁸ For just as Jonah became a sign to the Ninevites, so also the Son of Man will be to this generation.²⁹⁹ For just as Jonah was in the belly of the huge fish for three days and three nights, so the Son of Man will be three days and three nights in the heart of the earth.³⁰⁰ The men of Nineveh will stand up in the judgment with this generation and condemn it, because they repented at the preaching of Jonah. But one even greater than Jonah is here.³⁰¹ The Queen of the South will be raised up in the judgment with this generation and will condemn it, because she came from the ends of the earth to hear the wisdom of Solomon. But one even greater than Solomon is here."³⁰²

"When an unclean spirit has gone out of someone, it passes through dry places looking for rest, but it does not find it. Then it says, 'I will return to the home I came from,³⁰³ the one I left.'³⁰⁴ And when it has returned, it finds the place empty, swept, and put in order. Then it takes along with it seven other spirits more evil than itself, and they enter in and live there. So the last condition of that person becomes worse than the first.³⁰⁵ That is how it will be for this evil generation too."³⁰⁶

A Lamp and a Lampstand

"No one lights a lamp and puts it in a hidden place or under a basket, but on a stand so that those who come in may see the light. Your eye is the lamp of the body. When your eye is good, your whole body is full of light. But when it is bad, your body is full of darkness. Therefore, see to it that the light that is in you is not darkness. So if your whole body is full of light, without any dark part, it will be completely full of light, as when a lamp shines on you with bright light."³⁰⁷

Jesus' Mother and Brothers

Then his mother and his brothers arrived,³⁰⁸ but they could not get near him because of the crowd³⁰⁹ sitting around him.³¹⁰

While they were standing outside, they sent word to Jesus, calling for him.³¹¹ Someone said to him, "Look, your mother and your brothers are standing outside, wanting to talk to you."³¹²

But he replied to the one who told him, "Who is my mother? And who are my brothers?"³¹³ He looked at those who sat around him in a circle,³¹⁴ reached out his hand toward his disciples and said, "See, my mother and my brothers! For whoever does the will of my Father in heaven is my brother and sister and mother."³¹⁵

Woes and Warnings

After Jesus spoke, a Pharisee invited him to have a meal with him. He went in and reclined at the table. When the Pharisee saw this, he was amazed that he did not first wash[a] before the meal. But the Lord said to him, "Now you Pharisees clean the outside of the cup and dish, but inside you are full of greed and wickedness. Fools! Didn't the one who made the outside also make the inside? But give those things that are inside as a gift to the poor, and see, everything will be clean for you. But woe to you Pharisees, because you give a tenth of mint and rue and every herb, but you neglect justice and the love of God. You should have done these things without neglecting the others. Woe to you Pharisees, because you love the best seat in the synagogues and the greetings in the marketplaces. Woe to you, because you are like unmarked graves, and people walk over them without realizing it."

One of the legal experts answered him, "Teacher, by saying these things you are insulting us too."

But Jesus said, "Woe to you legal experts too, because you load people down with burdens too difficult to carry, and you yourselves do not touch these burdens with one of your fingers. Woe to you because you build monuments for the prophets, but your fathers killed them. So you are witnesses and agree with what your fathers did,

---

[a] Greek *baptizo* (translated *baptize* in other contexts)

because they killed them, and you build their monuments. For this reason the wisdom of God also said, 'I will send them prophets and apostles. Some of them they will kill and persecute, so that this generation may be held responsible for the blood of all the prophets that has been shed from the foundation of the world, from the blood of Abel to the blood of Zechariah, who was killed between the altar and the sanctuary.' Yes, I tell you, it will be charged against this generation. Woe to you legal experts, because you took away the key of knowledge. You yourselves did not enter, and you hindered those who were trying to enter."

When he went away from there, the experts in the law and the Pharisees began to oppose him fiercely and to question him closely about many things. They were plotting against him to trap him in something he said.[a] 316

Warning Against Hypocrisy

Meanwhile, when a crowd of many thousands gathered together so that they were trampling on one another, he began to speak first to his disciples: "Be on your guard against the yeast of the Pharisees, which is hypocrisy. There is nothing concealed that will not be revealed, or hidden that will not be made known. So then, whatever you have said in the dark will be heard in the light, and what you have whispered in the ear in the inner rooms will be proclaimed on the housetops.317

Fear God, Not People

"I tell you, my friends, do not be afraid of those who kill the body and after that are not able to do any more. But I will show you the one you should fear. Fear him who, after he has killed the body, has authority to throw it into hell.[b] Yes, I tell you, fear him!

"Are not five sparrows sold for two small coins?[c] And not one of them is forgotten in God's sight. Why, even the very hairs of your head are all numbered. So stop being afraid. You are worth more than many sparrows.318

Confess Christ

"I tell you, whoever confesses me before other people, the Son of Man will also confess him before the angels of God. But whoever denies me in the presence of other people will be denied in the presence of the angels of God. Everyone who speaks a word against the Son of Man will be forgiven. But anyone who blasphemes against the Holy Spirit will not be forgiven. When they bring you before synagogues, rulers, and authorities, do not worry about how you will defend yourself, or what you will say, for the Holy Spirit will teach you in that very hour what you should say."319

---

[a] Some witnesses to the text add *so they could accuse him*.
[b] *Gehenna*
[c] Greek *assarion*, less than a half hour's wage

The Rich Fool

Someone from the crowd said to him, "Teacher, tell my brother to divide the inheritance with me." But Jesus said to him, "Man, who appointed me to be a judge or an arbitrator over you?"

Then he said to them, "Watch out and be on guard against all greed, because a man's life is not measured by how many possessions he has."

He told them a parable: "The land of a certain rich man produced very well. He was thinking to himself, 'What will I do, because I do not have anywhere to store my crops?' He said, 'This is what I will do. I will pull down my barns and build bigger ones, and there I will store all my grain and goods. And I will tell my soul, "Soul, you have many goods stored up for many years. Take it easy. Eat, drink, and be merry."'

"But God said to him, 'You fool, this night your soul will be demanded from you. Now who will get what you have prepared?'

"That is how it will be for anyone who stores up treasure for himself and is not rich toward God."[320]

Do Not Worry

Jesus said to his disciples, "For that reason I tell you, stop worrying about your life, about what you will eat, or about your body, what you will wear. Certainly life is more than food, and the body is more than clothing. Consider the ravens: They do not sow or reap; they have no warehouse or barn; and yet God feeds them. How much more valuable are you than birds! And who of you by worrying can add a single moment to his lifespan? Since you are not able to do this little thing, why do you worry about the rest? Consider how the wild flowers grow. They do not labor or spin. But I tell you, not even Solomon in all his glory was dressed like one of these. If this is how God clothes the grass in the field, which is alive today and tomorrow is thrown into the furnace, how much more will he clothe you, you of little faith? Do not constantly chase after what you will eat or what you will drink. Do not be worried about it. To be sure, the nations of the world chase after all of these things, but your Father knows that you need them. Instead, continue to seek the kingdom of God, and all these things will be added to you. Do not be afraid, little flock, because your Father is pleased to give you the kingdom. Sell your possessions and give to the needy. Provide money bags for yourselves that do not become old, a treasure in the heavens that will not fail, where no thief comes near and no moth destroys. For where your treasure is, there your heart will be also.[321]

Be Ready!

"Be dressed, ready for service, and keep your lamps burning. Be like people waiting for their master to return from a wedding banquet, so that when he comes and knocks they can immediately open the door for him. Blessed are those servants, whom the master will find watching when he comes. Amen I tell you: He will dress himself and have them recline at the table, and he will come and serve them. Even if he comes in the second or third watch,[a] they will be blessed if he finds them alert. But know this: If the master of the house had known at what hour the thief was coming, he would have watched and not allowed his house to be broken into. You also be ready, because the Son of Man is coming at an hour when you are not expecting him."

Peter said, "Lord, are you telling this parable to us or to everybody?"

The Lord said, "Who then is the faithful and wise manager,[b] whom the master will put in charge of his servants to give them their food allowance at the proper time? Blessed is that servant whom his master will find doing so when he comes. Truly I tell you: He will put him in charge of all his possessions. But if that servant says in his heart, 'My master is staying away for a long time.' And he begins to beat the male and female servants, to eat and drink and become drunk, then the master of that servant will arrive on a day when he was not expected and at an hour that his servant does not know. The master will cut him in two and assign him a place with the unbelievers. That servant who knew his master's will and did not prepare or act according to what his master wanted, will be punished severely. But the one who did not know, and did something worthy of punishment, will be punished lightly. From everyone to whom much was given, much will be expected. From the one who was entrusted with much, much more will be asked.[322]

Division

"I came to throw fire on the earth, and how I wish it were already ignited. But I have a baptism to undergo, and how distressed I am until it is finished! Do you think that I came to bring peace on the earth? No, I tell you, but rather division. Yes, from now on there will be five divided in one household: three against two, and two against three. They will be divided: father against son, and son against father; mother against daughter, and daughter against mother; mother-in-law against her daughter-in-law, and daughter-in-law against her mother-in-law."[c] [323]

Interpret the Time

He also said to the crowds, "Whenever you see a cloud rising in the west, you immediately say that a rainstorm is coming, and so it happens. And whenever a south wind blows, you say that it is going to be hot, and it happens. Hypocrites! You know how to interpret the appearance of the earth and the sky, but how is it that you do not know how to interpret this present time? Why don't you judge for yourselves what is right? Indeed, as you are going with your adversary to the magistrate, make an effort on the way to reach a settlement with him. Otherwise, he may drag you off to the judge, and the judge may hand you over to the officer,

---

[a] That is, in the middle of the night
[b] Or *steward*
[c] Micah 7:6

and the officer may throw you into prison. I tell you, you will never get out of there until you have paid the last cent."a 324

Repent

At that time there were some present who told Jesus about the Galileans whose blood Pilate had mixed with their sacrifices. He answered them, "Do you think that these Galileans were worse sinners than all the other Galileans because they suffered these things? I tell you, no. But unless you repent, you will all perish too. Or those eighteen who were killed when the tower in Siloam fell on them—do you think that they were worse sinners than all the people living in Jerusalem? I tell you, no. But unless you repent, you will all perish too."325

Parable of the Fig Tree

He told them this parable: "A man had a fig tree planted in his vineyard. He came looking for fruit on it, but he did not find any. So he said to the gardener, 'Look, for three years now I have come looking for fruit on this fig tree, and I have found none. Cut it down. Why even let it use up the soil?' But the gardener replied to him, 'Sir, leave it alone this year also, until I dig around it and put fertilizer on it. If it produces fruit next year, fine. But if not, then cut it down.'"326

The Parable of the Sower

That same day Jesus left the house and was sitting by the sea.327 Jesus began to teach.328 A large crowd gathered around him. So he stepped into a boat and sat down, while all the people stood on the shore. He told them many things in parables, saying: "Listen, a sower went out to sow. As he sowed, some seed fell along the path, and the birds came and ate it. Other seed fell on rocky ground, where it did not have much soil. Immediately the seed sprang up, because the soil was not deep. But when the sun rose, the seed was scorched. Because it had no root, it withered away. Other seed fell among thorns. The thorns grew up and choked it,329 so it did not produce fruit. Still other seed fell on good ground and yielded fruit, sprouting and growing and producing a crop: some thirty, some sixty, and some one hundred times as much as was sown." Then Jesus said, "Whoever has ears to hear, let him hear."330

Jesus Explains the Parable of the Sower

When Jesus was alone, those who were around him with the Twelve asked him about the parables.331 The disciples came and said to him, "Why do you speak to them in parables?332 What does this parable mean?"333

He answered them, "To you it has been given to know the mysteries of the kingdom of heaven, but it has not been given to them,334 to those who are outside.335 For whoever has will be given even more, and he will have an abundance. But

---

a Literally *lepton*. One *lepton* was a coin worth about 1/128 of an agricultural worker's daily wages.

whoever does not have, even what he has will be taken away from him. This is why I speak to them in parables, because even though they see, they do not see; and even though they hear, they do not hear or understand.³³⁶ In them the prophecy of Isaiah is fulfilled which says,

> You will hear clearly, but you will never understand. You will see clearly, but you will never perceive. Because this people's heart has grown callous, their ears are hard of hearing. They have closed their eyes. Otherwise they would see with their eyes, hear with their ears, understand with their heart, turn, and I would heal them.ª ³³⁷

"But blessed are your eyes because they see and your ears because they hear. Amen I tell you: Many prophets and righteous people longed to see what you are seeing, but they did not see it. They longed to hear what you are hearing, but they did not hear it.³³⁸

Then he asked them, "Do you not understand this parable? How then will you understand any of the parables?³³⁹ So listen carefully to the parable of the sower.³⁴⁰ The seed is the word of God.³⁴¹ When anyone hears the word of the kingdom and does not understand it, the Evil One comes and snatches away what has been sown in his heart,³⁴² to keep [him] from believing and being saved.³⁴³ This is the seed that was sown along the path. The seed that was sown on rocky ground is the person who hears the word and immediately receives it with joy, yet he is not deeply rooted and does not endure. When trouble or persecution comes because of the word, he immediately falls away. The seed that was sown among the thorns is the one who hears the word, but the worry of this world, the deceitfulness of wealth,³⁴⁴ and pleasures of life³⁴⁵ choke the word, and it produces no fruit.³⁴⁶ [It does] not mature. And the seeds in the good ground are the ones who hear the word with an honest and good heart,³⁴⁷ accept³⁴⁸ and understand the word,³⁴⁹ hold on to it tightly, and produce fruit as they patiently endure.³⁵⁰ Indeed he continues to produce fruit: some a hundred, some sixty, and some thirty times more than was sown."³⁵¹

A Lamp and a Lampstand

He also said to them, "A lamp is not brought out to be put under a basket or under a bed, is it? Isn't it placed on a lampstand? For there is nothing hidden that will not be revealed, and nothing concealed that will not come to light. If anyone has ears to hear, let him hear."³⁵²

He went on to tell them, "Pay attention to what you hear. With the same measure you use, it will be measured to you, and more will be given to you. Yes, whoever has will be given more. And whoever does not have, even what he has will be taken away from him."³⁵³

ª Isaiah 6:9-10

Seed Sprouts and Grows

He said, "The kingdom of God is like this: A man scatters seed on the ground, and while he sleeps and rises, night and day, the seed sprouts and grows, though he does not know how. The ground produces fruit on its own: first the blade, then the head, then the full grain in the head. When the crop is ready, he swings the sickle without delay, because the harvest has come."[354]

The Parable of the Weeds

He presented another parable to them: "The kingdom of heaven is like a man who sowed good seed in his field. But while people were sleeping, his enemy came and sowed weeds among the wheat and went away. When the plants sprouted and produced heads of grain, the weeds also appeared. The servants of the owner came and said to him, 'Sir, did you not sow good seed in your field? Where did the weeds come from?' He said to them, 'An enemy did this.' The servants asked him, 'Do you want us to go and gather up the weeds?' 'No,' he answered, 'because when you gather up the weeds, you might pull up the wheat along with them. Let both grow together until the harvest, and at harvest time I will tell the reapers, "First, gather up the weeds, bind them in bundles, and burn them. Then, gather the wheat into my barn."'"[355]

Mustard Seed and Yeast

He presented another parable to them.[356] He said, "To what should we compare the kingdom of God? Or with what parable may we picture it?[357] The kingdom of heaven is like a mustard seed, which a man took and planted in his field. It is one of the smallest of seeds. But when it grows, it is larger than the other plants and becomes a tree, so that the birds of the air come and nest in its branches[358] under its shade."[359]

He spoke another parable to them: "The kingdom of heaven is like yeast, which a woman took and mixed into a bushel [a] of flour until the whole batch was leavened."[360]

With many similar parables he continued to speak the word to them, as much as they were able to hear. He did not speak to them without a parable. But when he was alone with his disciples, he explained everything to them.[361] This was to fulfill what was spoken through the prophet:

> I will open my mouth in parables,
> I will utter things hidden since the foundation of the world.[b] [362]

---

[a] *Three seahs*
[b] Psalm 78:2

Jesus Explains the Parable of the Weeds

Then Jesus sent the people away and went into the house. His disciples came to him and said, "Explain to us the parable of the weeds in the field."

He answered them, "The one who sows the good seed is the Son of Man. The field is the world. The good seeds are the sons of the kingdom. The weeds are the sons of the Evil One. The enemy who sowed them is the Devil. The harvest is the end of the world. The reapers are angels. Therefore, just as the weeds are gathered up and burned with fire, so it will be at the end of the world. The Son of Man will send out his angels, and they will pull out of his kingdom everything that causes sin[a] and those who continue to break the law. The angels will throw them into the fiery furnace where there will be weeping and gnashing of teeth. Then the righteous will shine like the sun in the kingdom of their Father. Whoever has ears to hear, let him hear.[363]

The Treasure, the Pearl, and the Net

"The kingdom of heaven is like a treasure hidden in a field, which a man found and hid again. In his joy, he goes away and sells all that he has and buys that field.

"Again, the kingdom of heaven is like a merchant seeking fine pearls. When he found one very valuable pearl, he went and sold all that he had and bought it.

"Again, the kingdom of heaven is like a dragnet that was cast into the sea and gathered fish of every kind. When the net was filled, they pulled it onto the shore. They sat down and gathered the good fish into containers, but threw the bad ones away. That is how it will be at the end of the world. The angels will go out and separate the wicked from the righteous who are among them. And they will throw the wicked into the fiery furnace where there will be weeping and gnashing of teeth."

Jesus said to them, "Did you understand all these things?"

They answered him, "Yes."

He said to them, "Therefore every expert in the law who has been trained as a disciple in the kingdom of heaven is like the owner of a house who brings out of his treasure both new things and old things."

When Jesus had finished these parables, he left that place.[364]

Follow Jesus

When Jesus saw a large crowd gathering around him, he gave orders to go over to the other shore.

Then an expert in the law came and said to him, "Teacher, I will follow you wherever you go."

Jesus said to him, "Foxes have holes, and birds of the air have nests, but the Son of Man has nowhere to lay his head."

Another of his disciples said to him, "Lord, first let me go and bury my father."

But Jesus told him, "Follow me, and let the dead bury their own dead."[365]

---

[a] Greek *skandalon* can refer to a temptation to sin.

Jesus Calms the Storm

On that day, when evening came,366 Jesus got into a boat with his disciples and told them, "Let's go over to the other side of the lake." So they set out.367 After leaving the crowd behind, the disciples took him along in the boat, just as he was. Other small boats also followed him.368 Suddenly369 a great windstorm arose, and the waves were splashing into the boat, so that the boat was quickly filling up. Jesus himself was in the stern, sleeping on a cushion.370 They went and woke him, saying, "Lord, save us! We're going to die!"371 They said, "Teacher, don't you care that we are about to drown?"372

He said to them, "Why are you so afraid? Do you still lack faith?"373 Then he got up, rebuked the wind, and said to the sea, "Peace! Be still!" The wind stopped, and there was a great calm.374

They were afraid and375 filled with awe and said to one another, "Who then is this? Even the wind and the sea obey him!"376

Two Demon-Possessed Men and a Herd of Pigs

They sailed down to the region of the Gerasenes,[a] which is across from Galilee.377 When [Jesus] arrived at the other side, in the region of the Gergesenes378—as soon as [he] stepped379 ashore380 out of the boat381—two demon-possessed men coming from the tombs met him there. They were very dangerous, so that nobody could pass that way. Suddenly they cried out, "What do we have to do with you, Son of God? Have you come here to torment us before the time?"382

[One of them in particular] for a long time had not worn any clothes. He did not live in a house but in the tombs.383 Nobody could bind him anymore, not even with a chain.384 In fact, the unclean spirit had seized him many times. He was kept under guard, and although he was bound with chains and shackles, he would break the restraints and was driven by the demon into deserted places.385 Nobody had the strength to subdue him. Night and day, in the tombs and in the mountains, he was constantly crying out and cutting himself with stones.386 When he saw Jesus from a distance, he ran and bowed down in front of him. He cried out with a loud voice, "What do I have to do with you, Jesus, Son of the Most High God? I beg you to swear by God not to torment me." For Jesus had said to him, "Come out of the man, you unclean spirit!"

Jesus asked him, "What is your name?"

"My name is Legion," he replied, "because we are many." He begged Jesus repeatedly that he would not send them out of the region387 to the abyss.388

There was a large herd of pigs there feeding on the hillside. The demons begged him, "Send us to the pigs so we may enter them."

Jesus gave them permission.389 He told them, "Go!"

So the demons came out of the men and went into the pigs.390 Then the herd of about two thousand pigs rushed down the steep bank into the sea and drowned.

---

[a] Some witnesses to the text read *Gadarenes*; others read *Gergesenes*.

Those who were feeding the pigs ran and reported this in the city and the countryside.³⁹¹

People went out to see what had happened. They came to Jesus and found the man from whom the demons had gone out, sitting at Jesus' feet. He was clothed and in his right mind, and the people were afraid. Those who saw it told them how the demon-possessed man was saved. The whole crowd of people from the surrounding country of the Gerasenes^a asked Jesus to leave them, because they were gripped with great fear.

As Jesus got into the boat and started back, the man from whom the demons had gone out begged to be with him. ³⁹² But Jesus would not let him. Instead, he told him, "Go home to your people, and tell them everything the Lord has done for you and how he had mercy on you."

The man left and began to proclaim in the Decapolis everything Jesus had done for him. And everyone was amazed.³⁹³

Jesus got into a boat, crossed over, and came to his own town.³⁹⁴ When Jesus returned, the crowd welcomed him, because they were all waiting for him.³⁹⁵

Jesus Sends Out the Twelve

Jesus called the Twelve^b together and gave them power and authority over all demons and to cure diseases. He sent them out to proclaim the kingdom of God and to heal the sick. He said to them, "Take nothing for the journey—no staff, no bag, no bread, no money."³⁹⁶

Jesus sent these twelve out and commanded them, "Do not go among the Gentiles, and do not enter any town of the Samaritans. Go instead to the lost sheep of the house of Israel. As you go, preach this message: 'The kingdom of heaven is near!' Heal the sick. Raise the dead. Cleanse lepers. Drive out demons. Freely you have received; freely give. Do not take gold, silver, or bronze in your money belts. Do not take a bag for the journey, or two coats, sandals, or a staff, because the worker deserves his support. Whenever you enter a town or village, find out who is worthy and stay there until you leave. As you enter the household, give it your greeting. If the household is worthy, let your peace rest on it. But if it is not worthy, let your peace return to you. If anyone does not receive you or listen to your words, shake the dust off your feet as you leave that house or that town³⁹⁷ as a testimony against them.³⁹⁸ Amen I tell you: It will be more bearable for the land of Sodom and Gomorrah on the day of judgment than for that town.

"Look, I am sending you out as sheep among wolves. So be as shrewd as snakes and as innocent as doves. Be on guard against people. They will hand you over to councils, and they will whip you in their synagogues. You will be brought into the presence of governors and kings for my sake, as a testimony to them and to the Gentiles. Whenever they hand you over, do not be worried about how you will

---

^a Some witnesses to the text read *Gadarenes*; others read *Gergesenes*.
^b Some witnesses to the text read *twelve apostles*.

respond or what you will say, because what you say will be given to you in that hour. In fact you will not be the ones speaking, but the Spirit of your Father will be speaking through you.

"Brother will hand over his brother to death, and a father will do the same with his child. Children will rise up against parents and have them put to death. You will be hated by all people because of my name, but whoever endures to the end will be saved. And when they persecute you in one town, flee to the next. Amen I tell you: You will not finish going through the cities of Israel before the Son of Man comes.

"A disciple is not above his teacher, nor is a servant above his master. It is enough for the disciple to be like his teacher and the servant like his master. If the master of the house was called Beelzebul, how much more the members of his household!

"So do not be afraid of them, because there is nothing concealed that will not be revealed, and nothing hidden that will not be made known. What I tell you in the dark, speak in the daylight; and what you hear whispered in your ear, proclaim from the housetops. Do not fear those who kill the body but cannot kill the soul. Rather, fear the one who is able to destroy both soul and body in hell.

"Are not two sparrows sold for a small coin?[a] Yet not one of them will fall to the ground without the knowledge and consent of your Father. And even the hairs of your head are all numbered. So do not be afraid. You are worth more than many sparrows.

"Everyone who confesses me before others, I will also confess before my Father who is in heaven. But whoever denies me before others, I will also deny before my Father who is in heaven.

"Do not think that I came to bring peace to the earth. I did not come to bring peace, but a sword. For I came to turn a man against his father, a daughter against her mother, and a daughter-in-law against her mother-in-law. A man's enemies will be the members of his own household.[b]

"Whoever loves father or mother more than me is not worthy of me, and whoever loves son or daughter more than me is not worthy of me. Whoever does not take up his cross and follow me is not worthy of me. Whoever finds his life will lose it, and whoever loses his life for my sake will find it.

"Whoever receives you receives me, and whoever receives me receives him who sent me. Whoever receives a prophet because he is a prophet will receive a prophet's reward. Whoever receives a righteous man because he is a righteous man will receive a righteous man's reward. Whoever gives one of these little ones even a cup of cold water to drink because he is my disciple—Amen I tell you—he will never lose his reward."[399]

After Jesus had finished instructing his twelve disciples, he moved on from there to teach and preach in their towns.[400] They set out and went throughout the villages, proclaiming the good news and healing everywhere.[401] They went out and preached

---

[a] Greek *assarion*, less than a half hour's wage
[b] Micah 7:6

that people should repent. They also drove out many demons. They anointed many sick people with oil and healed them.[402]

Recalling the Death of John the Baptist

At that time, Herod the tetrarch heard[403] about this because Jesus' name had become well known.[404] He said to his servants, "This is John the Baptist,[405] the man I beheaded![406] He has risen from the dead! That is why these powers are working in him."[407]

But Herod said, "I beheaded John, but who is this, about whom I hear such great things?" So he wanted to see him. But Herod said, "I beheaded John, but who is this, about whom I hear such great things?" So he wanted to see him.[408]

For it was Herod who had sent men to arrest John. He had him bound in prison because Herod had married Herodias, the wife of his brother Philip. Indeed, John had been telling him, "It is not lawful for you to have your brother's wife."[409]

Herodias held a grudge against John and wanted to put him to death, but she could not, because Herod feared John.[410] Although Herod wanted to put him to death, he feared the crowd, because they regarded him as a prophet.[411] He knew that John was a righteous and holy man, so he kept him safe. When Herod listened to John, he was perplexed in many ways, yet he gladly kept listening to him.

An opportune day came when it was Herod's birthday. He gave a banquet for his nobles, the military officers, and the prominent men of Galilee. When the daughter of Herodias came in and danced, she pleased Herod and his guests. The king said to the girl, "Ask me whatever you want, and I will give it to you." With an oath he promised her, "Whatever you ask of me, I will give you, up to half of my kingdom."

She went out and said to her mother, "What should I ask for?"

Herodias said, "The head of John the Baptizer."

The girl hurried right back to the king and made her request: "I want you to give me the head of John the Baptist on a platter right now."

The king was very sad. But because of his oaths and his dinner guests, he did not want to refuse her. The king sent an executioner at once and ordered him to bring John's head. He went, beheaded John in prison, brought his head on a platter, and gave it to the girl. Then the girl gave it to her mother.

When John's disciples heard about this, they came and took his body and laid it in a tomb.[412] Then they went and reported this to Jesus.[413]

Jesus Feeds More Than Five Thousand

When Jesus heard this, he withdrew from there.[414] The apostles returned,[415] gathered around Jesus, and reported to him all that they had done and taught. He said to them, "Come away by yourselves to a secluded place and rest a while." For there were so many people coming and going that they did not even have a chance to eat. They went away in the boat to a deserted place by themselves.[416] He took them and withdrew privately[417] to the other side of the Sea of Galilee (or Tiberias)[418] to a town called Bethsaida.[419] A large crowd followed him because they saw the miraculous signs he was performing on those who were sick.[420] Many people saw them leave and knew where they were going. They ran there on foot from all the towns and arrived ahead of them. When Jesus stepped out of the boat, he saw a large crowd. His heart went out to them because they were like sheep without a shepherd.[421] Jesus went up on the hillside and sat down there with his disciples. The Jewish Passover Festival was near.[422] He welcomed [the crowd] and spoke to them about the kingdom of God.[423] He began to teach them many things. It was already late in the day when his disciples came to him and said, "This is a deserted place and it is already very late. Send them away so they can go into the surrounding country and villages and buy themselves something to eat."[424]

But Jesus said to them, "They do not need to go away. You give them something to eat."[425] He asked Philip, "Where can we buy bread for these people to eat?" But Jesus was saying this to test him, for he himself knew what he was going to do.

Philip answered him, "Two hundred denarii[a] worth of bread would not be enough for each of them to have just a little."[426]

He said to them, "How many loaves do you have? Go see."[427]

One of his disciples, Andrew, Simon Peter's brother, said to him, "There's a boy here who has five barley loaves and two fish, but what is that for so many people?"[428]

"Bring them here to me," he replied.[429]

He said to his disciples, "Have them sit down in groups of about fifty each." They did so and got them all to sit down.[430]

There was plenty of grass in that place, so[431] they sat down [on the green grass] in groups of hundreds and fifties. Jesus took the five loaves and the two fish, looked up to heaven, and blessed the loaves and broke them. Then he kept giving pieces to his disciples to set in front of them,[432] as much as they wanted.[433] He also divided the two fish among them all. They all ate and were satisfied.

When the people were full, he told his disciples, "Gather the pieces that are left over so that nothing is wasted." So they gathered them and filled twelve baskets with pieces from the five barley loaves[434] and fish[435] left over by those who had eaten.[436] Those who ate were about five thousand men, not even counting women and children.[437]

When the people saw the miraculous sign Jesus did, they said, "This really is the Prophet who is coming into the world."[438]

Jesus Walks on Water

When Jesus realized that they intended to come and take him by force to make him king, he withdrew again to the mountain by himself.[439]

Immediately Jesus urged the disciples to get into the boat and to go ahead of him[440] to Capernaum across the sea[441] [from] Bethsaida,[442] while he dismissed the crowd. After he had dismissed the crowd, he went up onto the mountain by himself

---

[a] Or *two hundred days' wages*. A denarius was worth about one day's wage.

to pray. When evening came, he was there alone.⁴⁴³ It was already dark, and Jesus had not yet come to them. A strong wind started to blow, and the sea became rough.⁴⁴⁴ By then the boat was quite a distance from shore⁴⁴⁵ —they had rowed about three or four miles—⁴⁴⁶ in the middle of the sea,⁴⁴⁷ being pounded by the waves.⁴⁴⁸ He saw them straining at the oars, because the wind was against them. About the fourth watch of the night,[a] he went to them, walking on the sea. He was ready to pass by them.⁴⁴⁹

When the disciples saw him walking on the sea, they were terrified and cried out in fear, "It's a ghost!" But Jesus spoke to them at once, saying, "Take heart! It is I! Do not be afraid."

Peter answered him and said, "Lord, if it is you, command me to come to you on the water."

Jesus said, "Come!"

Peter stepped down from the boat, walked on the water, and went toward Jesus. But when he saw the strong wind, he was afraid. As he began to sink, he cried out, "Lord, save me!"

Immediately Jesus stretched out his hand, took hold of him, and said to him, "You of little faith, why did you doubt?"⁴⁵⁰ Then they were willing to take him into the boat.⁴⁵¹ He climbed into the boat with them, and the wind stopped.⁴⁵² And immediately the boat reached the shore where they were heading.⁴⁵³ They were completely amazed, because they had not understood about the loaves. Instead, their hearts were hardened.⁴⁵⁴ Those who were in the boat worshipped him, saying, "Truly you are the Son of God!"⁴⁵⁵

When they had crossed over, they landed at Gennesaret and anchored there. As soon as they stepped out of the boat, people recognized Jesus. They ran around that whole region and began to bring sick people on their stretchers to where they heard he was. Wherever he entered villages, cities, or the countryside, they were laying sick people in the marketplaces and pleading with him that they might just touch the edge of his garment. And all who touched it were made well.⁴⁵⁶

Bread from Heaven

The next day, the crowd that stayed on the other side of the sea noticed that only one boat[b] was there. They also knew that Jesus had not stepped into the boat with his disciples, but they had gone away without him. Other boats from Tiberias came to shore near the place where they ate the bread after the Lord gave thanks. When the crowd saw that neither Jesus nor his disciples were there, they got into the boats and went to Capernaum looking for Jesus. When they found him on the other side of the sea, they asked him, "Rabbi, when did you get here?"

Jesus answered them, "Amen, Amen, I tell you: You are not looking for me because you saw the miraculous signs, but because you ate the loaves and were filled. Do

---

[a] Between 3 AM and 6 AM
[b] Some witnesses to the text add *which his disciples entered*.

not continue to work for the food that spoils, but for the food that endures to eternal life, which the Son of Man will give you. For on him God the Father has placed his seal of approval."

So they said to him, "What should we do to carry out the works of God?"

Jesus answered them, "This is the work of God: that you believe in the one he sent."

Then they asked him, "So what miraculous sign are you going to do, that we may see it and believe you? What miraculous sign are you going to perform? Our fathers ate the manna in the wilderness, just as it is written, 'He gave them bread from heaven to eat.'"[a]

Jesus said to them, "Amen, Amen, I tell you: Moses did not give you the bread from heaven, but my Father gives you the real bread from heaven. For the bread of God is the one who comes down from heaven and gives life to the world."

"Sir," they said to him, "give us this bread all the time!"

"I am the Bread of Life," Jesus told them. "The one who comes to me will never be hungry, and the one who believes in me will never be thirsty. But I said to you that you have also seen me, and you do not believe. Everyone the Father gives me will come to me, and the one who comes to me I will never cast out. For I have come down from heaven, not to do my will, but the will of him who sent me. And this is the will of him who sent me: that I should lose none of those he has given me, but raise them up on the Last Day. For this is the will of my Father: that everyone who sees the Son and believes in him may have eternal life. And I will raise him up on the Last Day."

So the Jews started grumbling about him, because he said, "I am the bread that came down from heaven." They asked, "Isn't this Jesus, the son of Joseph, whose father and mother we know? So how can he say,[b] 'I have come down from heaven'?"

Jesus answered them, "Stop grumbling among yourselves. No one can come to me unless the Father who sent me draws him. And I will raise him up on the Last Day. It is written in the Prophets, 'They will all be taught by God.'[c] Everyone who listens to the Father and learns from him comes to me. I am not saying that anyone has seen the Father except the one who is from God. He is the one who has seen the Father. Amen, Amen, I tell you: The one who believes in me[d] has eternal life.

"I am the Bread of Life. Your fathers ate manna in the wilderness, and they died. This is the bread that comes down from heaven, so that anyone may eat it and not die. I am the living bread which came down from heaven. If anyone eats this bread, he will live forever. The bread that I will give for the life of the world is my flesh."

At that, the Jews argued among themselves, "How can this man give us his[e] flesh to eat?"

---

[a] Psalm 78:24
[b] Some witnesses to the text read *How can he now say.*
[c] Isaiah 54:13
[d] A few witnesses to the text omit *in me.*
[e] Some witnesses to the text omit *his.*

So Jesus said to them, "Amen, Amen, I tell you: Unless you eat the flesh of the Son of Man and drink his blood, you do not have life in yourselves. The one who eats my flesh and drinks my blood has eternal life, and I will raise him up on the Last Day. For my flesh is real food, and my blood is real drink. The one who eats my flesh and drinks my blood remains in me, and I in him. Just as the living Father sent me and I live because of the Father, so the one who feeds on me will live because of me. This is the bread that came down from heaven, not like your[a] fathers ate and died. The one who eats this bread will live forever."

He said these things while teaching in the synagogue in Capernaum. When they heard it, many of his disciples said, "This is a hard teaching! Who can listen to it?"

But Jesus, knowing in himself that his disciples were grumbling about this, asked them, "Does this cause you to stumble in your faith? What if you would see the Son of Man ascending to where he was before? The Spirit is the one who gives life. The flesh does not help at all. The words that I have spoken to you are spirit and they are life. But there are some of you who do not believe." For Jesus knew from the beginning those who would not believe and the one who would betray him. He said, "This is why I told you that no one can come to me unless it is given to him by my Father."

After this, many of his disciples turned back and were not walking with him anymore. So Jesus asked the Twelve, "You do not want to leave too, do you?"

Simon Peter answered him, "Lord, to whom will we go? You have the words of eternal life. We have come to believe and know that you are the Holy One of God."[b]

Jesus answered them, "Did I not choose you, the Twelve? Yet one of you is a devil!" He meant Judas, son of Simon Iscariot, one of the Twelve, because Judas was going to betray Jesus.

After this, Jesus moved around in Galilee. He did not want to travel in Judea because the Jews were trying to find a way to kill him.457

Up to Jerusalem

Now the Jewish Festival of Shelters[c] was near. So his brothers said to him, "You should leave here and go to Judea so your disciples there can also see the works you are doing. Indeed, no one acts in secret who wants to be known in public. If you are doing these things, show yourself to the world." For even his own brothers did not believe in him.

So Jesus told them, "The right time for me has not arrived yet, but any time is the right time for you. The world cannot hate you, but it hates me, because I testify about it, that its works are evil. You go up to the festival. I am not going up to this festival yet,[d] because the right time for me has not yet arrived."

---

[a] Some witnesses to the text read *the manna* before *your*.
[b] Some witnesses to the text read the same as Matthew 16:16, replacing *Holy One of God* with *Christ, the Son of the living God*.
[c] Traditionally *Tabernacles*
[d] Some witnesses to the text omit *yet*.

After he said this, he stayed in Galilee. However, after his brothers had gone up to the festival, then he also went up, not openly but in a private way.[458]

Chapter VII: Before Abraham Was Born, I Am.
In Judea for the Feast of Shelters

At the Feast of Shelters[a]

At the festival, the Jews kept looking for him. They asked, "Where is he?" And there was widespread whispering about him in the crowds. Some were saying, "He's a good man." Others were saying, "No, he deceives the people." Yet no one spoke openly about him for fear of the Jews.

When the festival was already half over, Jesus went up to the temple courts and began to teach. The Jews were amazed and asked, "How does this man know what is written without being instructed?"

Jesus answered them, "My teaching is not mine, but it comes from him who sent me. If anyone wants to do his will, he will know whether my teaching is from God or if I speak on my own. The one who speaks on his own is seeking his own glory. But he who seeks the glory of the one who sent him—that is the one who is true, and there is no unrighteousness in him. Didn't Moses give you the law? Yet none of you does what the law tells you. Why are you trying to kill me?"

"You have a demon!" the crowd answered. "Who is trying to kill you?"

Jesus answered them, "I did one work, and you are all amazed. Consider this: Because Moses has given you circumcision (not that it comes from Moses, but from the fathers), you circumcise a man even on the Sabbath. If a man receives circumcision on the Sabbath so that the law of Moses may not be broken, are you angry at me because I made a man completely well on the Sabbath? Stop judging by outward appearance. Instead make a right judgment."

Some of the people from Jerusalem were saying, "Isn't this the man they want to kill? Yet, look! He's speaking openly, and they don't say a thing to him. Certainly the rulers have not concluded that he is the Christ, have they? But we know where this man is from. When the Christ comes, no one will know where he is from."

Then Jesus called out as he was teaching in the temple courts, "Yes, you know me, and you know where I am from. Yet I have not come on my own, but the one who sent me is real. You do not know him. I know him because I am from him, and he sent me."

---

[a] Traditionally *Tabernacles*

So they tried to arrest him, but no one laid a hand on him, because his time had not yet come.

But many in the crowd believed in him and asked, "When the Christ comes, he won't do more miraculous signs than this man, will he?"

The Pharisees heard the crowd whispering these things about him, so the chief priests and the Pharisees sent guards to arrest him.

Then Jesus said, "I am going to be with you only a little while longer. Then I am going away to the one who sent me. You will be looking for me and will not find me, and where I am going to be, you cannot come."

Then the Jews said to one another, "Where does this man intend to go that we will not find him? He does not intend to go to the Jews scattered among the Greeks and teach the Greeks, does he? What does he mean by saying, 'You will be looking for me and will not find me, and where I am going to be, you cannot come'?"

On the last and most important day of the festival, Jesus stood up and called out, "If anyone is thirsty, let him come to me and drink! As the Scripture has said, streams of living water will flow from deep within the person who believes in me." By this he meant the Spirit, whom those who believed in him were going to receive. For the Holy[a] Spirit had not yet come, because Jesus had not yet been glorified.

After hearing his words, some of the people said, "This is truly the Prophet." Others said, "This is the Christ." But some said, "Surely the Christ does not come from Galilee, does he? Doesn't the Scripture say that the Christ comes from David's descendants and from the little town of Bethlehem where David lived?" So the people were divided because of him. Some of them wanted to arrest him, but no one laid hands on him.

Then the guards came to the chief priests and Pharisees, who asked them, "Why didn't you bring him in?"

The guards answered, "No one ever spoke the way this man does!"

So the Pharisees answered them, "You have not been deceived too, have you? Have any of the rulers or Pharisees believed in him? But this crowd, which does not know the law, is cursed!"

One of them, Nicodemus, who had come to Jesus earlier, asked, "Does our law condemn a man before we hear from him and find out what he's doing?"

"You are not from Galilee too, are you?" they replied. "Search and you will see that a prophet does not come from Galilee."

Then each of them went home.[b] 459

---

[a] Some witnesses to the text omit *Holy*.

[b] Some witnesses to the text omit 7:53–8:11 or include these verses in other places within John's Gospel. The witnesses that include these verses are early and widespread throughout most of the early church.

The Adulteress

But Jesus went to the Mount of Olives. Early in the morning, he came back into the temple courts. And all the people kept coming to him. He sat down and taught them.

Then the scribes and Pharisees brought a woman caught in adultery and had her stand in the center. "Teacher," they said to him, "this woman was caught in the act of committing adultery. In the Law, Moses commanded us to stone such women. So what do you say?" They asked this to test him, so that they might have evidence to accuse him.

Jesus bent down and started writing on the ground with his finger. But when they kept on asking him for an answer, he stood up and said to them, "Let the one among you who is without sin be the first to throw a stone at her." Then he stooped down again and wrote on the ground.

When they heard this, they went away one by one, beginning with the older men. Jesus was left alone with the woman in the center. Jesus stood up and said to her, "Woman, where are they? Has no one condemned you?"

"No one, Lord," she answered.

Then Jesus said, "Neither do I condemn you. Go, and from now on do not sin anymore."[460]

Jesus Is the Light of the World

When Jesus spoke to them again, he said, "I am the Light of the World. Whoever follows me will never walk in darkness, but will have the light of life."

So the Pharisees said to him, "You testify about yourself. Your testimony is not valid."

"Even if I testify about myself," Jesus replied, "my testimony is valid, because I know where I came from and where I am going. But you do not know where I came from or where I am going. You judge according to the flesh. I am not judging anyone. But even if I were to judge, my judgment would be true, because I am not alone, but I am with the Father who sent me. Even in your Law it is written that the testimony of two people is valid. I am one who testifies about myself, and the Father who sent me testifies about me."

Then they asked him, "Where is your Father?"

"You do not know me or my Father," Jesus answered. "If you knew me, you would also know my Father."

He spoke these words while teaching in the temple area near the offering box. But no one arrested him, because his time had not arrived yet.

So he told them again, "I am going away. You will look for me, and you will die in your sin. Where I am going, you cannot come."

So the Jews asked, "He won't kill himself, will he, because he says, 'Where I am going, you cannot come'?"

"You are from below," he told them. "I am from above. You are of this world. I am not of this world. That is why I told you that you will die in your sins. For if you do not believe that I am the one, you will die in your sins."

"Who are you?" they asked.

Jesus replied, "What I have been telling you from the beginning. I have many things to say and to judge concerning you. But the one who sent me is true. And what I heard from him, these are the things I am telling the world." They did not understand that he was talking to them about the Father.

So Jesus said to them, "When you lift up the Son of Man, then you will know that I am the one, and that I do nothing on my own. But I speak exactly as the Father taught me. The one who sent me is with me. He has not left me alone, because I always do what pleases him."

As he was saying these things, many believed in him.

So Jesus said to the Jews who had believed him, "If you remain in my word, you are really my disciples. You will also know the truth, and the truth will set you free."

"We are Abraham's descendants," they answered, "and we have never been slaves of anyone. How can you say, 'You will be set free'?"

Jesus answered, "Amen, Amen, I tell you: Everyone who keeps committing sin is a slave to sin. But a slave does not remain in the family forever. A son does remain forever. So if the Son sets you free, you really will be free. I know you are Abraham's descendants. Yet you are looking for a way to kill me, because there is no place for my word in you. I am telling you what I have seen at the side of the Father. As for you, you do what you have heard[a] at the side of your father."

"Our father is Abraham!" they answered.

"If you were Abraham's children," Jesus told them, "you would do the works of Abraham. But now you are looking for a way to kill me, a man who has told you the truth, which I heard at the side of God. Abraham did not do this. You are doing the works of your father."

"We were not born of sexual immorality!" they said. "We have one Father: God."

Jesus replied, "If God were your Father, you would love me, because I came from God and I am here. Indeed, I have not come on my own, but he sent me. Why do you not understand my message? It is because you are not able to listen to my word. You belong to your father, the Devil, and you want to do your father's desires. He was a murderer from the beginning and did not remain standing in the truth, because there is no truth in him. Whenever he lies, he speaks from what is his, because he is a liar and the father of lying. But because I tell the truth, you do not believe me. Who of you can convict me of sin? If I am telling the truth, why don't you believe me? Whoever belongs to God listens to what God says. The reason you do not listen is that you do not belong to God."

The Jews responded, "Are we not right in saying that you are a Samaritan and have a demon?"

---

[a] Some witnesses to the text read *seen*.

Jesus answered, "I do not have a demon. On the contrary, I honor my Father, and you dishonor me. I do not seek my own glory. There is one who seeks it, and he is the judge. Amen, Amen, I tell you: If anyone holds on to my word, he will certainly never see death."

So the Jews said to him, "Now we know that you have a demon. Abraham died, and so did the prophets. Yet you say, 'If anyone holds on to my word, he will certainly never taste death.' You are not greater than our father, Abraham, are you? He died. And the prophets died. Who do you think you are?"

Jesus answered, "If I glorify myself, my glory is nothing. It is my Father who glorifies me, about whom you say, 'He is our God.' Yet you do not really know him, but I do know him. If I said, 'I do not know him,' I would be a liar like you. But I do know him, and I hold on to his word. Your father Abraham was glad that he would see my day. He saw it and rejoiced."

The Jews replied, "You aren't even fifty years old, and you have seen Abraham?"

Jesus said to them, "Amen, Amen, I tell you: Before Abraham was born, I am." Then they picked up stones to throw at him. But Jesus was hidden and left the temple area.[a] 461

A Blind Man Sees

As Jesus was passing by, he saw a man blind from birth. His disciples asked him, "Rabbi, who sinned, this man or his parents, that he was born blind?"

Jesus answered, "It was not that this man sinned, or his parents, but that God's works might be revealed in connection with him. I[b] must do the works of him who sent me while it is day. Night is coming when no one can work. As long as I am in the world, I am the Light of the World."

After saying this, Jesus spit on the ground, made some mud with the saliva, and spread the mud on the man's eyes. "Go," Jesus told him, "wash in the pool of Siloam" (which means "Sent"). So he went and washed, and came back seeing.

His neighbors and those who had seen him before this as a beggar asked, "Isn't this the one who used to sit and beg?"

Some said, "He is the one." Others said, "No, but he looks like him." He kept saying, "I am the one!"

So they asked him, "How were your eyes opened?"

He answered, "The man who is called Jesus made mud, spread it on my eyes, and told me, 'Go to Siloam and wash.' So I went and washed, and then I could see."

"Where is he?" they asked.

"I don't know," he said.

They brought this man who had been blind to the Pharisees. Now it was a Sabbath day when Jesus made the mud and opened his eyes. So the Pharisees also asked him how he received his sight.

---

[a] Some witnesses to the text add *He went through the middle of them and so went on his way*. See Luke 4:30.

[b] Some witnesses to the text read *We*.

"He put mud on my eyes," the man told them. "I washed, and now I see."

Then some of the Pharisees said, "This man is not from God because he does not keep the Sabbath." Others were saying, "How can a sinful man work such miraculous signs?"

There was division among them, so they said to the blind man again, "What do you say about him, because he opened your eyes?"

The man replied, "He is a prophet."

The Jews still did not believe that he had been blind and received his sight, until they summoned the parents of the man who had received his sight. They asked them, "Is this your son, the one you say was born blind? How is it, then, that he can see now?"

"We know that this is our son," his parents answered, "and that he was born blind. But we do not know how he can see now, or who opened his eyes. Ask him. He is old enough. He will speak for himself." His parents said these things because they were afraid of the Jews. For the Jews had already agreed that anyone who confessed that Jesus was the Christ would be put out of the synagogue. That is why his parents said, "He is old enough. Ask him."

So for a second time they summoned the man who had been blind. They told him, "Give glory to God. We know that this man is a sinner."

He answered, "I do not know if he is a sinner. One thing I do know: I was blind, and now I see."

Then they asked him, "What did he do to you? How did he open your eyes?"

He answered, "I already told you, and you did not listen. Why do you want to hear it again? You don't want to become his disciples too, do you?"

They ridiculed him and said, "You are his disciple, but we are disciples of Moses. We know that God has spoken to Moses. But this man—we do not know where he comes from."

"That's amazing!" the man answered. "You do not know where he comes from, yet he opened my eyes. We know that God does not listen to sinners. But he does listen to anyone who worships God and does his will. From the beginning of time, no one has ever heard of anyone opening the eyes of someone born blind. If this man were not from God, he could do nothing."

They answered him, "You were entirely born in sinfulness! Yet you presume to teach us?" And they threw him out.

Jesus heard that they had thrown him out. When he found him, he asked, "Do you believe in the Son of God?"[a]

"Who is he, sir," the man replied, "that I may believe in him?"

Jesus answered, "You have seen him, and he is the very one who is speaking with you."

Then he said, "Lord, I believe!" and he knelt down and worshipped him.

Jesus said, "For judgment I came into this world, in order that those who do not see will see, and those who do see will become blind."

---

[a] Some witnesses to the text read *Son of Man*.

Some of the Pharisees who were with him heard this and asked, "We are not blind too, are we?"

Jesus told them, "If you were blind, you would not hold on to sin. But now that you say, 'We see,' your sin remains."[462]

The Good Shepherd

"Amen, Amen, I tell you: Anyone who does not enter the sheep pen by the door, but climbs in by some other way, is a thief and a robber. The one who enters by the door is the shepherd of the sheep. The doorkeeper opens the door for him, and the sheep listen to his voice. He calls his own sheep by name and leads them out. When he has brought out all his own sheep, he walks ahead of them. The sheep follow him because they know his voice. They will never follow a stranger, but will run away from him, because they do not know the voice of strangers." Jesus used this illustration in speaking to the people, but they did not understand what he was telling them.

So Jesus said again, "Amen, Amen, I tell you: I am the door for the sheep. All who came before me[a] were thieves and robbers, but the sheep did not listen to them. I am the door. Whoever enters through me will be saved. He will come in and go out, and find pasture.

"A thief comes only to steal and kill and destroy. I came that they may have life and have it abundantly.

"I am the Good Shepherd. The Good Shepherd lays down his life for the sheep. The hired man, who is not a shepherd, does not own the sheep. He sees the wolf coming, leaves the sheep, and runs away. Then the wolf attacks the sheep and scatters them. Because he works for money, he does not care about the sheep.

"I am the Good Shepherd. I know my sheep and my sheep know me (just as the Father knows me and I know the Father). And I lay down my life for the sheep. I also have other sheep that are not of this sheep pen. I must bring them also, and they will listen to my voice. Then there will be one flock and one shepherd. This is why the Father loves me, because I lay down my life so that I may take it up again. No one takes it from me, but I lay it down on my own. I have the authority to lay it down, and I have the authority to take it up again. This is the commission I received from my Father."

There was a division among the Jews again because of these words. Many of them were saying, "He has a demon and is out of his mind! Why listen to him?" Others said, "These are not the sayings of someone demon-possessed. Can a demon open the eyes of the blind?"[463]

Commandments and Traditions

The Pharisees and some of the experts in the law came from Jerusalem and gathered around Jesus. They saw some of his disciples eating bread with unclean

---

[a] Some witnesses to the text omit *before me*.

(that is, unwashed) hands. In fact, the Pharisees and all the Jews do not eat unless they scrub their hands with a fist,[a] holding to the tradition of the elders. When they come from the marketplace, they do not eat unless they wash.[b] And there are many other traditions they adhere to, such as the washing[c] of cups, pitchers, kettles, and dining couches.[d] The Pharisees and the experts in the law asked Jesus, "Why do your disciples not walk according to the tradition of the elders? Instead they eat bread with unclean hands."

He answered them, "Isaiah was right when he prophesied about you hypocrites. As it is written:

> These people honor me with their lips, but their heart is far from me.
> They worship me in vain, teaching human rules as if they were doctrines."[e]

"You abandon God's commandment but hold to human tradition like the washing of pitchers and cups, and you do many other such things."[f] He continued, "You have a fine way of setting aside God's commandment to keep[g] your own tradition. For example, Moses said, 'Honor your father and your mother,'[h] and 'Whoever speaks evil of his father or mother must be put to death.'[i] But you say, 'If a man tells his father or mother, "Whatever help you might have received from me is *corban*"'[j] (which means an offering), then you no longer let him do anything for his father or mother. So you nullify the word of God by your tradition that you have handed down. You do many things like that."[464]

Then he summoned the crowd and said to them, "Listen and understand. What goes into the mouth does not make a person unclean, but it is what comes out of the mouth that defiles a person.[465] If anyone has ears to hear, let him hear!"

After he had left the crowd and entered a house,[466] the disciples came and said to him, "Do you know that the Pharisees took offense when they heard this saying?"

He answered, "Every plant which my heavenly Father did not plant will be uprooted. Let them go. They are blind guides of the blind.[k] And if the blind are guiding the blind, both will fall into a pit."[467]

Peter replied and said to him, "Explain the parable to us."[468]

[Jesus] said, "Are you lacking in understanding too? Do you not understand that whatever goes into a man from the outside cannot make him unclean? For it does

---

[a] Or *up to the wrist*. This refers to a method of ceremonial washing.
[b] Greek *baptizo* (translated *baptize* in other contexts)
[c] Greek *baptismos* (translated *baptism* in other contexts)
[d] A few witnesses to the text omit *and dining couches*.
[e] Isaiah 29:13
[f] A few witnesses to the text omit the last part of verse 8 (*like the washing ...*).
[g] Some witnesses to the text read *establish*.
[h] Exodus 20:12; Deuteronomy 5:16
[i] Exodus 21:17; Leviticus 20:9
[j] *Corban* is a Hebrew word for an offering devoted to God.
[k] A few witnesses to the text omit *of the blind*.

not enter his heart but goes into his stomach and goes out of him into the latrine—in this way all foods are purified."[a]

He continued, "What comes out of a man, that is what makes a man unclean. In fact, from within, out of people's hearts, come evil thoughts, sexual sins, theft, murder, adultery, greed, wickedness, deceit, unrestrained immorality, envy, slander, arrogance, and foolishness,[469] false testimonies and blasphemies. These are the things that defile a person. But to eat with unwashed hands does not defile a person."[470]

---

[a] Or *latrine." (In this way all foods are purified.)* The punctuation in the text indicates Jesus spoke the last sentence of verse 19. The parentheses in this footnote would indicate that the last sentence was an inspired comment by Mark.

Chapter VIII: Your Faith Is Great!
In Tyre, Sidon, and the Decapolis

The Faith of a Gentile Woman

Jesus got up and[471] withdrew[472] from there to the region of Tyre and Sidon. He entered a house and did not want anyone to know it, but he could not remain hidden. Instead, when[473] a Canaanite woman from that territory[474] whose little daughter had an unclean spirit heard about him, she immediately came and fell down at his feet. This woman was a Greek, of Syro-Phoenician origin. She asked him to drive the demon out of her daughter,[475] and kept crying out, "Have mercy on me, Lord, Son of David! A demon is severely tormenting my daughter!"

But he did not answer her a word.

His disciples came and pleaded, "Send her away, because she keeps crying out after us."

He answered, "I was sent only to the lost sheep of the house of Israel."

But she came and knelt in front of him, saying, "Lord, help me."[476]

He answered her, "It is not good to take the children's bread and throw it to their little dogs."

"Yes, Lord," she said, "yet their little dogs also eat the crumbs that fall from their masters' table."

Then Jesus answered her, "Woman,[477] because of this statement, go![478] Your faith is great![479] The demon has gone out of your daughter.[480] It will be done for you, just as you desire." And her daughter was healed at that very hour.[481]

She went home, found the child lying on the bed and the demon gone.

Jesus left the region of Tyre again and went through Sidon to the Sea of Galilee,[482] along the sea[483] within the region of the Decapolis.[484] He went up onto the mountain and sat there. Large crowds came to him, bringing with them the lame, the blind, the crippled, those unable to speak, and many others. They put them down at his feet, and he healed them. As a result, the crowd was amazed when they saw the mute speaking, the crippled healed, the lame walking, and the blind seeing. And they glorified the God of Israel.[485]

"Ephphatha! Be opened!"

They brought a man to him who was deaf and had a speech impediment. They pleaded with Jesus to place his hand on him. Jesus took him aside in private, away from the crowd. He put his fingers into the man's ears. Then he spit and touched the man's tongue. After he looked up to heaven, he sighed and said, "Ephphatha!" (which means "Be opened!") Immediately the man's ears were opened, his tongue was set free, and he began to speak plainly. Jesus gave the people strict orders to tell no one, but the more he did so, the more they kept proclaiming it. They were amazed beyond measure and said, "He has done everything well. He even makes the deaf hear and the mute speak!"[486]

Jesus Feeds More Than Four Thousand

In those days, when there was again a large crowd and they had nothing to eat, Jesus called his disciples and said to them, "I feel compassion for the crowd because they have already stayed with me three days and do not have anything to eat. If I send them home hungry, they will faint on the way. Some of them have come from a long distance."

His disciples replied, "Where can anyone get enough bread to feed these people here in this deserted place?"

He asked them, "How many loaves do you have?"[487]

They said, "Seven, and a few small fish."

He instructed the crowd to sit down on the ground.[488] Then he took the seven loaves, gave thanks, and broke them. He gave the pieces to his disciples to distribute to the crowd, and they did so. They also had a few small fish. He blessed them and said that these should be distributed as well. The people ate and were satisfied. They picked up seven basketfuls of broken pieces that were left over.[489] Those who ate numbered four thousand men, without counting the women and children.[490] Then he sent them away. Right after that, Jesus got into the boat with his disciples and went to the region of Dalmanutha[491] (Magadan).[492]

The Pharisees and Sadducees came to Jesus and[493] began to argue with him. To test him, they asked him for a sign from heaven. He sighed deeply in his spirit and said, "Why does this generation seek a sign? Amen I tell you: No such sign will be given to this generation."[494] He answered them, "When it is evening you say, 'It will be fair weather because the sky is red.' In the morning you say, 'It will be stormy weather today because the sky is red and threatening.' You know how to interpret the appearance of the sky, but you cannot interpret the signs of the times! An evil and adulterous generation seeks a sign, but no sign will be given to it except the sign of Jonah."[495] After he left them and got back into the boat, he crossed to the other side.[496]

Chapter IX: You Are the Christ.
From Bethsaida to Caesarea Philippi

Watch Out for the Teaching of the Pharisees and Sadducees

When his disciples came to the other side, they had forgotten to take bread along[497] except for one loaf that they had with them in the boat.[498] Jesus said to them, "Watch out and be on guard against the yeast of the Pharisees and Sadducees,[499] and the yeast of Herod."[500]

They were discussing this among themselves and said, "It is because we did not bring any bread."

Since Jesus knew what they were saying, he said, "You of little faith! Why are you discussing among yourselves the fact that you brought no bread? Do you still not understand[501] or comprehend? Do you have a hardened heart? You have eyes—do you not see? You have ears—do you not hear? Do you not remember? When I broke the five loaves for the five thousand, how many basketfuls of broken pieces did you pick up?"

"Twelve," they told him.

"And when I broke the seven loaves for the four thousand, how many basketfuls of broken pieces did you pick up?"

"Seven," they said.

He said to them, "Do you still not comprehend?[502] How is it that you do not understand that I was not talking to you about bread? But be on guard against the yeast of the Pharisees and Sadducees."

Then they understood that he was not warning them about the yeast in bread, but about the teaching of the Pharisees and Sadducees.[503]

Jesus Heals a Blind Man

They came to Bethsaida, and some people brought him a blind man and begged him to touch him. He took hold of the blind man's hand and led him out of the village. When he had spit on his eyes, he placed his hands on him and asked him, "Do you see anything?"

The man looked up and said, "I see people. To me they look like trees walking."

Then Jesus placed his hands on his eyes again. The man opened his eyes and his sight was restored. He could see everything clearly. Jesus sent him home, saying, "Do not go into the village."[504]

Jesus Is the Christ

Jesus went away with his disciples to the villages of Caesarea Philippi. On the way[505] one time, when Jesus was praying alone and the disciples were with him, he asked them, "Who do the crowds say that I am?"[506]

They said, "Some say John the Baptist, others say Elijah, and others Jeremiah[507] one of the ancient prophets come back to life."[508]

He said to them, "But you, who do you say that I am?"

Simon Peter answered, "You are the Christ, the Son of the living God."

Jesus replied, "Blessed are you, Simon son of Jonah, for flesh and blood did not reveal this to you, but my Father who is in heaven. And I tell you that you are Peter, and on this rock I will build my church, and the gates of hell[a] will not overpower it.[b] I will give you the keys of the kingdom of heaven. Whatever you bind on earth will be[c] bound in heaven, and whatever you loose on earth will be loosed in heaven." Then he commanded the disciples not to tell anyone that he was the Christ.[509]

Jesus Predicts His Death and Resurrection

From that time, Jesus began to show his disciples that[510] the Son of Man[511] had to go to Jerusalem.[512]

He said, "The Son of Man must suffer many things and be rejected by the elders, chief priests, and experts in the law. He must be killed and be raised on the third day."[513] He was speaking plainly to them.[514]

Peter took him aside and began to rebuke him, saying, "May you receive mercy, Lord! This will never happen to you."[515]

But after turning around and looking at his disciples, Jesus rebuked Peter and said,[516] "Get behind me, Satan! You are a snare[d] to me because you are not thinking the things of God, but the things of men."[517]

Take Up the Cross

Then Jesus[518] called the crowd and his disciples together and said to them, "If anyone wants to follow me, let him deny himself, take up his cross[519] daily,[520] and follow me. For whoever wants to save his life will lose it. But whoever loses his life for my sake, and for the sake of the gospel, will save it. After all, what good is it for a man to gain the whole world and yet forfeit his soul? Or what can a man give in exchange for his soul? In fact, whoever is ashamed of me and my words in this

---

[a] Greek *hades*
[b] Or *stand up against it*
[c] Or *will have been*
[d] Or *stumbling block*

adulterous and sinful generation, the Son of Man will also be ashamed of him when he comes in[521] his glory, and the glory of the Father, and of the holy angels.[522] For the Son of Man will come in the glory of his Father together with his angels, and then he will repay everyone according to his actions. Amen I tell you: Some who are standing here will certainly not taste death until they see the Son of Man coming in his kingdom."[523]

The Transfiguration

After six days Jesus took Peter, James, and John[524] the brother of James[525] with him[526] to pray,[527] and led them up a high mountain where they were alone by themselves.[528] While he was praying,[529] he was transfigured in front of them. His face was shining like the sun.[530] His clothes became radiant, dazzling white;[531] as white as the light;[532] whiter than anyone on earth could bleach them. Just then, two men, Moses and Elijah, were talking with him! They appeared in glory and were talking about his departure,[a] which he was going to bring to fulfillment in Jerusalem.

Peter and those with him were weighed down with sleep, but when they were completely awake, they saw his glory and the two men standing with him.

As the men were leaving Jesus, Peter said to him, "Master, it is good for us to be here. Let's make three tents: one for you, one for Moses, and one for Elijah." He did not realize what he was saying. [533] He did not know what to say because they were terrified.[534]

While he was still speaking, suddenly a bright cloud overshadowed them.[535] They were afraid as they went into the cloud. Then a voice came out of the cloud, saying, "This is my Son, whom I love.[b] Listen to him!"[536] When the disciples heard this, they fell face down and were terrified. Jesus approached and as he touched them, he said, "Get up, and do not be afraid." When they opened their eyes, they saw no one except Jesus alone.

As they were coming down the mountain, Jesus commanded them, "Do not tell anyone what you have seen until the Son of Man has been raised from the dead."[537] They told no one in those days any of the things they had seen.[538] They kept the matter to themselves, discussing with one another what this "rising from the dead" meant.

They asked him, "Why do the experts in the law say that Elijah must come first?"[539]

Jesus answered them, "Yes, Elijah is coming and will restore all things,[c] but I tell you that Elijah has already come, and they did not recognize him. Instead they did to him whatever they desired. In the same way the Son of Man will also suffer at their hands." Then the disciples understood that he was talking to them about John the Baptist.[540]

---

[a] Or *exodus*
[b] A few witnesses to the text read *my chosen one* instead of *whom I love*.
[c] Malachi 4:5-6

Jesus Heals a Boy with a Demon

The next day, after they had come down from the mountain,[541] they returned to the other disciples. They saw a large crowd around them, and some experts in the law were arguing with them. As soon as all the people in the crowd saw Jesus, they were very excited and ran to greet him. He asked them, "What are you arguing about with them?"[542]

Just then a man from the crowd called out, "Teacher, I beg you to look at my son, because he is my only child."[543] [The] man approached Jesus and knelt in front of him. "Lord," he said, "have mercy on my son.[544] See, a spirit takes hold of him, and suddenly he screams.[545] [It] makes him unable to speak. Wherever it seizes him, it throws him down, and he foams at the mouth, grinds his teeth, and becomes rigid.[546] He often falls into the fire or into the water.[547] It hardly ever leaves him and constantly tortures him. I begged your disciples to drive it out, but they could not.[548] They were not able to cure him."

Jesus answered, "O unbelieving and perverse generation! How long must I be with you? How long must I put up with you? Bring him here to me."[549]

They brought the boy to Jesus. As soon as the spirit saw him, it threw the boy into a convulsion. He fell on the ground and rolled around, foaming at the mouth.

Jesus asked the boy's father, "How long has this been happening to him?"

"From childhood," he said. "It has often thrown him into the fire and into the water to kill him. But if you can do anything, have compassion on us and help us."

"If you can?"[a] Jesus said to him. "All things are possible for the one who believes."

The child's father immediately cried out and said with tears,[b] "I do believe. Help me with my unbelief!"

When Jesus saw that a crowd was quickly gathering, he rebuked the unclean spirit. "You mute and deaf spirit," he said, "I command you to come out of him and never enter him again!"

The spirit screamed, shook the boy violently, and came out. The boy looked so much like a corpse that many of them said, "He's dead!" But Jesus took him by the hand, raised him up, and he stood up.[550] They were all astonished at the majesty of God.[551]

When Jesus went into a house, his disciples asked him privately, "Why were we not able to drive it out?"[552]

He said to them, "Because of your little faith.[c] Amen I tell you: If you have faith like a mustard seed, you will tell this mountain, 'Move from here to there,' and it will move. Nothing will be impossible for you. But this kind does not go out except by prayer and fasting."[d] [553]

---

[a] Some witnesses to the text read *If you are able to believe*.
[b] A few witnesses to the text omit *with tears*.
[c] Some witnesses to the text read *your unbelief*.
[d] A few witnesses to the text omit verse 21.

Jesus Predicts His Death and Resurrection Again

They went on from there and passed through Galilee. He did not want anyone to know this, because he was teaching his disciples.

While everyone was amazed at all the things Jesus was doing, he said to his disciples, "Let these words sink into your ears[a] and remember this:[554] The Son of Man is about to be betrayed into the hands of men. They will kill him, but on the third day he will be raised." And they were greatly distressed.[555] They did not understand what he was saying. It was hidden from them so they did not grasp it. And they were afraid to ask him about this statement.[556]

---

[a] Or *put these words in your ears*

Chapter X: The Days Will Come.
From Galilee through Samaria to Judea and Perea

A Coin in a Fish's Mouth

When they came to Capernaum,[557] those who collected the temple tax[a] came to Peter and said, "Doesn't your teacher pay the temple tax?" He said, "Yes."

When he came into the house, Jesus spoke first, "What do you think, Simon? From whom do the kings of the earth collect tolls or a tax? From their own sons or from others?"

Peter said to him, "From others."

Jesus said to him, "Then the sons are exempt. But, so that we do not offend them, go to the sea, cast a hook, and take the first fish that you pull up. When you open its mouth, you will find a silver coin.[b] Take that coin and give it to them for me and for you."[558]

Who Is the Greatest?

At that time the disciples approached Jesus and asked, "Who then is the greatest in the kingdom of heaven?"[559]

When he was in the house, he asked them, "What were you arguing about on the way?" But they remained silent, because on the way they had argued with one another about who was the greatest.[560] Since Jesus knew the thoughts of their hearts,[561] [he] sat down, called the Twelve, and said to them, "If anyone wants to be first, he will be the last of all and the servant of all."[562]

Jesus called a little child, had him stand[563] next to him[564] in their midst. Taking the child in his arms, he said to them, "Whoever welcomes one of these little children in my name welcomes me. And whoever welcomes me, welcomes not just me but also him who sent me.[565] In fact, the one who is least among all of you is the one who is great."[566]

---

[a] The *two-drachma tax*
[b] A *stater* coin, worth four drachmas

Whoever Is Not Against Us Is for Us

John said in reply, "Master, we saw someone driving out demons in your name, and we tried to stop him, because he is not following you along with us."[567]

But Jesus said, "Do not try to stop him, because no one who does a miracle in my name will be able soon afterward to speak evil about me. Whoever is not against us is for us. Amen I tell you: Whoever gives you a cup of water to drink in my name, because you belong to Christ, will certainly not lose his reward."[568]

Do Not Cause Little Believers to Fall into Sin

"Amen I tell you: Unless you are turned and become like children, you will never enter the kingdom of heaven. Whoever humbles himself like this little child is the greatest in the kingdom of heaven. And whoever receives a little child like this one in my name receives me."

"But, if anyone causes one of these little ones who believe in me to sin,[a] it would be better for him to have a huge millstone hung around his neck and to be drowned in the depths of the sea. Woe to the world because of temptations to sin.[569]

Temptations to sin are sure to come, but woe to the one through whom they come![570] Watch yourselves.[571]

If your hand causes you to fall into sin, cut it off. It is better for you to enter life maimed, than to have two hands and go into hell,[b] into the unquenchable (eternal) fire, 'where their worm does not die, and the fire is not quenched.'[c] If your foot causes you to fall into sin, cut it off. It is better for you to enter life lame, than to have two feet and be thrown into hell,[d] 'where their worm does not die, and the fire is not quenched.' If your eye causes you to fall into sin, pluck it out[572] and throw it away from you.[573] It is better for you to enter the kingdom of God with one eye, than to have two eyes and be thrown into hell,[e] 'where their worm does not die, and the fire is not quenched.' For everyone will be salted with fire. Salt is good. But if the salt loses its flavor, how will you make it salty again? Have salt in yourselves, and be at peace with one another."[574]

See to it that you do not look down on one of these little ones, because I tell you that their angels in heaven always see the face of my Father who is in heaven. For the Son of Man came to save what was lost.[f] [575]

---

[a] Or *stumble*. The Greek *skandalizo* could mean to stumble into sin or fall from faith.

[b] Or *Gehenna*

[c] Isaiah 66:24 is quoted in verses 44, 46, and 48. A few witnesses to the text omit verses 44 and 46.

[d] Or *Gehenna*

[e] Or *Gehenna*

[f] Some witnesses to the text omit verse 11. See Luke 19:10.

Increase Our Faith

"If your brother sins, rebuke him. If he repents, forgive him. Even if he sins against you seven times in a day, and seven times returns to you and says, 'I repent,' forgive him."

The apostles said to the Lord, "Increase our faith."

The Lord said, "If you had faith like a mustard seed, you could tell this mulberry tree, 'Be uprooted and planted in the sea,' and it would obey you. Which one of you who has a servant plowing or taking care of sheep will say to him when he comes in from the field, 'Come at once and recline at the table'? Won't the master tell him instead, 'Prepare my supper, and after you are properly dressed, serve me while I eat and drink. After that you may eat and drink'? He does not thank the servant because he did what he was commanded to do, does he? So also you, when you have done all that you were commanded, say, 'We are unworthy servants. We have only done what we were supposed to do.'"[576]

The Lost Sheep

All the tax collectors and sinners were coming to Jesus to hear him. But the Pharisees and the experts in the law were complaining, "This man welcomes sinners and eats with them."

He told them this parable:[577] "What do you think? If a man has a hundred sheep, and one of them wanders away, will he not leave the ninety-nine on the hills and go looking for the one that wandered away? If[578] and when he finds it, he joyfully puts it on his shoulders and goes home. Then he calls together his friends and his neighbors, telling them, 'Rejoice with me, because I have found my lost sheep!'[579] Amen I tell you—he rejoices more over that one sheep than over the ninety-nine that did not wander away. In the same way, your Father in heaven does not want even one of these little ones to perish.[580] I tell you, there will be more joy in heaven over one sinner who repents than over ninety-nine righteous people who do not need to repent.[581]

The Lost Coin

"Or what woman who has ten silver coins,[a] if she loses one coin, would not light a lamp, sweep the house, and search carefully until she finds it? And when she finds it, she calls together her friends and neighbors and says, 'Rejoice with me, because I have found the lost coin.' In the same way, I tell you, there is joy in the presence of the angels of God over one sinner who repents."[582]

The Lost Son

Jesus said, "A certain man had two sons. The younger of them said to his father, 'Father, give me my share of the estate.' So he divided his property between them. Not many days later, the younger son gathered together all that he had and traveled

---

[a] These silver coins were Greek drachmas, each worth about a day's wage.

to a distant country. There he wasted his wealth with reckless living. After he had spent everything, there was a severe famine in that country, and he began to be in need. He went and hired himself out to one of the citizens of that country, who sent him into his fields to feed pigs. He would have liked to fill his stomach with the carob pods that the pigs were eating, but no one gave him anything.

"When he came to his senses, he said, 'How many of my father's hired servants have more than enough bread, and I am dying from hunger! I will get up, go to my father, and tell him, "Father, I have sinned against heaven and in your sight. I am no longer worthy to be called your son. Make me like one of your hired servants."'

"He got up and went to his father. While he was still far away, his father saw him and was filled with compassion. He ran, hugged his son, and kissed him. The son said to him, 'Father, I have sinned against heaven and in your sight. I am no longer worthy to be called your son.'

"But the father said to his servants, 'Quick, bring out the best robe and put it on him. Put a ring on his finger and sandals on his feet. Bring the fattened calf and kill it. Let us eat and celebrate, because this son of mine was dead and is alive again. He was lost and is found.' Then they began to celebrate.

"His older son was in the field. As he approached the house, he heard music and dancing. He called one of the servants and asked what was going on. The servant told him, 'Your brother is here! Your father killed the fattened calf, because he has received him back safe and sound.' The older brother was angry and refused to go in. His father came out and began to plead with him.

"He answered his father, 'Look, these many years I've been serving you, and I never disobeyed your command, but you never gave me even a young goat so that I could celebrate with my friends. But when this son of yours arrived after wasting your property with prostitutes, you killed the fattened calf for him!'

"The father said to him, 'Son, you are always with me, and all that I have is yours. But it was fitting to celebrate and be glad, because this brother of yours was dead and is alive again. He was lost and is found.'"[583]

The Shrewd Manager

Jesus also said to his disciples, "There was a rich man who had a manager who was accused of wasting his possessions. The rich man called him in and said to him, 'What is this that I hear about you? Give an account of your management, because you can no longer be manager.'

"The manager said to himself, 'What will I do, since my master is taking away the management position from me? I am not strong enough to dig. I am ashamed to beg. I know what I will do, so that when I am removed from my position as manager, people will receive me into their houses.'

"He called each one of his master's debtors to him. He asked the first, 'How much do you owe my master?' He said, 'Six hundred gallons[a] of olive oil.' He said to him,

---

[a] Or *one hundred baths*. A *bath* was about six gallons.

'Take your bill, sit down quickly, and write three hundred.' Then he said to another, 'How much do you owe?' And he said, 'Six hundred bushels[a] of wheat.' He said to him, 'Take your bill and write four hundred and eighty.'

"The master commended the dishonest manager because he had acted shrewdly. For the children [b] of this world are more shrewd in dealing with their own generation[c] than the children of the light are. I tell you, make friends for yourselves with unrighteous *mammon*,[d] so that when it runs out, they will welcome you into the eternal dwellings. The person who is faithful with very little is also faithful with much. And the person who is unrighteous with very little is also unrighteous with much. So if you have not been faithful with unrighteous *mammon*, who will entrust you with what is really valuable? If you have not been faithful with what belongs to someone else, who will give you something to be your own? No servant can serve two masters. Indeed, either he will hate the one and love the other, or he will be devoted to the one and despise the other. You cannot serve both God and *mammon*."

The Pharisees, who loved money, also heard all these things and sneered at him. He said to them, "You are the ones who justify yourselves in the sight of people, but God knows your hearts. In fact, what is highly regarded among people is an abomination in God's sight. The Law and the Prophets were until John. Since that time the good news of the kingdom of God is proclaimed, and everyone is trying to force his way into it.[e]

"It is easier for heaven and earth to pass away than for even one part of a letter in the Law to fail. Anyone who divorces his wife and marries another is committing adultery, and the man who marries a woman divorced from her husband is committing adultery.[584]

The Rich Man and Poor Lazarus

"There was a rich man who was dressed in purple and fine linen, living in luxury every day. A beggar named Lazarus had been laid at his gate. Lazarus was covered with sores and longed to be fed with what fell from the rich man's table. Besides this, the dogs also came and licked his sores. Eventually the beggar died, and the angels carried him to Abraham's side. The rich man also died and was buried. In hell,[f] where he was in torment, he lifted up his eyes and saw Abraham far away and Lazarus at his side. He called out and said, 'Father Abraham, have mercy on me! Send Lazarus to dip the tip of his finger in water and cool my tongue, because I am in misery in this flame.'

---

[a] Or *one hundred cors*. A *cor* was about six bushels.
[b] Or *people*
[c] Or *kind of people*
[d] *Mammon* is an Aramaic word that is transliterated in the Greek. It refers to *worldly wealth* (sometimes personified). It also appears in verses 11 and 13, and Matthew 6:24. It may also be translated *money*, but a different word for money is used in verse 14.
[e] Or *everyone is urgently invited into it*
[f] Greek *hades*

"But Abraham said, 'Son, remember that in your lifetime you received your good things, and Lazarus received bad things. But now he is comforted here, and you are in misery. Besides all this, a great chasm has been set in place between us and you, so that those who want to cross from here to you cannot, nor can anyone cross over from there to us.'

"He said, 'Then I beg you, father, send him to my father's home, because I have five brothers—to warn them, so that they will not also come to this place of torment.'

"Abraham said, 'They have Moses and the Prophets. Let them listen to them.'

"'No, father Abraham,' he said, 'but if someone from the dead goes to them, they will repent.'

"Abraham replied to him, 'If they do not listen to Moses and the Prophets, they will not be convinced even if someone rises from the dead.'"[585]

Show Your Brother His Sin

"If your brother sins against you, go and show him his sin just between the two of you. If he listens to you, you have regained your brother. But if he will not listen, take one or two others along with you, so that 'every matter[a] may be established by the testimony of two or three witnesses.'[b] If he refuses to listen to them, tell it to the church. And, if he refuses to listen even to the church, then treat him as an unbeliever or a tax collector. Amen I tell you: Whatever you bind on earth will be[c] bound in heaven, and whatever you loose on earth will be loosed in heaven. Amen I tell you again: If two of you on earth agree to ask for anything, it will be done for them by my Father who is in heaven. In fact where two or three have gathered together in my name, there I am among them."[586]

The Unmerciful Servant

Then Peter came up and asked Jesus, "Lord, how many times must I forgive my brother when he sins against me? As many as seven times?"

Jesus said to him, "Not seven times, but I tell you as many as seventy-seven times.[d] For this reason the kingdom of heaven is like a king who wanted to settle accounts with his servants. When he began to settle them, a man who owed him ten thousand talents[e] was brought to him. Because the man was not able to pay the debt, his master ordered that he be sold, along with his wife, children, and all that he owned to repay the debt.

---

[a] Or *word, fact, charge,* or *statement*
[b] Deuteronomy 19:15
[c] Or *will have been*
[d] Or *seventy times seven*
[e] *Ten thousand talents* was an enormous amount equal to sixty million days' wages. Each *talent* was worth six thousand *denarii*. A *denarius* was one day's wage.

"Then the servant fell down on his knees in front of him, saying, 'Master, be patient with me, and I will pay you everything!' The master of that servant had pity on him, released him, and forgave him the debt.

"But when that servant went out, he found one of his fellow servants who owed him one hundred denarii.[a] He grabbed him and began choking him, saying, 'Pay me what you owe!'

"So his fellow servant fell down and begged him, saying, 'Be patient with me, and I will pay you back!' But he refused. Instead he went off and threw the man into prison until he could pay back what he owed.

"When his fellow servants saw what had happened, they were very distressed. They went and reported to their master everything that had taken place.

"Then his master called him in and said to him, 'You wicked servant! I forgave you all that debt when you begged me to. Should you not have had mercy on your fellow servant just as I had mercy on you?' His master was angry and handed him over to the jailers until he could pay back everything he owed.

"This is what my heavenly Father will also do to you unless each one of you forgives his brother from his heart."[587]

When Jesus had finished saying these things, [588] [and] when the days were approaching for him to be taken up, Jesus was determined[b] to go to Jerusalem.[589]

Ten Lepers Healed—One Thanks God

As Jesus was on his way to Jerusalem, he was passing along the border between Samaria and Galilee. When he entered a certain village, ten men with leprosy met him. Standing at a distance, they called out loudly, "Jesus, Master, have mercy on us!"

When he saw them, he said, "Go, show yourselves to the priests." As they went away they were cleansed.

One of them, when he saw that he was healed, turned back, glorifying God with a loud voice. He fell on his face at Jesus' feet, thanking him. And he was a Samaritan. Jesus responded, "Were not ten cleansed? Where are the other nine? Was no one found to return and give glory to God except this foreigner?" Then he said to him, "Get up and go your way. Your faith has saved you."[590]

The Kingdom of God Is Within You

The Pharisees asked Jesus when the kingdom of God would come. Jesus answered them, "The kingdom of God is not coming in a way you can observe, nor will people say, 'Look, here it is!' or 'Look, there it is!' because the kingdom of God is within[c] you."[591]

---

[a] This was one hundred days' wages, since one *denarius* was equal to one day's wage.
[b] Literally *set his face*
[c] Or *among*

Jesus Will Return

He said to the disciples, "The days will come when you will long to see one of the days of the Son of Man, and you will not see it. They will tell you, 'Look, there he is!' or 'Look, here he is!' Do not go out or chase after them, for the Son of Man in his day will be like the lightning that flashes and lights up the sky from one side to the other side. But first, he must suffer many things and be rejected by this generation. Just as it was in the days of Noah, so will it also be in the days of the Son of Man. They were eating and drinking, marrying and being given in marriage, until the day when Noah entered the ark. Then the flood came and destroyed them all. Likewise, just as it was in the days of Lot: They were eating and drinking, buying and selling, planting and building, but on the day when Lot went out from Sodom, fire and sulfur rained down from heaven and destroyed them all. It will be the same on the day the Son of Man is revealed. On that day, the person who is on the roof and has belongings in the house should not go down to get them. Likewise, the person in the field should not turn back for anything. Remember Lot's wife! Whoever tries to preserve his life will lose it, but whoever loses his life will keep it. I tell you, on that night there will be two people in one bed. One will be taken, and the other will be left. There will be two women grinding grain at the same place. One will be taken, and the other will be left."[a]

"Where, Lord?" they asked him.

He said to them, "Where the corpse is, there the vultures will be gathered."[592]

The Parable of the Persistent Widow

Jesus told them a parable about the need to always pray and not lose heart: "There was a judge in a certain town who did not fear God and did not care about people. There was a widow in that town, and she kept going to him, saying, 'Give me justice from my adversary!' For some time he refused, but after a while he said to himself, 'Even though I do not fear God or care about people, yet because this widow keeps bothering me, I will give her justice so that she will not wear me out with her endless pleading.'"

The Lord said, "Listen to what the unjust judge says. Will not God give justice to his chosen ones, who are crying out to him day and night? Will he put off helping them? I tell you that he will give them justice quickly. However, when the Son of Man comes, will he find faith on the earth?"[593]

The Pharisee and the Tax Collector

Jesus told this parable to certain people who trusted in themselves (that they were righteous) and looked down on others: "Two men went up to the temple courts to pray. One was a Pharisee, and the other was a tax collector. The Pharisee stood and prayed about himself like this: 'God, I thank you that I am not like other

---

[a] Some witnesses to the text include verse 36: *Two will be in the field: One will be taken, and the other will be left.* (See Matthew 24:40.)

people, robbers, evildoers, adulterers, or even like this tax collector. I fast twice a week. I give a tenth of all my income.'

"However the tax collector stood at a distance and would not even lift his eyes up to heaven, but was beating his chest and saying, 'God, be merciful to me, a sinner!'

"I tell you, this man went home justified rather than the other, because everyone who exalts himself will be humbled, but the one who humbles himself will be exalted."[594]

Jesus Is Determined to Go to Jerusalem

[Jesus] left Galilee and went to the region of Judea beyond the Jordan.[595]

He sent messengers ahead of him. They went and entered a Samaritan village to make preparations for him. But the people did not welcome him, because he was determined to go to Jerusalem. When his disciples James and John saw this, they said, "Lord, do you want us to call down fire from heaven to consume them?"[a]

But he turned and rebuked them. "You don't know what kind of spirit is influencing you. For the Son of Man did not come to destroy people's souls, but to save them."[b] Then they went to another village.[596]

Follow Jesus

As they went on the way, a man said to him, "I will follow you wherever you go."

Jesus said to him, "Foxes have holes, and birds of the air have nests, but the Son of Man has no place to lay his head."

He said to another man, "Follow me!"

But he said, "Lord, first let me go and bury my father."

Jesus told him, "Let the dead bury their own dead, but you go and proclaim the kingdom of God."

Another man also said, "I will follow you, Lord, but first let me say good-bye to those at my home."

Jesus told him, "No one who puts his hand to the plow and looks back is fit for the kingdom of God."[597]

Jesus Appoints Seventy-Two

After this, the Lord appointed seventy-two[c] others and sent them out two by two ahead of him[d] to every town and place where he was about to go.

He told them, "The harvest is plentiful, but the workers are few. So ask the Lord of the harvest to send out workers into his harvest field. Go your way. Look, I am sending you out as lambs among wolves. Do not carry a money bag or traveler's bag or sandals. Do not greet anyone along the way. Whenever you enter a house, first

---

[a] Some witnesses to the text add *just as Elijah did*.
[b] Some witnesses to the text omit this quotation.
[c] Some witnesses to the text read *seventy* (also in verse 17).
[d] Literally *before his face*

say, 'Peace be to this house.' And if a peaceful person is there, your peace will rest on him, but if not, it will return to you. Remain in that same house, eating and drinking what they give you, because the worker is worthy of his pay. Do not keep moving from house to house. Whenever you enter a town and they welcome you, eat what is set before you. Heal the sick who are in the town and tell them, 'The kingdom of God has come near you.'

"But whenever you enter a town and they do not welcome you, go out into its streets and say, 'Even the dust from your town that clings to our feet, we wipe off against you. Nevertheless know this: The kingdom of God has come near.' I tell you, it will be more bearable for Sodom on that day than for that town.

"Woe to you, Chorazin! Woe to you, Bethsaida! For if the miracles that were done in you had been done in Tyre and Sidon, they would have repented long ago, sitting in sackcloth and ashes. But it will be more bearable for Tyre and Sidon in the judgment than for you. And you, Capernaum, will you be lifted up to heaven? No, you will be brought down to hell.[a] Whoever listens to you listens to me. Whoever rejects you rejects me. And whoever rejects me rejects the one who sent me."

The seventy-two returned with joy, saying, "Lord, even the demons submit to us in your name!"

He told them, "I was watching Satan fall like lightning from heaven. Look, I have given you authority to trample on snakes and scorpions and over all the power of the enemy. And nothing will ever harm you. Nevertheless, do not rejoice that the spirits submit to you, but rejoice that your names have been written in heaven."

In that same hour, Jesus rejoiced in the Holy Spirit and said, "I praise you, Father, Lord of heaven and earth, that you have hidden these things from the wise and learned and have revealed them to little children. Yes, Father, because this was pleasing in your sight.

[b]"Everything was handed over to me by my Father. No one knows who the Son is except the Father, and no one knows who the Father is except the Son and anyone to whom the Son wants to reveal him."

Turning to the disciples, he said privately, "Blessed are the eyes that see what you see! Indeed, I tell you that many prophets and kings wanted to see the things that you are seeing, yet did not see them, and to hear the things that you are hearing, yet did not hear them."[598]

The Good Samaritan

Just then, an expert in the law stood up to test Jesus, saying, "Teacher, what must I do to inherit eternal life?"

"What is written in the law?" he asked him. "What do you read there?"

---

[a] Greek *hades*
[b] Some witnesses to the text add *Turning to his disciples, Jesus said.*

He replied, "Love the Lord your God with all your heart, with all your soul, with all your strength, and with all your mind;[a] and, love your neighbor as yourself."[b]

He said to him, "You have answered correctly. Do this, and you will live."

But he wanted to justify himself, so he asked Jesus, "And who is my neighbor?"

Jesus replied, "A man was going down from Jerusalem to Jericho. He fell among robbers who stripped him, beat him, and went away, leaving him half dead. It just so happened that a priest was going down that way. But when he saw the man, he passed by on the other side. In the same way, a Levite also happened to go there, but when he saw the man, he passed by on the other side. A Samaritan, as he traveled, came to where the man was. When he saw him, he felt sorry for the man. He went to him and bandaged his wounds, pouring oil and wine on them. He put him on his own animal, took him to an inn, and took care of him. The next day, when he left, he took out two denarii,[c] gave them to the innkeeper, and said, 'Take care of him. Whatever extra you spend, I will repay you when I return.' Which of these three do you think acted like a neighbor to the man who fell among robbers?"

"The one who showed mercy to him," he replied.

Then Jesus told him, "Go and do likewise."[599]

Mary and Martha

As they went on their way, Jesus came into a village, and a woman named Martha welcomed him into her home. She had a sister named Mary, who was sitting at the Lord's feet and was listening to his word. But Martha was distracted with all her serving. She came over and said, "Lord, don't you care that my sister has left me to serve alone? Tell her to help me."

The Lord answered and told her, "Martha, Martha, you are worried and upset about many things, but one thing is needed. In fact, Mary has chosen that better part, which will not be taken away from her."[600]

"I and the Father Are One"

Then the Festival of Dedication took place in Jerusalem. It was winter, and Jesus was walking in the temple area in Solomon's Colonnade.

So the Jews gathered around Jesus, asking, "How long will you keep us in suspense? If you are the Christ, tell us plainly."

Jesus answered them, "I did tell you, but you do not believe. The works I am doing in my Father's name testify about me. But you do not believe, because you are not my sheep, as I said to you.[d] My sheep hear my voice. I know them, and they follow me. I give them eternal life, and they will never perish. No one will snatch them out

---

[a] Deuteronomy 6:5

[b] Leviticus 19:18

[c] A *denarius* was one day's wage.

[d] Some witnesses to the text omit *as I said to you*.

of my hand. My Father, who has given them to me, is greater than all. No one can snatch them out of my Father's hand. I and the Father are one."

Again the Jews picked up stones to stone him. Jesus answered them, "I have shown you many good works from my Father. For which of these are you going to stone me?"

"We are not going to stone you for a good work," the Jews answered, "but for blasphemy, because although you are a man, you make yourself out to be God."

Jesus answered them, "Is it not written in your Law, 'I said you are gods'?[a] If he called those people 'gods,' to whom the word of God came, and the Scripture cannot be broken, what about the one whom the Father set apart and sent into the world? Do you accuse me of blasphemy because I said, 'I am God's Son'? If I am not doing the works of my Father, do not believe me. But if I am doing them, even if you do not believe me, believe the works so that you will know and understand[b] that the Father is in me, and I am in the Father."

So they tried to arrest him again, but he eluded their grasp. He went back across the Jordan to the place where John had been baptizing earlier, and he stayed there.

Many came to him and were saying, "John never did a miraculous sign, but everything John said about this man was true." And many believed in him there.[601]

Jesus Heals a Crippled Woman

Jesus was teaching in one of the synagogues on the Sabbath. And a woman was there who had a spirit that had disabled her for eighteen years. She was bent over and could not stand up straight. When Jesus saw her, he called her over and said, "Woman, you are freed from your disability." He placed his hands on her, and immediately she stood up straight and began to glorify God.

But the ruler of the synagogue was indignant that Jesus had healed on the Sabbath. He said to the crowd in response, "There are six days to do work. So come to be healed on those days and not on the Sabbath day!"

The Lord answered him, "Hypocrites! Doesn't each of you untie his ox or his donkey from the manger on the Sabbath and lead it to water? Here is this daughter of Abraham, whom Satan has bound for eighteen years! Shouldn't she be set free from this bondage on the Sabbath day?"

As he said these things, all his adversaries were put to shame. But the entire crowd was rejoicing over all the glorious things he was doing.

Mustard Seed and Yeast

Then Jesus asked, "What is the kingdom of God like, and to what will I compare it? It is like a mustard seed, which a man took and planted in his garden. It grew and became a large tree, and the birds of the air nested in its branches."

---

[a] Psalm 82:6
[b] Some witnesses to the text read *believe*.

Again he said, "To what will I compare the kingdom of God? It is like yeast, which a woman took and mixed into a bushel[a] of flour until it was all leavened."[602]

The Narrow Door

He went on his way from one town and village to another, teaching, and making his way to Jerusalem. Someone said to him, "Lord, are only a few going to be saved?"

He said to them, "Strive to enter through the narrow door, because many, I tell you, will try to enter and will not be able. Once the master of the house gets up and shuts the door, you will begin to stand outside and knock on the door, saying, 'Lord, open for us!' He will tell you in reply, 'I don't know you or where you come from.' Then you will begin to say, 'We ate and drank in your presence, and you taught in our streets.' And he will say, 'I don't know where you come from. Depart from me, all you evildoers.' There will be weeping and gnashing of teeth when you see Abraham, Isaac, and Jacob, and all the prophets in the kingdom of God, but you yourselves thrown outside. People will come from east and west, from north and south, and will recline at the table in the kingdom of God. And note this: Some are last who will be first, and some are first who will be last."[603]

Jesus Warns Jerusalem

In that very hour, some Pharisees came to him and said, "Leave, and go away from here, because Herod wants to kill you."

He said to them, "Go tell that fox, 'Look, I am going to drive out demons and heal people today and tomorrow, and on the third day I will reach my goal. Nevertheless, I must go on my way today and tomorrow and the next day, because it cannot be that a prophet would be killed outside Jerusalem!'

"Jerusalem, Jerusalem, the city that kills the prophets and stones those sent to her! How often I have wanted to gather your children together, as a hen gathers her chicks under her wings, but you were not willing! Look, your house is left to you desolate. I tell you, you will not see me until the time comes when you will say, 'Blessed is he who comes in the name of the Lord!'"[604]

Jesus in a Pharisee's Home

One Sabbath day, when Jesus went into the house of a leader of the Pharisees to eat bread, they were watching him closely.

Right in front of him was a man who was suffering from swelling of his body.[b] Jesus addressed the legal experts and Pharisees, saying, "Is it lawful to heal on the Sabbath or not?"

---

[a] *Three seahs*
[b] Or *dropsy* (hydropsy), an abnormal accumulation of fluid in the tissues of the body

But they were silent. So he took hold of the man, healed him, and let him go. He said to them, "Which of you, if your son[a] or an ox would fall into a well on a Sabbath day, would not immediately pull him out?"

And they could not reply to these things.

When he noticed how they were selecting the places of honor, he told the invited guests a parable. "When you are invited by someone to a wedding banquet, do not recline in the place of honor, or perhaps someone more distinguished than you may have been invited by him. The one who invited both of you may come and tell you, 'Give this man your place.' Then you will begin, with shame, to take the lowest place.

"But when you are invited, go and recline in the lowest place, so that when the one who invited you comes, he will tell you, 'Friend, move up to a higher place.' Then you will have honor in the presence of all who are reclining at the table with you.

"Yes, everyone who exalts himself will be humbled, and whoever humbles himself will be exalted."

He also said to the one who had invited him, "When you make a dinner or a supper, do not invite your friends, or your brothers, or your relatives, or rich neighbors, so that perhaps they may also return the favor and pay you back.

"But when you make a feast, invite the poor, the crippled, the lame, the blind, and you will be blessed, because they cannot repay you. Certainly, you will be repaid in the resurrection of the righteous."[605]

The Parable of the Great Banquet

When one of those at the table with him heard these things, he said to Jesus, "Blessed is the one who will feast in the kingdom of God!"

Jesus said to him, "A certain man made a great banquet and invited many people. When it was time for the banquet, he sent out his servant to tell those who were invited, 'Come, because everything is now ready.' But they all alike began to make excuses.

"The first one told him, 'I bought a field, and I need to go and see it. I ask you to excuse me.'

"Another one said, 'I bought five yoke of oxen, and I am going to try them out. I ask you to excuse me.'

"Still another said, 'I just got married, and so I am unable to attend.'

"The servant arrived and reported these things to his master. Then the master of the house was angry and said to his servant, 'Go out quickly into the streets and alleys of the town, and bring in here the poor, the crippled, the blind, and the lame.'

"The servant said, 'Master, what you commanded has been done, and there is still room.'

---

[a] Some witnesses to the text read *donkey*.

"Then the master said to the servant, 'Go out into the highways and hedges, and urge them to come in, so that my house may be filled. Yes, I tell you that none of those men who were invited will taste my banquet.'"[606]

The Cost

Large crowds were traveling with Jesus. He turned and said to them, "If anyone comes to me and does not hate his own father and mother, wife and children, brothers and sisters, yes, even his own life, he cannot be my disciple. Whoever does not carry his own cross and follow me cannot be my disciple. For which of you, if he wants to build a tower, does not first sit down and count the cost to see if he has enough to complete it? Otherwise, when he has laid a foundation and is not able to finish, everyone who sees it will begin to ridicule him, saying, 'This fellow began to build, but was not able to finish.' Or what king, as he goes out to confront another king in war, will not first sit down and consider if he is able with ten thousand to oppose the one who comes against him with twenty thousand? And if he is not able, he sends out a delegation and asks for terms of peace while his opponent is still far away. So then, any one of you who does not say farewell to all his own possessions cannot be my disciple. Salt is good, but if the salt has lost its flavor, how will it become salty again? It is not fit for the soil or for the manure pile. It is thrown away. The one who has ears to hear, let him hear."[607]

Marriage and Divorce

Large crowds followed[608] [and] gathered around him again and, as he usually did, he taught[609] and healed them there. Some Pharisees came in order to test him. They asked, "Is it lawful for a man to divorce his wife for any reason?"[610]

He replied, "What did Moses command you?"

They said, "Moses permitted a man to write a certificate of divorce and send her away."[a]

But Jesus told them, "He wrote this command for you because of your hard hearts. But from the beginning of creation, God made them male and female.[b] For this reason a man will leave his father and mother and be joined to his wife, and the two will become one flesh.[c] So they are no longer two but one flesh. Therefore, what God has joined together, let no one separate."

In the house his disciples asked him about this again.

He said to them,[611] "I tell you that whoever divorces his wife, except on the grounds of her sexual immorality, and marries another woman is committing adultery."[d]

---

[a] See Deuteronomy 24:1,3.
[b] Genesis 1:27; 5:2
[c] Genesis 2:24
[d] Some witnesses to the text add *And the one who marries the divorced woman also commits adultery.*

His disciples said to him, "If this is the relationship of a man with his wife, it is better not to marry."

But he said to them, "Not everyone can accept this saying, but only those to whom it has been given. For example, there are eunuchs who were born that way, and others who were castrated by people, and others who decided to remain unmarried because of the kingdom of heaven. The one who is able to accept this should accept it."[612]

Jesus Loves Little Children

Some people began bringing little children to Jesus[613]—even their babies)[614]—to have him place his hands on them and pray.[615] When the disciples saw this, they began to rebuke them.[616] When Jesus saw this, he was indignant. He said, "Let the little children come to me! Do not hinder them, because the kingdom of God belongs to such as these. Amen I tell you: Whoever will not receive the kingdom of God like a little child will never enter it." And he took the little children in his arms, laid his hands on them, and blessed them.[617] After he placed his hands on them, he left that place.[618]

Chapter XI: I Am the Resurrection and the Life.
Withdrawal to Ephraim after Raising Lazarus

The Rich Young Ruler

As Jesus was setting out on a journey,619 a certain ruler620 ran up to him and knelt in front of him. He asked,621 "Teacher, what good thing should I do that I may have eternal life?"

Jesus said to him, "Why do you ask me about what is good? Only one is good. But if you want to enter life, keep the commandments."

"Which ones?" the man asked him.

Jesus said, "'You shall not murder. You shall not commit adultery. You shall not steal. You shall not give false testimony. Honor your father and mother.' And, 'You shall love your neighbor as yourself.'"a

The young man said to him, "I have kept all these. What am I still lacking?"

Jesus told him, "If you want to be perfect, go, sell your possessions, and give to the poor, and you will have treasure in heaven. Then come, follow me." But when the young man heard this, he went away sad, because he had many possessions.622

When Jesus saw that the man became very sad,623 [he] looked around and said to his disciples, "How hard it will be for those who have riches to enter the kingdom of God!"

The disciples were amazed at his words. But Jesus told them again, "Children, how hard it is for those who trust in their riches to enter the kingdom of God! It is easier for a camel to go through the eye of a needle than for a rich man to enter the kingdom of God."

They were even more astonished and said to one another, "Who then can be saved?"

Jesus looked at them and said, "For people, it is impossible, but not for God, because all things are possible for God."

Peter began to say to him,624 "Look, we have left everything and followed you! What then will we have?"

Jesus said to them, "Amen I tell you: In the renewal, when the Son of Man sits on his glorious throne, you who have followed me will also sit on twelve thrones, judging the twelve tribes of Israel. Everyone who has left homes or brothers or

---

a Exodus 20:12-16; Deuteronomy 5:16-20; Leviticus 19:18

sisters or father or mother or children or fields, because of my name, will receive a hundred times as much and will inherit eternal life. Many who are first will be last, and many who are last will be first."[625]

The Workers in the Vineyard

"Indeed the kingdom of heaven is like a landowner who went out early in the morning to hire workers for his vineyard. After agreeing to pay the workers a denarius for the day, he sent them into his vineyard. He also went out about the third hour[a] and saw others standing unemployed in the marketplace. To these he said, 'You also go into the vineyard, and I will give you whatever is right.' So they went. Again he went out about the sixth and the ninth hour and did the same thing. When he went out about the eleventh hour, he found others standing unemployed. He said to them, 'Why have you stood here all day unemployed?'

"They said to him, 'Because no one hired us.'

"He told them, 'You also go into the vineyard.' When it was evening, the owner of the vineyard said to his foreman, 'Call the workers and pay them their wages, starting with the last group and ending with the first.'

"When those who were hired around the eleventh hour came, they each received a denarius. When those who were hired first came, they thought they would receive more. But they each received a denarius too. After they received it, they began to grumble against the landowner: 'Those who were last worked one hour, and you made them equal to us who have endured the burden of the day and the scorching heat!'

"But he answered one of them, 'Friend, I am doing you no wrong. Did you not make an agreement with me for a denarius? Take what is yours and go. I want to give to the last one hired the same as I also gave to you. Can't I do what I want with my own money? Or are you envious because I am generous?' In the same way, the last will be first, and the first, last."[626]

Jesus Raises Lazarus

Now a certain man named Lazarus was sick. He was from Bethany, the village of Mary and her sister Martha. This Mary, whose brother Lazarus was sick, was the same Mary who anointed the Lord with perfume and wiped his feet with her hair.

So the sisters sent a message to Jesus, saying, "Lord, the one you love is sick!"

When Jesus heard it, he said, "This sickness is not going to result in death, but it is for the glory of God, so that the Son of God may be glorified through it."

Jesus loved Martha and her sister and Lazarus. Yet when he heard that Lazarus was sick, he stayed in the place where he was two more days.

Then afterwards he said to his disciples, "Let's go back to Judea."

The disciples said to him, "Rabbi, recently the Jews were trying to stone you. And you are going back there again?"

---

[a] 9 AM

Jesus answered, "Are there not twelve hours of daylight? If anyone walks around during the day, he does not stumble because he sees this world's light. But if anyone walks around at night, he stumbles because there is no light on him."

He said this and then told them, "Our friend Lazarus has fallen asleep, but I am going there to wake him up."

Then the disciples said, "Lord, if he has fallen asleep, he will get well."

Jesus had been speaking about his death, but they thought he was merely talking about ordinary sleep. So Jesus told them plainly, "Lazarus is dead. And I am glad for your sake that I was not there, so that you may believe. But let us go to him."

Then Thomas (called the Twin[a]) said to his fellow disciples, "Let's go too, so that we may die with him."

When Jesus arrived, he found that Lazarus had already been in the tomb for four days.

Bethany was near Jerusalem, about two miles away. Many Jews had come to Martha and Mary to comfort them concerning their brother.

When Martha heard that Jesus was coming, she went to meet him, while Mary was sitting in the house.

Martha said to Jesus, "Lord, if you had been here, my brother would not have died. But even now I know that whatever you ask from God, God will give you."

Jesus said to her, "Your brother will rise again."

Martha replied, "I know that he will rise in the resurrection on the Last Day."

Jesus said to her, "I am the resurrection and the life. Whoever believes in me will live, even if he dies. And whoever lives and believes in me will never perish.[b] Do you believe this?"

"Yes, Lord," she told him. "I believe[c] that you are the Christ, the Son of God, who was to come into the world."

After she said this, Martha went back to call her sister Mary. She whispered, "The Teacher is here and is calling for you."

When Mary heard this, she got up quickly and went to him. Now Jesus had not yet gone into the village, but was still where Martha met him. The Jews who were with Mary in the house consoling her saw that she got up quickly and left. So they followed her, supposing[d] she was going to the tomb to weep there. When Mary came to where Jesus was and saw him, she fell at his feet and said, "Lord, if you had been here, my brother would not have died."

When Jesus saw her weeping, and the Jews who came with her also weeping, he was deeply moved in his spirit and troubled.

He asked, "Where have you laid him?"

They told him, "Lord, come and see."

Jesus wept.

---

[a] Greek *Didymus* is the equivalent of *Thomas* in Hebrew/Aramaic, both meaning *Twin*.
[b] Literally *not die into eternity*
[c] Or *have believed*
[d] Some of the witnesses to the text read *saying that*.

Then the Jews said, "See how he loved him!" But some of them said, "Could not he who opened the eyes of the blind man have kept this man from dying?"

Jesus was deeply moved again as he came to the tomb. It was a cave, and a stone was lying against it. "Take away the stone," he said.

Martha, the dead man's sister, told him, "Lord, by this time there will be an odor, because it has been four days."

Jesus said to her, "Did I not tell you that if you believe, you will see the glory of God?" So they took away the stone.

Jesus looked up and said, "Father, I thank you that you heard me. I knew that you always hear me, but I said this for the benefit of the crowd standing here, so that they may believe that you sent me." After he said this, he shouted with a loud voice, "Lazarus, come out!"

The man who had died came out with his feet and his hands bound with strips of linen and his face wrapped with a cloth. Jesus told them, "Loose him and let him go."627

The Plot

Therefore many of the Jews who came to Mary and saw what Jesus did believed in him. But some of them went to the Pharisees and told them what Jesus had done. So the chief priests and the Pharisees called a meeting of the Sanhedrin. They asked, "What are we going to do, because this man is doing many miraculous signs? If we let him go on like this, everyone will believe in him. Then the Romans will come and take away both our place and our nation."

But one of them, Caiaphas, who was high priest that year, said to them, "You know nothing at all. You do not even consider that it is better for us[a] that one man die for the people than that the whole nation perish." He did not say this on his own, but, as high priest that year, he prophesied that Jesus was going to die for the nation, and not only for that nation, but also in order to gather into one the scattered children of God.

So from that day on they plotted to kill him. Therefore Jesus no longer walked about openly among the Jews. Instead he withdrew into a region near the wilderness, to a town called Ephraim. And he stayed there with his disciples.628

---

[a] Some witnesses to the text read *you*.

Chapter XII: The Son of Man Handed Over
To Jerusalem for the Final Passover

The Final Passover Is Near

The Jewish Passover was near, and many went up to Jerusalem from the country to purify themselves before the Passover. They kept looking for Jesus and asking one another as they stood in the temple area, "What do you think? He certainly won't come to the Festival, will he?" The chief priests and the Pharisees had given orders that if anyone knew where Jesus was, he should report it so that they could arrest Jesus.[629]

Again Jesus Predicts His Death and Resurrection

They were on the road, going up to Jerusalem, and Jesus was leading them. The disciples were amazed, and the others who followed were afraid. He took the Twelve aside again and began to tell them what was going to happen to him.[630] "Look, we are going up to Jerusalem, and everything that is written through the prophets about the Son of Man will be accomplished.[631] The Son of Man will be handed over to the chief priests and experts in the law, and they will condemn him to death. They will hand him over to the Gentiles to mock, flog, and crucify him. On the third day he will be raised."[632]

They did not understand any of these things. What he said was hidden from them, and they did not understand what was said.[633]

Then the mother of Zebedee's sons,[634] James and John,[635] came to him with her sons, kneeling and asking something of him. He said to her, "What do you want?"[636]

James and John said, "Teacher, we wish that you would do for us whatever we ask."

He said to them, "What do you want me to do for you?"[637]

[Their mother] said to him, "Promise that in your kingdom these two sons of mine may sit, one on your right hand and one on your left hand[638] in your glory."

But Jesus said to them, "You do not know what you are asking. Can you drink the cup that I am going to drink or be baptized with the baptism that I am going to be baptized with?"

"We can," they replied.

Jesus told them, "You will drink the cup that I am going to drink and be baptized with the baptism that I am going to be baptized with. But to sit at my right or at my left is not for me to give; rather, these places belong to those for whom they have been prepared[639] by my Father."[640]

When the ten heard this, they were angry with James and John.

Jesus called them together and said, "You know that those who are considered rulers over the Gentiles lord it over them, and their great ones exercise authority over them. But that is not the way it is to be among you. Instead, whoever wants to be great among you will be your servant, and whoever wants to be first among you will be a slave of all. For even the Son of Man did not come to be served, but to serve, and to give his life as a ransom for many."[641]

Jesus Heals Two Blind Men

They came to Jericho. As Jesus and his disciples and a large crowd were leaving Jericho,[642] there were two blind men sitting by the road.[643] When [one of them],[644] Bartimaeus the son of Timaeus,[645] heard a crowd go by, he asked what was happening. They told him that Jesus the Nazarene was passing by. He called out, "Jesus, Son of David, have mercy on me!" Those who were at the front of the crowd rebuked him, telling him to be quiet.[646] But they shouted even louder, "Have mercy on us, Lord, Son of David!"[647]

Jesus stopped and said, "Call him."

They called the blind man, saying, "Cheer up! Get up. He is calling you!"

He tossed aside his outer garment, jumped up, and went to Jesus.

"What do you want me to do for you?" Jesus asked [them].

The blind man replied, "*Rabboni*,[a] I want to see again."[648]

They told him, "Lord, open our eyes."

Jesus was moved with compassion and touched their eyes.[649] [He] said to him, "Receive your sight."[650] Jesus told him, "Go. Your faith has made you well."[651] Immediately he received his sight and began following Jesus, glorifying God. All the people, when they saw this, gave praise to God.[652]

Zacchaeus

Jesus entered Jericho and was passing through. A man named Zacchaeus was there. He was a chief tax collector, and he was rich. He was trying to see who Jesus was, but since he was short, he could not see because of the crowd. He ran on ahead and climbed up into a sycamore tree to see Jesus, because he was about to pass by that way. When Jesus came to the place, he looked up and said to him, "Zacchaeus, hurry and come down, for I must stay at your house today." He came down quickly and welcomed Jesus joyfully. When the people saw it, they were all grumbling because he went to be a guest of a sinful man.

---

[a] *Rabboni* means *my rabbi* (my teacher, my master).

Zacchaeus stood up and said to the Lord, "Look, Lord, I am going to give half of my possessions to the poor. And if I have cheated anyone out of anything, I will pay back four times as much."

Jesus said to him, "Today, salvation has come to this house, because he too is a son of Abraham. For the Son of Man came to seek and to save the lost."[653]

Parable of the Ten Minas

As they were listening to these things, Jesus went on to tell a parable, because he was near Jerusalem, and the people thought that the kingdom of God was going to appear at once. So he said, "A man of noble birth traveled to a distant country to receive a kingdom for himself and then to return. He called ten of his servants and gave them ten minas.[a] 'Conduct business until I return,' he said to them.

"But his subjects hated him and sent a delegation after him, saying, 'We do not want this man to be king over us.'

"When he returned after receiving the kingdom, he summoned the servants to whom he had given the money. He wanted to find out what they had gained by conducting business.

"The first one came to him and said, 'Master, your mina has earned ten more minas.'

"He said to him, 'Well done, good servant! Because you were faithful in a very small matter, you will have authority over ten cities.'

"The second one came and said, 'Master, your mina has produced five more minas.'

"So he said to him, 'You will be over five cities.'

"And another one came and said, 'Master, here is your mina that I laid away in a piece of cloth. For I was afraid of you, since you are a demanding man. You take what you did not deposit and reap what you did not sow.'

"He said to him, 'You wicked servant, I will judge you with your own words! You knew that I am a demanding man, taking what I did not deposit and reaping what I did not sow. Then why did you not put my money in the bank? Then, when I returned, I could have collected it with interest!'

"He said to those standing there, 'Take the mina away from him and give it to the one who has the ten minas.'

"But they said to him, 'Master, he already has ten minas!'

"'I tell you that to everyone who has, more will be given, but from the one who does not have, even what he has will be taken away. Now as for those enemies of mine who did not want me to be king over them, bring them here and kill them in front of me.'"[654]

After Jesus had said these things, he went on ahead, going up to Jerusalem.[655]

---

[a] A *mina* was worth one hundred drachmas, or about one hundred days' wages.

Mary Anoints Jesus

Six days before the Passover, Jesus came to Bethany, the home of Lazarus, who had died, the one Jesus raised from the dead. They gave a dinner for him there. Martha was serving, and Lazarus was one of those reclining at the table with him.

Then Mary took about twelve ounces[a] of very expensive perfume (pure nard) and anointed Jesus' feet and wiped his feet with her hair. The house was filled with the fragrance of the perfume.

But one of his disciples, Judas Iscariot, who was going to betray him, said, "Why wasn't this perfume sold for three hundred denarii[b] and given to the poor?" He did not say this because he cared for the poor, but because he was a thief. He held the money box and used to steal what was put into it.

Jesus replied, "Leave her alone. She intended to keep this for the day of my burial. Indeed, the poor you always have with you, but you are not always going to have me."

A large crowd of the Jews learned that he was there. They came not only because of Jesus, but also to see Lazarus, whom he raised from the dead. So the chief priests made plans to kill Lazarus too, because it was on account of him that many of the Jews were leaving them and believing in Jesus.[656]

The King Comes to Jerusalem

The next day, the large crowd that had come for the Festival heard that Jesus was on his way to Jerusalem.[657]

As they approached Jerusalem, at Bethphage and Bethany, on the Mount of Olives, he sent two of his disciples and told them, "Go into the village ahead of you. As soon as you enter it,[658] you will find a donkey tied there along with her colt. Untie them and bring them to me.[659] If anyone asks you, 'Why are you doing this?' say, 'The Lord needs it, and he will send it back here without delay.'"[660]

This took place to fulfill what was spoken through the prophet:

> Tell the daughter of Zion: Look, your King comes to you, humble, and riding on a donkey, on a colt, the foal of a donkey.[c] [661]

At first, his disciples did not understand these things. But when Jesus was glorified, then they remembered that these things had been written about him and that they did these things for him.[662]

Those who were sent ahead went and found things just as he had told them.[663] They found a colt on the street, tied at a door; and they untied it.[664] As they were untying the colt, its owners said to them,[665] "What are you doing, untying that colt?" The disciples answered them just as Jesus had instructed them, and the men let them go.[666]

---

[a] Greek *litra* is the Roman pound (327.45 grams or 11.55 ounces, by weight).
[b] Or *three hundred days' wages*. A denarius was worth about one day's wage.
[c] Isaiah 62:11; Zechariah 9:9

Then they brought the colt to Jesus.⁶⁶⁷ They brought the donkey and the colt, laid their outer clothing on them, and he sat on it.⁶⁶⁸ As he went along,⁶⁶⁹ a very large crowd spread their outer clothing on the road. Others were cutting⁶⁷⁰ palm⁶⁷¹ branches from the trees and spreading them out on the road.⁶⁷² The crowd that was with him when he called Lazarus out of the tomb and raised him from the dead kept telling what they had seen. This is another reason a crowd met him: They heard he had done this miraculous sign.

So the Pharisees said to one another, "You see? You are accomplishing nothing. Look! The world has gone after him."⁶⁷³

The crowds who went in front of him and those who followed kept shouting,⁶⁷⁴

> Hosanna!ᵃ
> Blessed is he who comes in the name of the Lordᵇ ⁶⁷⁵—the King of Israel!⁶⁷⁶
> Blessed is the coming kingdom of our father David!
> Hosanna in the highest!⁶⁷⁷

As he was approaching the slope of the Mount of Olives, the whole crowd of disciples began to praise God joyfully, with a loud voice, for all the miracles they had seen, saying, "Blessed is the King who comes in the name of the Lord!ᶜ Peace in heaven and glory in the highest!"

Some of the Pharisees from the crowd said to him, "Teacher, rebuke your disciples!"

He replied, "I tell you, if these people would be silent, the stones would cry out."

As he came near, he saw the city and wept over it. He said, "If you, yes you, had only known on this dayᵈ the things that would bring peace to you. But now, it is hidden from your eyes. In fact, the days will come upon you when your enemies will build an embankment against you, surround you, and hem you in on every side. Within your walls, they will dash you and your children to the ground. And within your walls, they will not leave one stone on top of another, because you did not recognize the time when God came to help you."ᵉ ⁶⁷⁸

When he entered Jerusalem, the whole city was stirred up, asking, "Who is this?" And the crowds were saying, "This is Jesus, the prophet from Nazareth in Galilee."⁶⁷⁹

Jesus went into the temple courts in Jerusalem and looked around at everything. Since it was already late, he went out to Bethany with the Twelve.⁶⁸⁰

Jesus Curses a Fig Tree

As he returned to the city early in the morning⁶⁸¹ the next day, after they had set out from Bethany, Jesus was hungry. When he saw a fig tree in leaf in the distance, he went to see if he might find anything on it. When he came to it, he found nothing

---

ᵃ *Hosanna* means *save us* or *help us, we pray*.
ᵇ Psalm 118:25-26
ᶜ Psalm 118:26
ᵈ Some witnesses to the text read *this your day*.
ᵉ *The time when God came to help you* is literally *the time of your visitation*.

but leaves, since it was not the season for figs. Jesus said to it, "May no one ever eat fruit from you again!" And his disciples were listening.⁶⁸²

Jesus Cleanses His Father's House

They came to Jerusalem. Jesus went into the temple area and began to drive out those who were selling and buying in the temple courts. He overturned the tables of the money changers and the chairs of those who were selling doves. He would not allow anyone to carry any merchandise through the temple courts. He began to teach them: "Is it not written: 'My house will be called a house of prayer for all nations'?ᵃ But you have made it 'a den of robbers'!"ᵇ ⁶⁸³

Every day he was teaching in the temple courts, but the chief priests, the experts in the law, and the leaders of the people continued to look for a way to put him to death. They could not find any way to do it, because all the people were clinging to him and listening.⁶⁸⁴ Indeed they were afraid of him, because the whole crowd was amazed at his teaching.⁶⁸⁵

The blind and the lame came to him in the temple, and he healed them. But when the chief priests and the experts in the law saw the wonders he performed and heard the children calling out in the temple, "Hosanna to the Son of David!" they were indignant. They said to him, "Do you hear what they are saying?"

"Yes," Jesus told them, "Have you never read,

> From the lips of little children and nursing babies
>   you have prepared praise?"ᶜ

He left them, went out of the city to Bethany, and spent the night there. ⁶⁸⁶ (When evening came, Jesus and his disciples would leave the city.)⁶⁸⁷

The Withered Fig Tree

As they passed by in the morning, they saw the fig tree withered down to the roots. Peter remembered and said, "Rabbi, look! The fig tree that you cursed has withered."⁶⁸⁸ When the disciples saw it, they were amazed and asked, "How did the fig tree wither so quickly?"⁶⁸⁹

Jesus replied, "Have faith in God. Amen I tell you: Whoever says to this mountain, 'Be lifted up and thrown into the sea,' and does not doubt in his heart, but believes that what he says will happen, it will be done for him. Therefore I tell you, everything that you ask for in prayer, believe that you have received it, and it will be yours. Whenever you stand praying, if you have anything against anyone, forgive him, so that your Father in heaven may forgive you your sins. But if you do not forgive, your Father in heaven will not forgive your sins."ᵈ ⁶⁹⁰

ᵃ Isaiah 56:7
ᵇ Jeremiah 7:11
ᶜ Psalm 8:2
ᵈ A few witnesses to the text do not include verse 26.

Chapter XII: The Son of Man Handed Over

Jesus' Authority Is Questioned

They went into Jerusalem again. As he was walking in the temple courts,[691] teaching the people and preaching the good news,[692] the chief priests and experts in the law came to him with the elders.

They asked him, "By what authority are you doing these things? Or who gave you this authority to do these things?"

Jesus replied, "I will ask you one question. Answer me, and I will tell you by what authority I am doing these things. The baptism of John—was it from heaven or from men? Answer me."

They discussed this with one another, saying, "If we say, 'From heaven,' he will say, 'Then why did you not believe him?'[693] But if we say, 'From men,' all the people will stone us, for they are convinced that John was a prophet."[694] So they answered Jesus, "We don't know."

Jesus said to them, "Neither will I tell you by what authority I am doing these things."[695]

Two Sons

"What do you think? A man had two sons. He went to the first and said, 'Son, go work today in my vineyard.' He answered, 'I will not,' but later he changed his mind and went. He came to the second and said the same thing. The second son answered, 'I will go, sir,' but he did not go. Which of the two did the will of his father?"

They said to him, "The first."

Jesus said to them, "Amen I tell you: The tax collectors and the prostitutes are entering the kingdom of God ahead of you. For John came to you in the way of righteousness, but you did not believe him. However, the tax collectors and prostitutes did believe him. Even when you saw this, you did not change your mind and believe him.[696]

The Parable of the Wicked Tenants

"Listen to another parable. There was a landowner who[697] planted a vineyard, put a fence around it, dug a pit for the winepress, and built a watchtower. Then he rented it out to some tenant farmers and went on a journey. When it was time, he sent a servant to the tenants to receive his share of the vineyard's produce. They took him, beat him, and sent him away empty-handed. Again, he sent another servant to them. But they hit him on the head and treated him shamefully. Then he sent another servant, but they killed that one. He also sent many others; some they beat, and others they killed.[698]

The owner of the vineyard said, 'What should I do? I will send my son, whom I love. Perhaps they will respect him.'

"But when the tenant farmers saw him, they talked it over with one another. They said, 'This is the heir. Let's kill him, so that the inheritance will be ours.'[699] They seized him, killed him, and threw him out of the vineyard.[700] So when the landowner comes, what will he do to those tenant farmers?"

They told him, "He will bring those wretches to a wretched end. Then he will lease out the vineyard to other tenants who will give him his fruit when it is due."

Jesus said to them, "Have you never read in the Scriptures:

> The stone the builders rejected has become the cornerstone.
> This was the Lord's doing, and it is marvelous in our eyes?[a]

"That is why I tell you the kingdom of God will be taken away from you and given to a people that produces its fruit. Whoever falls on this stone will be broken to pieces, and it will crush anyone on whom it falls."

When the chief priests and the Pharisees heard his parables, they knew that he was talking about them. Although they were looking for a way to arrest him, they were afraid of the crowds because the people regarded him as a prophet.[701]

The Parable of the Wedding Banquet

Jesus spoke to them again in parables. He said, "The kingdom of heaven is like a certain king who prepared a wedding banquet for his son. He sent out his servants to summon those who were invited to the wedding banquet, but they did not want to come.

"Then he sent out other servants and said, 'Tell those who are invited: Look, I have prepared my dinner. My oxen and my fattened cattle have been butchered, and everything is ready. Come to the wedding banquet!'

"But those who were invited paid no attention and went off, one to his own farm, another to his business. The rest seized the king's servants, mistreated them, and killed them. As a result, the king was very angry. He sent his army and killed those murderers and burned their town.

"Then he said to his servants, 'The wedding banquet is ready, but those who were invited were not worthy. So go to the main crossroads and invite as many as you find to the wedding banquet.' Those servants went out to the roads and gathered together everyone they found, both good and bad, and the wedding hall was filled with guests. But when the king came in to see the guests, he saw a man there who was not wearing wedding clothes. He said to him, 'Friend, how did you get in here without wearing wedding clothes?' The man was speechless. Then the king told the servants, 'Tie him hand and foot and throw him into the outer darkness where there will be weeping and gnashing of teeth.' For many are called, but few are chosen."[702]

Paying Taxes to Caesar

Then the Pharisees went out and plotted together.[703] They watched him carefully and sent spies, who pretended to be sincere, so that they could trap Jesus in something he said, and then deliver him up to the power and authority of the governor.[704] They sent their disciples to him along with the Herodians. "Teacher," they said, "we know that you are truthful and teach the way of God in accord with

---

[a] Psalm 118:22-23

the truth. You are not concerned about gaining anyone's approval because you are not swayed by appearances. So tell us, what do you think? Is it lawful to pay taxes to Caesar or not?[705] Should we pay it or not?"[706]

But Jesus knew their evil purpose[707]—their hypocrisy,[708] their deceit—[709] and said, "Why are you testing me, hypocrites? Show me the coin used for the tax,[710] a denarius, so that I can look at it."[711]

They brought him a denarius.

He asked them, "Whose image and inscription is this?"

"Caesar's," they replied to him.

Then he said to them, "Therefore give to Caesar the things that are Caesar's, and to God the things that are God's."[712]

They were not able to trap him in what he said in the presence of the people. They were amazed at his answer and became silent.[713] Then they left him and went away.[714]

The God of the Living

That same day some Sadducees (who say there is no resurrection) came to him. They asked him a question: "Teacher, Moses said, 'If a man dies without having children, his brother should marry his wife and raise up offspring for his brother.'[a] Now there were seven brothers among us. The first one died after he married her, and since he had no children, he left his wife to his brother. It was the same with the second brother, the third, and all the way to the seventh. Last of all, the woman died. So then, in the resurrection, whose wife will she be of the seven, since they all married her?"

"You are mistaken," Jesus replied, "since you do not know the Scriptures or the power of God.[715] Jesus said to them, "The people of this age marry and are given in marriage. But those who are considered worthy to experience that age and the resurrection from the dead neither marry nor are given in marriage. In fact, they cannot die any more, for they are like the angels[716] of God in heaven.[717] They are sons of God, because they are sons of the resurrection.[718] And concerning the resurrection of the dead, have you never read[719] in the book of Moses, in the passage about the burning bush, how God told him, 'I am the God of Abraham, the God of Isaac, and the God of Jacob'?[b] He is not the God of the dead, but of the living[720] for all are alive to him.[721] You are badly mistaken."[722]

When the crowds heard his answer, they were amazed at his teaching.[723] Some of the experts in the law answered, "Teacher, you have spoken well." Then they no longer dared to ask him anything.[724]

---

[a] Deuteronomy 25:5
[b] Exodus 3:6,15

Love God and Your Neighbor

When they heard that he had silenced the Sadducees, the Pharisees met together. One of them who was an expert in the law asked him a question, trying to trap him. "Teacher, which is the greatest commandment of the Law?"725

Jesus answered, "The most important is: 'Hear, O Israel, the Lord, our God, the Lord is one. You shall love the Lord your God with all your heart, with all your soul, with all your mind, and with all your strength.'ᵃ The second is this: 'You shall love your neighbor as yourself.'ᵇ There is no other commandment greater than these.726 All the Law and the Prophets dependᶜ on these two commandments."

The expert in the law said to him, "Well said, teacher. You have spoken correctly on the basis of the truth that he is one, and there is no other besides him.ᵈ To love him with all your heart, with all your understanding, and with all your strength, and to love your neighbor as yourself, is more important than all whole burnt offerings and sacrifices."ᵉ

When Jesus saw that he had answered wisely, he said to him, "You are not far from the kingdom of God." After that, no one dared to ask him any more questions.727

David's Son and David's Lord

While Jesus was teaching in the temple courts,728 the Pharisees were gathered together. Jesus asked them a question: "What do you think about the Christ? Whose son is he?"

They said to him, "The Son of David."

He said to them, "Then how729 in the book of Psalms730 can David in the Spirit call him Lord, saying,731

> The Lord said to my Lord, 'Sit at my right hand,
>   until I make your enemies a footstool under your feet.'ᶠ

"So if David calls him Lord, how is he his son?"732

The large crowd listened to him with delight.733 No one was able to answer him a word, and from that day on no one dared to ask him any more questions.734

Do Not Do as They Do

Then Jesus spoke to the crowds and to his disciples. He said, "The experts in the law and the Pharisees sit in Moses' seat. So practice and observe whatever they tell you. But do not do as they do, because they do not practice what they preach. They

---

ᵃ Deuteronomy 6:4-5
ᵇ Leviticus 19:18
ᶜ Or *hang*
ᵈ See Deuteronomy 6:4; 4:35; Isaiah 45:21.
ᵉ Deuteronomy 6:5; Leviticus 19:18
ᶠ Psalm 110:1

tie up heavy loads, burdens that are hard to carry, and place them on people's shoulders, but they will not lift a finger to help them. They do all their works to be seen by people. They make their phylacteries[a] wide and lengthen the fringes of their garments. They love the place of honor at feasts, the best seats in the synagogues, the greetings in the marketplaces.[735] They devour widows' houses and offer long prayers to look good. These men will receive greater condemnation.[736] [They love] being called 'Rabbi' by people. But you are not to be called 'Rabbi,' for you have one Teacher, and you are all brothers. Also do not call anyone on earth your 'Father,' for you have one Father, and he is in heaven. And you are not to be called 'leaders,' for you have one Leader, the Christ. But the greatest among you will be your servant. Whoever exalts himself will be humbled, and whoever humbles himself will be exalted."[737]

Woes and Warnings

"But woe to you, experts in the law and Pharisees, you hypocrites! You shut the kingdom of heaven right in front of people's faces. You yourselves do not enter, nor do you permit those who are trying to enter to do so.[b] Woe to you, experts in the law and Pharisees, you hypocrites! You travel the sea and the land to make one convert, and then when he is converted, you make him twice as much a son of hell as you are."

"Woe to you, blind guides, who say, 'Whoever swears by the temple, it is nothing; but whoever swears by the gold of the temple, he is obligated.' You blind fools! After all, which is greater: the gold or the temple that sanctifies the gold? And you say, 'Whoever swears by the altar, it is nothing; but whoever swears by the gift that is on it, he is obligated.' You blind men! After all, which is greater: the gift or the altar that sanctifies the gift? So whoever swears by the altar, swears by it and by everything on it. Also, whoever swears by the temple, swears by it and by him who dwells in it. And whoever swears by heaven, swears by God's throne and by him who sits on it."

"Woe to you, experts in the law and Pharisees, you hypocrites! You give ten percent of your mint, dill, and cumin, but you have neglected the more important matters of the law: justice, mercy, and faith. You should have done these things and not failed to do the other things. Blind guides, you strain out a gnat but swallow a camel!"

"Woe to you, experts in the law and Pharisees, you hypocrites! You clean the outside of a cup and dish, but inside they are full of greed and self-indulgence. Blind Pharisee, first clean the inside of the cup and dish so that the outside may become clean too."

---

[a] *Phylacteries* were small leather boxes attached by a leather strap to the forehead or left arm. In each box were pieces of parchment inscribed with quotations from Exodus 13:1-10; 13:11-16; Deuteronomy 6:4-9; 11:13-21. See Deuteronomy 6:8 for this custom.

[b] Many early witnesses to the text omit verse 14. See Mark 12:40 and Luke 20:47 where inclusion is certain.

"Woe to you, experts in the law and Pharisees, you hypocrites! You are like whitewashed tombs that appear beautiful on the outside, but on the inside are full of dead people's bones and every kind of uncleanness. In the same way, on the outside you seem righteous to people, but on the inside you are full of hypocrisy and wickedness."

"Woe to you, experts in the law and Pharisees, you hypocrites! You build the tombs of the prophets and decorate the monuments of the righteous, and you say, 'If we had lived in the days of our fathers, we would not have joined with them in shedding the blood of the prophets.' By saying this you testify against yourselves that you are sons of those who murdered the prophets. Fill up, then, the measure of your fathers. You serpents, you offspring of vipers, how will you escape being condemned to hell?"

"Look, this is why I am sending you prophets, wise men, and experts in the law. Some of them you will kill and crucify, and some of them you will flog in your synagogues and persecute from town to town. As a result, you will be held responsible for all the righteous blood shed on the earth, from the blood of righteous Abel to the blood of Zechariah son of Berekiah, whom you murdered between the sanctuary and the altar. Amen I tell you: All these things will come upon this generation."

"Jerusalem, Jerusalem, who kills the prophets and stones those sent to her! How often I have wanted to gather your children together as a hen gathers her chicks under her wings, but you were not willing! Look, your house is left to you desolate. For I tell you, you will certainly not see me again until you say, 'Blessed is he who comes in the name of the Lord!'"[a] [738]

The Poor Widow's Offering

Jesus sat down opposite the offering box and was watching how the crowd put money into it. Many rich people put in large amounts. One poor widow came and put in two small bronze coins,[b] worth less than a penny.[c] He called his disciples together and said to them, "Amen I tell you: This poor widow put more into the offering box than all the others. For they all gave out of their surplus, but she, out of her poverty, put in everything—all that she had to live on."[739]

The Destruction of Jerusalem and the End of the World

As Jesus left the temple and was walking away, his disciples came up to him to call his attention to the temple buildings,[740] how it was decorated with beautiful stones and offerings. [741] One of his disciples said to him, "Teacher, look what impressive stones these are, and what impressive buildings!"

---

[a] Psalm 118:26
[b] Literally *lepta*. One lepton was a coin worth about 1/128 of an agricultural worker's daily wages.
[c] Literally *quadrans*. One quadrans was a coin worth about 1/64 of an agricultural worker's daily wages.

Chapter XII: The Son of Man Handed Over

Jesus said to them, "Do you see these large buildings?[742] These things that you see here—[743]Amen I tell you:[744] The days will come when[745] there will not be one stone here left on top of another. They will all be thrown down."

As he was sitting on the Mount of Olives opposite the temple, Peter, James, John, and Andrew asked him privately, "Tell us, when will these things happen, and what will be the sign when all these things[746]—your coming and the end of the world—[747]are about to be fulfilled?"

Jesus began by telling them, "Be careful that no one deceives you. Many will come in my name, saying, 'I am[748] the Christ,'[749] and 'The time is near,'[750] and they will deceive many people.[751] Do not follow them."

"Whenever you hear of wars and rumors of wars,[752] and revolutions, do not be terrified, for these things must happen first, but the end will not be right then."

Then he said to them, "Nation will rise against nation, and kingdom against kingdom. There will be great earthquakes, famines, and plagues in various places.[753] These are the beginning of birth pains.[754] There will be horrifying sights and great signs from heaven.[755] But be on your guard![756] Before all these things, they will lay their hands on you,[757] hand you over to be persecuted,[758] and they will put you to death. [759] People will hand you over to councils, and you will be beaten in synagogues. You will stand in the presence of rulers and kings for my sake as a witness to them.[760] It will turn out to be your opportunity to testify.[761] And the gospel must first be preached to all the nations.[762] Whenever they arrest you and hand you over, do not worry beforehand what you should say,[763] how to defend yourselves, for I will give you words and wisdom that none of your adversaries will be able to withstand or contradict.[764] Say whatever is given to you in that hour, because you will not be the ones speaking; instead it will be the Holy Spirit.[765] You will be betrayed even by parents, brothers,[a] relatives, and friends.[766] Brother will betray brother to death, and a father, his child. Children will rise up against their parents and put them to death.[767] You will be hated by everyone because of my name.[768] Then many will fall away from faith. They will betray each other and hate each other. Many false prophets will appear and deceive many people. Because lawlessness will increase, the love of many will grow cold. But whoever endures to the end will be saved.[769] Not a hair of your head will perish. By patient endurance you will gain your lives. [770] This gospel of the kingdom will be proclaimed throughout the whole world as a testimony to all nations, and then the end will come."[771]

"Therefore[772] when you see Jerusalem surrounded by armies, then know that its desolation is near.[773] When you see the abomination that causes desolation[b],[774] that was spoken of through the prophet Daniel, standing in the holy place,[775] where it should not be[776]—let the reader understand—then those who are in Judea should

---

[a] Greek *adelphoi*. Depending on the context, this plural word may refer to *brothers* or *siblings* (including any sisters). See Luke 14:26 where the text literally says *brothers and sisters*.

[b] Daniel 9:18; 11:31; 12:11

flee to the mountains.⁷⁷⁷ Let those who are inside the city get out. Let those who are in the country not enter the city.⁷⁷⁸ The one who is on the housetop should not go down or enter to take anything out of his house. The one who is in the field should not return to get his clothes.⁷⁷⁹ For these are days of vengeance, to fulfill all that has been written.⁷⁸⁰ How terrible it will be for those who are pregnant and nursing infants in those days!⁷⁸¹ Pray that your flight will not take place in the winter or on a Sabbath. For at that time⁷⁸² there will be great distress⁷⁸³ in the land and wrath against this people—⁷⁸⁴of such a kind as has not happened from the beginning of the creation until now, and surely never will be again.⁷⁸⁵ They will fall by the edge of the sword and be taken captive to all nations. Jerusalem will be trampled on by Gentiles until the times of the Gentiles are fulfilled.⁷⁸⁶ If the Lord had not shortened those days, no one would be saved. But for the sake of the elect, whom he has chosen, he has shortened the days."

"Then if someone tells you, 'Look, here is the Christ!' or, 'Look, there he is!' do not believe it. For false Christs and false prophets will rise up and perform signs and wonders to deceive even the elect, if it were possible. So be on your guard. I have told you everything in advance."⁷⁸⁷

"So if they tell you, 'Look! There he is in the wilderness,' do not go out there, or 'Look! Here he is in the inner rooms,' do not believe it. Just as the lightning flashes from the east and shines as far as the west, so it will be when the Son of Man comes. Wherever the carcass may be, there the vultures will gather."⁷⁸⁸

"But after that distress in those days,⁷⁸⁹ there will be signs in the sun, moon, and stars.⁷⁹⁰ The sun will be darkened, and the moon will not give its light. The stars will be falling from the sky.⁷⁹¹ And on the earth nations will be in anguish, in perplexity at the roaring of the sea and the surging waves, people fainting from fear and expectation of the things coming on the world,⁷⁹² for the powers of the heavens will be shaken."⁷⁹³

"Then the sign of the Son of Man will appear in the sky. And at that time all the nations of the earth will mourn.⁷⁹⁴ Then you will see the Son of Man coming on clouds with great power and glory.[a] ⁷⁹⁵ At that time he will send out his angels and gather his elect from the four winds, from the farthest end of the earth to the farthest end of the sky.⁷⁹⁶ But when these things begin to happen, stand up and lift up your heads, because your redemption is near."⁷⁹⁷

"Learn this lesson from the fig tree. When its branch has become tender and produces leaves, you know that summer is near. In the same way, when you see all these things, know that he is near, right at the doors. Amen I tell you: This generation[b] will certainly not pass away until all these things take place. Heaven and earth will pass away, but my words will never pass away."⁷⁹⁸

---

[a] See Daniel 7:13.
[b] Or *kind of people,* or *race*

Be Ready!

"No one knows when that day and hour will be, not the angels of heaven, not even the Son, but only the Father.⁷⁹⁹ Watch! Be alert and pray, because you do not know when the time will come. It is like a man going away on a journey. When he left his home, he put his servants in charge and assigned what each one was to do. He also commanded the doorkeeper to keep watch. Therefore keep watch, because you do not know when the owner of the house is coming: whether in the evening, or at midnight, or when the rooster crows, or early in the morning. If he comes suddenly, do not let him find you sleeping. What I say to you, I say to everyone: Keep watch!"⁸⁰⁰

"Just as it was in the days of Noah, so it will be when the Son of Man returns. In fact, in the days before the flood people were eating and drinking, marrying and giving in marriage, until the very day that Noah entered the ark. And they did not realize what was coming until the flood came and took them all away. That is how it will be when the Son of Man returns."

"At that time two men will be in the field; one will be taken and one will be left. Two women will be grinding at the mill; one will be taken and one will be left. So be alert, because you do not know on what day your Lord is coming. But understand this: If the master of the house had known at what time of night the thief was coming, he would have stayed awake and would not have let his house be broken into. You also need to be ready for this reason: The Son of Man is coming at an hour when you do not expect him."

"Who then is the faithful and wise servant, whom his master has put in charge of his household, to give them their food at the proper time? Blessed is that servant whom his master finds doing this when he returns. Amen I tell you: He will put him in charge of all that he has. But if that servant is wicked and says in his heart, 'My master is staying away a long time,' and he begins to beat his fellow servants and eats and drinks with drunkards, the master of that servant will return on a day when he does not expect it and at an hour he does not know. The master will cut him in two and assign him a place with the hypocrites, where there will be weeping and gnashing of teeth."⁸⁰¹

"Watch yourselves or else your hearts will be weighed down with carousing, drunkenness, and the worries of this life, and that day may come on you suddenly.ᵃ For it will come like a trap on all those who dwell on the face of the whole earth. Stay alert all the time, praying that you may be able to escape all these things that are going to happen and that you may be able to stand before the Son of Man."⁸⁰²

The Parable of the Ten Virgins

"At that time the kingdom of heaven will be like ten virgins who took their lamps and went out to meet the bridegroom. Five of them were foolish, and five were wise. When the foolish ones took their lamps, they did not take any oil with them; but the

---

a   A few witnesses to the text read *suddenly like a trap. Yes, it will come on all those ...*

wise took oil in their containers with their lamps. While the bridegroom was delayed, they all became drowsy and fell asleep. But at midnight there was a shout, 'Look, the bridegroom! Come out to meet him!' Then all those virgins got up and trimmed their lamps. The foolish ones said to the wise, 'Give us some of your oil because our lamps are going out.' But the wise answered, 'No, there may not be enough for us and for you. Instead, go to those who sell oil and buy some for yourselves.' But while they were away buying oil, the bridegroom came. Those who were ready went in with him to the wedding banquet, and the door was shut. Later, the other virgins also came and said, 'Lord, Lord, let us in.' But he answered, 'Amen I tell you: I do not know you.' Therefore, keep watch, because you do not know the day or the hour."[803]

The Parable of the Talents

"You see, the kingdom of heaven is like a man going on a journey. He called his servants and entrusted his possessions to them. To one he gave five talents,[a] to another two talents, and to still another one talent, each according to his own ability. Then he went on his journey. The servant who had received the five talents immediately put them to work and gained five more talents. In the same way, the servant who had received the two talents gained two more. But the servant who had received one talent went away, dug a hole in the ground, and hid his master's money."

"After a long time the master of those servants came and settled accounts with them. The servant who received the five talents came and brought five more talents. He said, 'Master, you entrusted five talents to me. See, I have gained five more talents.'"

"His master said to him, 'Well done, good and faithful servant! You were faithful with a few things. I will put you in charge of many things. Enter into the joy of your master.'"

"The servant who received the two talents came and said, 'Master, you entrusted me with two talents. See, I have gained two more talents.'"

"His master said to him, 'Well done, good and faithful servant! You were faithful with a few things. I will put you in charge of many things. Enter into the joy of your master.'"

"Then the servant who received one talent came and said, 'Master, I knew that you are a hard man, reaping where you did not plant and gathering where you did not scatter seed. Since I was afraid, I went away and hid your talent in the ground. See, you have what is yours.'"

"His master answered him, 'You wicked and lazy servant! You knew that I reap where I did not plant and gather where I did not scatter seed? Well then, you should have deposited my money with the bankers so that when I came I would get my money back with interest. Take the talent away from him and give it to the servant

---

[a] Each *talent* was worth six thousand *denarii*. A *denarius* was one day's wage.

who has the ten talents. Because everyone who has will be given more, and he will have an abundance. But the one who does not have, even what he has will be taken away from him. Throw that worthless servant into the outer darkness, where there will be weeping and gnashing of teeth.'"[804]

Jesus Will Judge the World

"When the Son of Man comes in his glory, and all the angels with him, he will sit on his glorious throne. All the nations will be gathered in his presence, and he will separate them one from another, as a shepherd separates the sheep from the goats. He will put the sheep on his right and the goats on his left. Then the King will say to those on his right, 'Come, you who are blessed by my Father, inherit the kingdom prepared for you from the foundation of the world. For I was hungry and you gave me food to eat. I was thirsty and you gave me something to drink. I was a stranger and you welcomed me. I was lacking clothes and you clothed me. I was sick and you took care of me. I was in prison and you visited me.'"

"Then the righteous will answer him, 'Lord, when did we see you hungry and feed you, or thirsty and give you a drink? When did we see you a stranger and welcome you, or lacking clothes and clothe you? When did we see you sick or in prison and visit you?'"

"The King will answer them, 'Amen I tell you: Just as you did it for one of the least of these brothers of mine, you did it for me.'"

"Then he will say to those on his left, 'Depart from me, you who are cursed, into the eternal fire, which is prepared for the Devil and his angels. For I was hungry and you did not give me food to eat. I was thirsty and you did not give me anything to drink. I was a stranger and you did not welcome me, lacking clothes and you did not clothe me, sick and in prison and you did not take care of me.'"

"Then they will also answer, 'Lord, when did we see you hungry or thirsty or a stranger or lacking clothes or sick or in prison and did not serve you?'"

"At that time he will answer them, 'Amen I tell you: Just as you did not do it for one of the least of these, you did not do it for me.' And they will go away to eternal punishment, but the righteous to eternal life."[805]

The Plot to Kill Jesus

When Jesus had finished saying all these things, he said to his disciples, "You know that after two days it will be the Passover, and the Son of Man will be handed over to be crucified."[806] (It was two days before the Passover and the Festival of Unleavened Bread.)[807]

Then the chief priests and the elders of the people assembled in the palace of the high priest, whose name was Caiaphas. They plotted together how to arrest Jesus by stealth and kill him[808] because they were afraid of the people.[809] But they said, "Not during the Festival, or else there might be a riot among the people."[810]

Judas Plans to Betray Jesus

Then Satan entered Judas, called Iscariot, who was one of the Twelve. He went away and spoke with the chief priests and officers of the temple guard about how he could betray Jesus to them,[811] and said, "What are you willing to give me if I hand him over to you?"[812] When they heard this, they were glad and promised to give him money.[813] They paid him thirty pieces of silver.[814] He promised to do it, and[815] from that time on[816] was looking for an opportunity to betray Jesus to them away from the crowd.[817]

During the days, Jesus was teaching in the temple courts, and each night he would go out and spend the night on the Mount of Olives. And all the people came early in the morning to listen to him in the temple courts.[818]

Before the Passover Festival, Jesus knew that the time had come for him to leave this world and go to the Father. Having loved those who were his own in the world, he loved them to the end.[a] [819]

The day of Unleavened Bread[820] (the first day of the Festival)[821] arrived, when it was necessary to sacrifice the Passover lamb.[b] Jesus sent Peter and John, saying, "Go prepare the Passover for us, so that we may eat it."

They said to him, "Where do you want us to prepare it?"

He told them, "Just as you enter the city, a man carrying a jar of water will meet you. Follow him into the house that he enters. Tell the owner of the house, 'The Teacher says to you,[822] "My time is near.[823] Where is the guest room[824] at your house,[825] where I may eat the Passover with my disciples?"' He will show you a large, furnished upper room. Make preparations there."[826]

His disciples left and went into the city and found things just as he had told them; and they prepared the Passover.[827]

Death and Glory

Now there were some Greeks among those who went up to worship at the Festival. They came to Philip, who was from Bethsaida in Galilee, and asked him, "Sir, we want to see Jesus." Philip went to tell Andrew. Andrew came with Philip and told Jesus.

Jesus answered them, "The time has come for the Son of Man to be glorified. Amen, Amen, I tell you: Unless a kernel of wheat falls to the ground and dies, it continues to be one kernel. But if it dies, it produces much grain. Anyone who loves his life destroys it. And the one who hates his life in this world will hold on to it for eternal

---

[a] Or *to the fullest extent*

[b] [According to the Lord's command, the evening of Nisan 14 was the beginning of the Passover, while the evening of Nisan 15 began the Feast of Unleavened Bread. Nevertheless, by the time of Jesus incarnation, it was (and arguably to this day still is) customary for the Jews to reckon the two festivals as one 8-day festival. Likewise, Josephus writes, "We keep a feast for eight days, which is called the *Feast of Unleavened Bread*" (*Antiquities* 2.14.6 311-317). Here, then, reference to Nisan 14 as the first day of the Festival, or "The Day of Unleavened Bread", is not unexpected.]

life. If anyone serves me, let him follow me. And where I am, there my servant will be also. If anyone serves me, the Father will honor him."

"Now my soul is troubled. And what shall I say? 'Father, save me from this hour'? No, this is the reason I came to this hour. Father, glorify your name!"

A voice came from heaven: "I have glorified my name, and I will glorify it again."

The crowd standing there heard it and said it thundered. Others said an angel talked to him. Jesus answered, "This voice was not for my sake but for yours."

"Now is the judgment of this world. Now the ruler of this world will be thrown out. And I, when I am lifted up from the earth, will draw all people to myself." He said this to indicate what kind of death he was going to die.

The crowd answered him, "We have heard from the Scriptures that the Christ will remain forever. So how can you say, 'The Son of Man must be lifted up'? Who is this Son of Man?"

Then Jesus told them, "The light will be with you just a little while longer. Keep on walking while you have the light, so that darkness does not overtake you. The one who walks in the darkness does not know where he is going. While you have the light, believe in the light, so that you may become sons of light."

Jesus spoke these words, and then went away and was hidden from them.

Even though Jesus had done so many miraculous signs in their presence, they still did not believe in him. This was to fulfill the word of Isaiah the prophet, who said:

> Lord, who has believed our message?
> And to whom has the arm of the Lord been revealed?[a]

For this reason they could not believe, because Isaiah also said:

> He has blinded their eyes
>   and hardened their heart,
>   so that they would not see with their eyes,
>   or understand with their heart,
>   or turn—and I would heal them.[b]

Isaiah said these things when[c] he saw Jesus' glory and spoke about him.

Nevertheless, even many of the rulers believed in him, but because of the Pharisees they were not confessing him, so that they would not be put out of the synagogue. For they loved praise from people more than praise from God.

Then Jesus called out, "The one who believes in me does not believe in me only, but in him who sent me. And the one who sees me sees him who sent me. I have come into the world as a light, so that everyone who believes in me would not remain in darkness. If anyone hears my words but does not hold on to them, I do not judge him, for I did not come to judge the world, but to save the world. The one who rejects me and does not receive my words does have a judge. The word which

---

[a] Isaiah 53:1
[b] Isaiah 6:10
[c] Some witnesses to the text read *because*.

I spoke is what will judge him on the Last Day, because I have not spoken on my own, but the Father himself who sent me has given me a command regarding what I am to say and what I am to speak. And I know that his command is eternal life. So the things I speak are exactly what the Father told me to speak."[828]

Jesus Celebrates the Passover

When it was evening, he arrived with the Twelve.[829]

By the time the supper took place, the Devil had already put the idea into the heart of Judas, son of Simon Iscariot, to betray Jesus.[830]

When the hour had come, Jesus reclined at the table with the twelve apostles.[831] He said to them, "I have eagerly desired to eat this Passover with you before I suffer, for I tell you, I will not eat it again until it is fulfilled in the kingdom of God."

He took a cup, gave thanks, and said, "Take this and divide it among yourselves, for I tell you, from now on I will not drink of the fruit of the vine until the kingdom of God comes."[832]

No Greater Love—in Service

Jesus knew that the Father had given all things into his hands, and that he had come from God and was going back to God. He got up from the supper and laid aside his outer garment. He took a towel and tied it around his waist. Then he poured water into a basin and began to wash his disciples' feet, drying them with the towel that was wrapped around him.

He came to Simon Peter, who asked him, "Lord, are you going to wash my feet?"

Jesus answered him, "You do not understand what I am doing now, but later you will understand."

Peter told him, "You will never, ever, wash my feet!"

Jesus replied, "If I do not wash you, you have no part with me."

"Lord, not just my feet," Simon Peter replied, "but also my hands and my head!"

Jesus told him, "A person who has had a bath needs only to wash his feet, but his body is completely clean. And you[a] are clean, but not all of you." Indeed, he knew who was going to betray him. That is why he said, "Not all of you are clean."

After Jesus had washed their feet and put on his outer garment, he reclined at the table again. "Do you understand what I have done for you?" he asked them. "You call me Teacher and Lord. You are right, because I am. Now if I, your Lord and Teacher, have washed your feet, you also ought to wash one another's feet. Yes, I have given you an example so that you also would do just as I have done for you. Amen, Amen, I tell you: A servant is not greater than his master, nor is a messenger greater than the one who sent him. If you know these things, you are blessed if you do them."

"I am not talking about all of you. I know those I have chosen. But this is so that the Scripture may be fulfilled: 'One who eats bread with me has raised his heel

---

[a] *You* is plural.

against me.'ª I am telling you this right now before it happens, so that when it does happen, you may believe that I am he."

"Amen, Amen, I tell you: Whoever receives anyone I send, receives me. And whoever receives me, receives the one who sent me."[833]

One Will Betray Jesus

After saying this,[834] while they were reclining and eating,[835] Jesus was troubled in his spirit and testified, "Amen, Amen, I tell you: One of you will betray me,[836] one who is eating with me.[837] The hand of him who is going to betray me is with mine on the table."[838]

The disciples were looking at each other, uncertain which of them he meant.[839] They were very sad and began to say to him one after another, "Surely, not I, Lord?"[840] He said to them, "It is one of the Twelve, one who is dipping bread with me in the dish.[841] Indeed, the Son of Man is going to go just as it has been written about him, but woe to that man by whom the Son of Man is betrayed![842] It would have been better for that man if he had not been born."[843]

They began to discuss with one another which of them it was who was going to do this.[844]

Judas, who betrayed him, replied, "Surely, not I, Rabbi?"

He said to him, "Yes, you are the one."ᵇ [845]

One of his disciples, the one Jesus loved, was reclining at Jesus' side. So Simon Peter motioned to him to find out which one he was talking about.

So leaning back against Jesus' side, he asked, "Lord, who is it?"

Jesus replied, "It is the one to whom I will give this piece of bread, after I have dipped it in the dish." Then he dipped the piece of bread and gave it to Judas, the son of Simon Iscariot. As soon as Judas took the bread, Satan entered into him.

So Jesus told him, "What you are about to do, do more quickly."

None of those reclining at the table understood why Jesus said this to him. Because Judas kept the money box, some thought that Jesus was telling him, "Buy what we need for the Festival," or to give something to the poor. As soon as Judas had taken the bread, he went out. And it was night.

After Judas left, Jesus said, "Now the Son of Man is glorified, and God is glorified in him.ᶜ If God is glorified in him,ᵈ God will also glorify the Son in himself and will glorify him at once."[846]

ª Psalm 41:9
ᵇ Or *It is what you yourself said*, or *You have said it yourself*.
ᶜ Or *Now the Son of Man was glorified, and God was glorified in him*.
ᵈ Some witnesses to the text omit *If God is glorified in him*.

The Lord's Supper

While they were eating, Jesus took bread, blessed and broke it, and gave it to the disciples. He said, "Take, eat, this is my body,[847] which is given for you. Do this in remembrance of me."

In the same way, he took the cup after the supper,[848] gave thanks, and gave it to them, saying "Drink from it all of you, for this is my blood of the new[a] testament,[b] which is poured out for many for the forgiveness of sins."[849] They all drank from it. He said to them, "Amen I tell you: I will certainly[850] not drink of this fruit of the vine from now until that day when I drink it new with you in my Father's kingdom."[851]

Who Is Greatest?

A dispute arose among the disciples about which of them was considered to be greatest. But he told them, "The kings of the Gentiles lord it over them, and those who have authority over them are called Benefactors. But it is not to be that way with you. Instead, let the greatest among you become like the youngest, and the one who leads like the one who serves. For who is greater, one who reclines at the table or one who serves? Isn't it the one who reclines at the table? But I am among you as one who serves. You are those who have remained with me in my trials. I am going to grant a kingdom to you, just as my Father granted to me, so that you may eat and drink at my table in my kingdom. And you will sit on thrones, judging the twelve tribes of Israel."[852]

Jesus Predicts Peter's Denial

"Dear children, I am going to be with you only a little longer. You will look for me, and just as I told the Jews, so I tell you now: Where I am going, you cannot come."

"A new commandment I give you: Love one another. Just as I have loved you, so also you are to love one another. By this everyone will know that you are my disciples, if you have love for one another."

Simon Peter said to him, "Lord, where are you going?"

Jesus answered, "Where I am going you cannot follow now, but you will follow later."

Peter asked, "Lord, why can't I follow you now? I will lay down my life for you!"

Jesus replied, "Will you really lay down your life for me?"[853]

The Lord said, "Simon, Simon, pay attention: Satan has asked to have you all, so that he may sift you as wheat. But I prayed for you, Simon, that your faith may not fail. And when you have returned to me, strengthen your brothers."

He said to him, "Lord, I am ready to go with you both to prison and to death!"

But Jesus replied,[854] "Amen, Amen, I tell you: The rooster will not crow until you have denied me three times."[855]

---

[a] A few early witnesses to the text omit *new*.
[b] As in *last will and testament*. See Galatians 3:15.

Then Jesus said to them, "This night you will all fall away on account of me, for it is written, 'I will strike the shepherd, and the sheep of the flock will be scattered.'[a] But after I have been raised, I will go ahead of you into Galilee."

Peter answered him, "Even if all fall away because of you, I will never fall away."[856]

But Jesus replied, "I tell you, Peter:[857] Today—this very night—before the rooster crows twice, you will deny me three times."

But Peter kept saying emphatically, "Even if I have to die with you, I will never deny you." And they all said the same thing.[858]

He said to them, "When I sent you out without money bag, traveler's bag, and sandals, did you lack anything?"

"Nothing," they said.

Then he told them, "But now, let the one who has a money bag take it, and likewise a traveler's bag. And let the one who has no sword sell his cloak and buy one. For I tell you that this Scripture must be fulfilled in me: 'He was counted with transgressors.'[b] Indeed, what is written about me is going to have its fulfillment."

They said, "Lord, look, here are two swords."

He said to them, "That is enough."[859]

No Greater Love—in Peace

"Do not let your heart be troubled. Believe in God; believe also in me. In my Father's house are many mansions.[c] If it were not so, I would have told you. I am going to prepare a place for you.[d] And if I go and prepare a place for you, I will come again and take you to be with me, so that you may also be where I am. You know where I am going, and you know the way."

"Lord, we don't know where you are going," Thomas replied, "so how can we know the way?"

Jesus said to him, "I am the Way and the Truth and the Life. No one comes to the Father, except through me. If you know me, you would also know my Father.[e] From now on you do know him and have seen him."

"Lord," said Philip, "show us the Father, and that is enough for us."

"Have I been with you so long," Jesus answered, "and you still do not know me, Philip? The one who has seen me has seen the Father. How can you say, 'Show us the Father'? Don't you believe that I am in the Father and the Father is in me? The words that I am telling you I am not speaking on my own, but the Father who remains in me is doing his works. Believe me that I am in the Father, and the Father is in me. Or else believe[f] because of the works themselves."

---

[a] Zechariah 13:7
[b] Isaiah 53:12
[c] Or *dwelling places*, referring to permanent residences
[d] Some witnesses to the text read *If it were not so, would I have told you that I am going away to prepare a place for you?*
[e] Some witnesses to the text read *If you have known me, you will also know my Father.*
[f] Some witnesses to the text add *me*.

"Amen, Amen, I tell you: The one who believes in me will do the works that I am doing. And he will do even greater works than these, because I am going to the Father. I will do whatever you ask in my name so that the Father may be glorified in the Son. If you ask me[a] for anything in my name, I will do it."

"If you love me, hold on to[b] my commands. I will ask the Father, and he will give you another Counselor to be with you forever. He is the Spirit of truth, whom the world cannot receive because it does not see him or know him. You know him because he stays with you and will be in you."

"I will not leave you as orphans; I am coming to you. In a little while the world will see me no longer, but you will see me. Because I live, you also will live. In that day you will know that I am in my Father, and you in me, and I in you. The one who has my commands and holds on to them is the one who loves me. And the one who loves me will be loved by my Father. I too will love him and show myself to him."

Judas (not Iscariot) said to him, "Lord, what has happened that you are going to show yourself to us and not to the world?"

Jesus answered him, "If anyone loves me, he will hold on to my word. My Father will love him, and we will come to him and make our home with him. The one who does not love me does not hold on to my words. The word that you are hearing is not mine, but it is from the Father who sent me."

"I have told you these things while staying with you. But the Counselor, the Holy Spirit, whom the Father will send in my name, will teach you all things and remind you of everything I told you."

"Peace I leave with you. My peace I give to you. Not as the world gives do I give to you. Do not let your heart be troubled, and do not let it be afraid. You heard me tell you, 'I am going away and I am coming to you.' If you loved me, you would be glad that I am going to the Father, because the Father is greater than I."

"I have told you now before it happens so that, when it does happen, you may believe. I will not speak with you much longer, because the ruler of this world is coming. He has no power over me. But I want the world to know that I love the Father and that I am doing exactly what the Father has instructed me."

"Get up. Let's leave this place."[860] After they sang a hymn, they went out.[861]

No Greater Love—in Good Fruit

"I am the true vine, and my Father is the gardener.[c] Every branch in me that does not bear fruit, he is going to cut off. And he prunes every branch that does bear fruit, so that it will bear more fruit."

"You are already clean because of the word I have spoken to you. Remain in me, and I am going to remain in you. A branch cannot bear fruit by itself; it must remain in the vine. Likewise, you cannot bear fruit unless you remain in me."

---

[a] Some witnesses to the text omit *me*.
[b] Some witnesses to the text read *you will hold on to*.
[c] Or *vinedresser*

"I am the Vine; you are the branches. The one who remains in me and I in him is the one who bears much fruit, because without me you can do nothing. If anyone does not remain in me, he is thrown away like a branch and withers. Such branches are gathered, thrown into the fire, and burned. If you remain in me and my words remain in you, ask whatever you wish, and it will be done for you. My Father is glorified by this: that you continue to bear much fruit and prove to be[a] my disciples."

"As the Father has loved me, so also I have loved you. Remain in my love. If you hold on to my commands, you will remain in my love, just as I have held on to my Father's commands and remain in his love. I have told you these things so that my joy would continue to be in you and that your joy would be complete."

"This is my command: Love one another as I have loved you. No one has greater love than this: that someone lays down his life for his friends. You are my friends if you continue to do the things I instruct you. I no longer call you servants, because a servant does not know what his master is doing. But I have called you friends, because everything that I heard from my Father, I have made known to you. You did not choose me, but I chose you and appointed you to go and bear fruit, fruit that will endure, so that the Father will give you whatever you ask in my name. These things I am instructing you, so that you love one another."

"If the world hates you, you know that it hated me first. If you were of the world, the world would love its own. However, because you are not of the world, but I have chosen you out of it, for that very reason the world hates you. Remember the saying I told you: 'A servant is not greater than his master.' If they persecuted me, they will persecute you too. If they held on to my word, they will hold on to yours as well. But they will do all these things to you on account of my name, because they do not know the one who sent me. If I had not come and spoken to them, they would have no sin. But now they have no excuse for their sin. The one who hates me also hates my Father. If I had not done the works among them that no one else did, they would not be guilty of sin. But now they have seen and hated both me and my Father. This was to fulfill the word which is written in their Law: 'They hated me for no reason.'"[b]

"When the Counselor comes, whom I will send to you from the Father—the Spirit of truth, who proceeds from the Father—he will testify about me. And you also are going to testify, because you have been with me from the beginning."[862]

No Greater Love—in Joy

"I have told you these things so that you will not fall away. They will put you out of the synagogues. In fact, a time is coming when anyone who murders you will think he is offering a service to God. They will do these things because they have not known the Father or me. But I have told you these things so that when their[c] time comes, you may remember that I told them to you. I did not tell you these things from the beginning, because I was with you."

---

a   Some witnesses to the text read *so will prove to be*.
b   Psalm 35:19; 69:4
c   Some witnesses to the text read *the*.

"But now I am going away to him who sent me, and not one of you asks me, 'Where are you going?' Yet because I have told you these things, sorrow has filled your heart. Nevertheless, I am telling you the truth: It is good for you that I go away. For if I do not go away, the Counselor will not come to you. But if I go, I will send him to you. When he comes, he will convict the world about sin, about righteousness, and about judgment: about sin, because they do not believe in me; about righteousness, because I am going to the Father and you will no longer see me; about judgment, because the ruler of this world has been condemned."

"I still have many things to tell you, but you cannot bear them now. But when he, the Spirit of truth, comes, he will guide you into[a] all truth. For he will not speak on his own, but whatever he hears he will speak. He will also declare to you what is to come. He will glorify me, because he will take from what is mine and declare it to you. Everything the Father has is mine. This is why I said that he takes from what is mine and will declare it to you."

"In a little while you are not going to see me anymore, and again in a little while you will see me, because I am going away to the Father."[b]

Therefore some of his disciples asked one another, "What does he mean when he tells us, 'In a little while you are not going to see me, and again in a little while you will see me,' and 'Because I am going away to the Father'?" So they kept asking, "What does he mean by 'a little while'? We don't understand what he's saying."

Jesus knew that they wanted to ask him about this, so he said to them, "Are you trying to determine with one another what I meant by saying, 'In a little while you are not going to see me, and again in a little while you will see me'? Amen, Amen, I tell you: You will weep and wail, but the world will rejoice. You will become sorrowful, but your sorrow will turn to joy. A woman giving birth has pain, because her time has come. But when she has delivered the child, she no longer remembers the anguish, because of her joy that a person has been born into the world."

"So you also have sorrow now. But I will see you again. Your heart will rejoice, and no one will take your joy away from you. In that day you will not ask me anything. Amen, Amen, I tell you: Whatever you ask the Father in my name, he will give you. Until now you have not asked for anything in my name. Ask, and you will receive, so that your joy may be made complete."

"I have told you these things using figurative language. A time is coming when I will no longer speak to you using figurative language, but I will tell you plainly about the Father. In that day you will ask in my name, and I am not telling you that I will make requests of the Father on your behalf. For the Father himself loves you, because you have loved me and have believed that I came from God. I came from the Father and have come into the world. Now I am going to leave the world and go to the Father."

---

[a] Some witnesses to the text read *in*.
[b] Some witnesses to the text omit *because I am going away to the Father*.

"Yes!" his disciples said. "Now you are speaking plainly and not using figurative language. Now we know that you know everything and do not need to have anyone ask you anything. For this reason we believe that you came from God."

Jesus answered them, "Now do you believe? Listen, a time is coming, in fact it is here, when you will be scattered, everyone to his own home. You will leave me all alone. Yet I am not going to be alone, because the Father is with me. I have told you these things, so that you may have peace in me. In this world you are going to have trouble. But be courageous! I have overcome the world."[863]

Jesus' High Priestly Prayer

After Jesus had spoken these things, he looked up to heaven and said, "Father, the time has come. Glorify your Son so that your Son may glorify you. For you gave him authority over all flesh, so that he may give eternal life to all those you have given him. This is eternal life: that they may know you, the only true God, and Jesus Christ, whom you sent. I have glorified you on earth by finishing the work you gave me to do. Now, Father, glorify me at your own side with the glory I had at your side before the world existed."

"I revealed your name to the men you gave me out of the world. They were yours; you gave them to me, and they have held on to your word. Now they know that everything you have given me comes from you. For I gave them the words you gave me, and they received them. They learned the truth that I came from you. They believed that you sent me."

"I pray for them. I am not praying for the world, but for those you have given me, because they are yours. All that is mine is yours, and what is yours is mine. And I am glorified in them. I am no longer going to be in the world, but they are still in the world, and I am coming to you. Holy Father, protect them by your name, which you gave me, so that they may be one as we are one. While I was with them, I kept those you gave me safe in your name.[a] I protected them and not one of them was destroyed, except the son of destruction, so that the Scripture might be fulfilled."

"But now I am coming to you, and I am saying these things in the world, so that they may be filled with my joy. I have given them your word. The world hated them, because they are not of the world, just as I am not of the world. I am not asking that you take them out of the world, but that you protect them from the Evil One. They are not of the world, just as I am not of the world."

"Sanctify them by the truth. Your word is truth. As you sent me into the world, I also sent them into the world. I sanctify myself for them, so they also may be sanctified by the truth."

"I am praying not only for them, but also for those who believe in me through their message. May they all be one, as you, Father, are in me and I am in you. May they also be one[b] in us, so that the world may believe that you sent me. I have given

---

[a] Some witnesses to the text read *I kept them safe in your name, which you gave me.*
[b] Some witnesses to the text omit *one*.

them the glory you gave me, so that they may be one, as we are one: I in them, and you in me. May they become completely one, so that the world may know that you sent me and loved them even as you loved me."

"Father, I want those you have given me to be with me where I am so that they may see my glory—the glory you gave me because you loved me before the world's foundation. Righteous Father, the world did not know you, but I knew you, and these men knew that you sent me. I made your name known to them and will continue to make it known, so that the love you have for me may be in them and that I may be in them."[864]

The Arrest

After saying these things,[865] Jesus left and went out to the Mount of Olives, as was his custom,[866] across the Kidron Valley,[a] where there was a garden[867] called Gethsemane.[868] When he reached the place,[869] he and his disciples went into it.[870] Jesus[871] told his disciples, "Sit here, while I go over there and pray.[872] Keep praying that you may not enter into temptation."[873] Then[874] he took with him Peter, and[875] James and John[876] (the two sons of Zebedee), and he began to be sorrowful and distressed. Then he said to them, "My soul is very sorrowful, even to the point of death. Stay here, and keep watch with me."[877]

Going forward a little,[878] he withdrew from them about a stone's throw [and] knelt down[879] on the ground.[880] He fell on his face,[881] and prayed that, if it were possible, the hour might pass from him. He also said, "*Abba*,[882] my[883] Father, everything is possible for you.[884] If you are willing,[885] take this cup away from me. Yet not what I will, but what you will."[886] An angel from heaven appeared to him and strengthened him.[887]

When he returned to the disciples, he found them sleeping. He said to Peter, "Simon, are you sleeping? Were you not strong enough to keep watch for one hour? Watch and pray that you may not enter into temptation. The spirit is willing, but the flesh is weak."[888]

He went away a second time and prayed,[889] saying the same thing,[890] "My Father, if it is not possible for this cup to pass from me[b] unless I drink it, may your will be done." Again[891] when he returned, he found them sleeping, for their eyes were heavy. They did not know what they should answer him.[892] He left them again, went away, and prayed a third time. He said the same words as before.[893] As he was in agony, he prayed more fervently. His sweat became like great drops of blood falling to the ground.[c] [894]

When he rose from prayer, he went to the disciples[895] the third time[896] and found them sleeping as a result of sorrow. He said to them, "Why are you sleeping?[897] Get up and keep praying so that you may not enter into temptation.[898] It is enough. The

---

[a] The Greek word translated *Valley* refers to a seasonal stream.
[b] Some witnesses to the text omit *from me*.
[c] A few witnesses to the text omit verses 43-44.

Chapter XII: The Son of Man Handed Over

hour has come. Look, the Son of Man is betrayed into the hands of sinners. Rise, let us go. Look, my betrayer is near."[899]

Just then, while he was still speaking, Judas, one of the Twelve, arrived.[900] Now Judas, who was betraying him, also knew the place, because Jesus often met there with his disciples.[901] So Judas took the company of soldiers and some guards from the chief priests and the Pharisees,[902] from the experts in the law and the elders[903] of the people.[904] [They] came there with lanterns, torches, and weapons,[905] with swords and clubs.[906]

Now his betrayer had given them a signal, saying, "The one I kiss is the man. Arrest him and lead him away under guard."[907] Immediately he went to Jesus and said, "Greetings, Rabbi!" and kissed him.[908] But Jesus said to him, "Judas, are you betraying the Son of Man with a kiss?"[909]

Jesus said to him, "Friend, why are you here?"[910]

Jesus, knowing everything that was going to happen to him, went out and asked them, "Who are you looking for?"

"Jesus the Nazarene," they replied.

"I am he," Jesus told them.

Judas, the betrayer, was standing with them. When Jesus told them, "I am he," they backed away and fell to the ground.

Then Jesus asked them again, "Who are you looking for?"

"Jesus the Nazarene," they said.

"I told you that I am he," Jesus replied. "So if you are looking for me, let these men go." This was to fulfill the statement he had spoken: "I did not lose any of those you have given me."[911]

When those who were around him saw what was about to happen, they said to him, "Lord, should we strike with a sword?"[912]

Then they advanced, took hold of Jesus, and arrested him.[913] Then Simon Peter, who had a sword, drew it, struck the high priest's servant, and cut off his right ear. The servant's name was Malchus.[914]

But Jesus responded, "Stop! No more of this!" Then he touched the servant's ear and healed him."[915]

Then Jesus said to [Peter], "Put your sword back into its place,[916] because all who take the sword will die by the sword. Do you not realize that I could call on my Father, and at once he would provide me with more than twelve legions[a] of angels? But then how would the Scriptures be fulfilled that say it must happen this way?[917] Shall I not drink the cup my Father has given me?"[918]

At that same time Jesus said to the[919] chief priests, the officers of the temple guard, and the elders, who had come out against him,[920] "Have you come out to arrest me with swords and clubs as if I were a robber? Day after day I was sitting in the temple courts teaching, and you did not arrest me. But all this has happened so that the writings of the prophets would be fulfilled.[921] This is your hour—when darkness rules."[922] Then all the disciples deserted him and fled.[923]

---

[a] A Roman *legion* contained as many as six thousand soldiers.

A certain young man was following him, wearing just a linen cloth over his naked body. They seized him, but he left behind the linen cloth and fled from them naked.⁹²⁴

Then the company of soldiers, their commander, and the Jewish guards⁹²⁵ seized [Jesus],⁹²⁶ arrested and bound him.⁹²⁷ They led him away, and brought him into the high priest's house.⁹²⁸

First they led him to Annas, because he was father-in-law to Caiaphas, who was the high priest that year. Now it was Caiaphas who had advised the Jews, "It is better that one man die for the people."⁹²⁹

Peter Denies Jesus

Peter followed him at a distance, right into the courtyard of the high priest. He was sitting with the guards and warming himself at the fire.

Simon Peter and another disciple kept following Jesus⁹³⁰ at a distance.⁹³¹ That disciple was known to the high priest, so he went into the high priest's courtyard with Jesus. But Peter stood outside by the door. So the other disciple, the one known to the high priest, went out and talked to the girl watching the door and brought Peter in.⁹³² He went inside and sat down with the guards to see how it would turn out.⁹³³

While Peter was in the courtyard below,⁹³⁴ the girl at the door⁹³⁵ (one of the servant girls of the high priest) came there.⁹³⁶ When they had lit a fire in the middle of the courtyard and sat down together, Peter sat down among⁹³⁷ the guards to see how it would turn out.⁹³⁸ [While] he was sitting with the guards and warming himself at the fire,⁹³⁹ [the] servant girl saw him sitting near the light.⁹⁴⁰ She looked directly at him and said, "You were also with the Nazarene, Jesus,⁹⁴¹ the Galilean!"⁹⁴² She looked closely at him and said, "This man also was with him.⁹⁴³ You are not one of this man's disciples too, are you?"

"I am not!" he said.⁹⁴⁴ "Woman, I do not know him."⁹⁴⁵ He denied it in front of everyone, saying,⁹⁴⁶ "I don't know or understand what you are saying," and he went out to the entryway. Then a rooster crowed.⁹⁴⁷

The servants and guards were standing around a fire of coals that they had made because it was cold. While they warmed themselves, Peter was standing with them, warming himself too.⁹⁴⁸

Jesus before Annas

The high priest questioned Jesus about his disciples and his teaching.

Jesus answered him, "I have spoken openly to the world. I always taught in a synagogue or at the temple, where all the Jews gather. I said nothing in secret. Why are you questioning me? Ask those who heard what I told them. Look, they know what I said."

When he said this, one of the guards standing there hit Jesus in the face. "Is that how you answer the high priest?" he demanded.

"If I said something wrong," Jesus answered, "testify about what was wrong. But if I was right, why did you hit me?"

Then Annas sent him bound to Caiaphas the high priest.⁹⁴⁹

Jewish Court

Those who had arrested Jesus led him away to Caiaphas.⁹⁵⁰ As soon as it was day, the council of the elders of the people met together, both the chief priests and experts in the law. They brought him into their Sanhedrin.⁹⁵¹

The chief priests and the whole Sanhedrin were looking for testimony against Jesus in order to put him to death, but they did not find any. Many testified falsely against him, but their testimonies did not agree. Some stood up and gave this false testimony against him: "We heard him say, 'I will destroy this temple made with hands, and in three days I will build another made without hands.'" Yet even on this point, their testimony did not agree.

The high priest stepped forwardᵃ and questioned Jesus, "Have you no answer? What is this they are testifying against you?"

But Jesus was silent and did not answer anything.

Again the high priest asked him,⁹⁵² "I place you under oath by the living God:⁹⁵³ Are you the Christ, the Son of the Blessed One?"

"I am," Jesus said.⁹⁵⁴ But he said to them, "If I tell you, you will not believe, and if I ask you, you will not answer me or release me.ᵇ ⁹⁵⁵But from now on, the Son of Man will be seated at the right hand of the power of Godᶜ ⁹⁵⁶ and coming with the clouds of heaven."⁹⁵⁷

Then the high priest tore his robes and said, "He has spoken blasphemy! Why do we need any more witnesses? See, you have just heard the blasphemy⁹⁵⁸ from his own mouth!⁹⁵⁹ What do you think?"⁹⁶⁰

They answered, "He is deserving of death!" Then they spit in his face.⁹⁶¹ They covered his face and struck him with their fists.⁹⁶² Some slapped him and said, "Prophesy to us, Christ! Who hit you?"⁹⁶³ The guards also took him and beat him.⁹⁶⁴

The Guards Mock Jesus

The men who were holding Jesus in custody mocked him while they were beating him. They blindfolded him and kept asking him, "Prophesy! Who hit you?" And they went on saying many other blasphemous things against him.⁹⁶⁵

Peter Denies Again

After a little while,⁹⁶⁶ when Peter went out to the entryway, someone else saw him and said to those who were there, "This fellow was with Jesus of Nazareth.⁹⁶⁷ You also are one of them!"⁹⁶⁸

---

a   Or *stood up in front* (literally *in the center*)
b   A few witnesses to the text omit *or release me*.
c   Psalm 110:1

When the servant girl saw him, once more she began to tell those standing there, "This is one of them."[969] Simon Peter continued to stand there warming himself. So they said to him, "You are not one of his disciples too, are you?"[970]

Again Peter denied it with an oath and said,[971] "Man, I am not![972] I do not know the man."[973]

After about one hour had passed, someone else was firmly insisting, "Truly this man was with him too, because he is a Galilean!"[974] Those who stood by came and said to Peter,[975] "Surely you are one of them,[976] because you are a Galilean.[977] Even your accent gives you away."[978] One of the servants of the high priest, a relative of the man whose ear Peter had cut off, said, "Didn't I see you with him in the garden?"[979]

Then[980] Peter[981] began to curse and to swear,[982] "Man, I don't know what you are talking about![983] "I do not know the man!"[984] At that very moment, while he was still speaking, the rooster crowed[985] for the second time.[986] The Lord turned and looked at Peter. Then Peter remembered the Lord's word, how he had said to him, "Before the rooster crows [987] twice [988] today you will deny me three times." He went outside,[989] broke down,[990] and wept bitterly.[991]

As soon as it was morning, the chief priests, along with the elders, the experts in the law, and the whole Sanhedrin, reached a decision[992] to put Jesus to death.[993] They bound him, led him[994] from Caiaphas to the Praetorium,[995] and handed him over to Pontius Pilate, the governor. [996] They did not enter the Praetorium themselves, so that they would not become ceremonially unclean. (They wanted to be able to eat the Passover meal.)[997]

The End of Judas

Then when Judas, who had betrayed him, saw that Jesus was condemned, he felt remorse. He brought back the thirty pieces of silver to the chief priests and elders and said, "I have sinned by betraying innocent blood." But they said, "What is that to us? That's your problem."

He threw the pieces of silver into the temple and left. Then he went out and hanged himself. The chief priests took the pieces of silver and said, "It is not lawful to put these into the treasury, since it is blood money." They reached a decision to buy the potter's field with the money, as a burial place for foreigners. So that field has been called The Field of Blood to this day. Then what was spoken through Jeremiah the prophet was fulfilled:

> They took the thirty pieces of silver, the price the sons of Israel had set for him, and they gave them for the potter's field, just as the Lord commanded me.[a] [998]

---

[a] See Zechariah 11:12-13; Jeremiah 19:1-13; 32:6-9.

Chapter XII: The Son of Man Handed Over

Jesus' Trial in Pilate's Court

So Pilate went out to [the Jews] and said, "What charge do you bring against this man?"

They answered him, "If this man were not a criminal, we would not have handed him over to you."[999]

Pilate told them, "Take him yourselves and judge him according to your law."

The Jews said, "It's not legal for us to put anyone to death." This happened so that the statement Jesus had spoken indicating what kind of death he was going to die would be fulfilled.[1000]

The whole group began to accuse him, saying, "We found this fellow misleading our nation, forbidding the payment of taxes to Caesar, and saying that he himself is Christ, a king."[1001]

Pilate went back into the Praetorium and summoned Jesus.[1002] He asked him, "Are you the King of the Jews?"[1003]

Jesus answered, "Are you saying this on your own, or did others tell you about me?"

Pilate answered, "Am I a Jew? Your own people and chief priests handed you over to me. What have you done?"

Jesus replied, "My kingdom is not of this world. If my kingdom were of this world, my servants would fight so that I would not be handed over to the Jews. But now my kingdom is not from here."

"You are a king then?" Pilate asked.[1004]

Jesus answered, "I am, as you say, a king.[1005] For this reason I was born, and for this reason I came into the world, to testify to the truth. Everyone who belongs to the truth listens to my voice."

"What is truth?" Pilate said to him.

After he said this, he went out again to the Jews.[1006] Pilate said to the chief priests and the crowds, "I find no basis for a charge against this man."[1007]

But they kept insisting, "He stirs up the people, teaching all through Judea, beginning from Galilee all the way here."[1008]

Pilate Sends Jesus to Herod

When Pilate heard this, he asked if the man was a Galilean. When he learned that he was under Herod's jurisdiction, he sent him to Herod, who was also in Jerusalem during those days.

When Herod saw Jesus, he was very glad. For a long time, he had wanted to see him, because he had heard many things about him. He hoped to see some miracle performed by him. He questioned him with many words, but Jesus gave him no answer. The chief priests and the experts in the law stood there, vehemently accusing him. Herod, along with his soldiers, treated him with contempt and ridiculed him. Dressing him in bright clothing, he sent him back to Pilate. Herod and Pilate became friends with each other on that day. Before this they had been enemies of each other.

Pilate called together the chief priests, the rulers, and the people, and said to them, "You brought this man to me as one who is misleading the people. Look, I have examined him in your presence. I have found in this man no basis for the charges you are bringing against him. Herod did not either, for he sent him back to us.[a] See, he has done nothing worthy of death. So I will have him flogged and release him."[1009]

When [Jesus] was accused by the chief priests and elders, he answered nothing. Then Pilate said to him,[1010] "Are you not going to answer anything?[1011] Don't you hear how many things they are testifying against you?"

But he did not answer him—not even one word, so that the governor was very surprised.[1012]

Barabbas or Jesus?

At the time of the Festival the governor had a custom to release to the crowd any one prisoner they wanted.[1013] At that time they were holding a notorious prisoner named Barabbas.[1014] Barabbas had been thrown in prison for a rebellion in the city and for murder.[1015] The crowd came up and began to ask Pilate to do for them what he usually did.[1016] So when they were assembled, Pilate said to them,[1017] "You have a custom that I release one prisoner to you at the Passover.[1018] Which one do you want me to release to you? Barabbas—or Jesus, who is called Christ?[1019] Do you want me to release the King of the Jews for you?"[1020] For Pilate knew that they had handed Jesus over to him because of envy.

While he was sitting on the judgment seat, Pilate's wife sent him a message. "Have nothing to do with that righteous man," she said, "since I have suffered many things today in a dream because of him."[1021] But the chief priests and the elders persuaded the crowd to ask for Barabbas and to have Jesus put to death.[1022]

Then they shouted back, "Not this man, but Barabbas![1023] Release Barabbas to us!"[1024]

Pilate addressed them again, because he wanted to release Jesus.[1025] The governor asked them, "Which of the two do you want me to release to you?"[1026]

Pilate said to them, "Then what should I do with[1027] Jesus, who is called Christ[1028] the man you call the King of the Jews?"[1029]

They all[1030] kept shouting, "Crucify! Crucify him!"[1031]

The governor asked them, "Which of the two do you want me to release to you?" "Barabbas!" they said.

But Pilate said to them[1032] the third time,[1033] "Why? What has he done wrong?[1034] I have found no grounds for sentencing him to death. So I will whip him and release him." But they kept pressuring him with loud voices, demanding that he be crucified.[1035] They kept shouting even louder: "Crucify him!"[1036] And their voices[b] were overwhelming.[1037]

---

[a] Some witnesses to the text read *For I sent you to him*.
[b] Some witnesses to the text add *and the voices of the high priests*.

When Pilate saw that he was accomplishing nothing and that instead it was turning into a riot, he took water, washed his hands in front of the crowd, and said, "I am innocent of this righteous man's blood. It is your responsibility."

And all the people answered, "Let his blood be on us and on our children!"[1038]

Since he wanted to satisfy the crowd,[1039] Pilate decided that what they demanded would be done.[1040] He released Barabbas to them,[1041] but he handed Jesus over to their will.[1042]

Soldiers Mock Jesus

Then Pilate took Jesus and had him flogged.[1043] The soldiers led him away inside the palace, which is the Praetorium, and called together the whole cohort[a] of soldiers.[1044] They stripped him and put a[1045] scarlet[1046] purple[1047] robe on him. They twisted together a crown of thorns and put it on his head.[1048] The soldiers began to salute him.[1049] They put a staff in his right hand, knelt in front of him, and mocked him by saying, "Hail, King of the Jews!"[1050] And they kept hitting him in the face.[1051] They spit on him, took the staff, and hit him repeatedly on his head.[1052]

"Behold the Man!"

Pilate went outside again and said to them, "Look, I am bringing him out to you to let you know that I find no basis for a charge against him."

So Jesus came out wearing the crown of thorns and the purple robe. Pilate said to them, "Behold the man!"

When the chief priests and guards saw him, they shouted, "Crucify! Crucify!"

Pilate told them, "Take him yourselves and crucify him, for I find no basis for a charge against him."

The Jews answered him, "We have a law, and according to that law he ought to die, because he claimed to be the Son of God."

When Pilate heard this statement, he was even more afraid. He went back inside the palace again and asked Jesus, "Where are you from?"

But Jesus gave him no answer.

So Pilate asked him, "Are you not talking to me? Don't you know that I have the authority to release you or to crucify you?"

Jesus answered, "You would have no authority over me at all if it had not been given to you from above. Therefore the one who handed me over to you has the greater sin."

From then on Pilate tried to release Jesus. But the Jews shouted, "If you let this man go, you are no friend of Caesar! Anyone who claims to be a king opposes Caesar!"

When Pilate heard these words, he brought Jesus outside. He sat down on the judge's seat at a place called the Stone Pavement, or Gabbatha in Aramaic. It was

---

[a] A Roman cohort was about six hundred soldiers.

about the sixth hour[a] on the Preparation Day for the Passover. Pilate said to the Jews, "Here is your king!"

They shouted, "Away with him! Away with him! Crucify him!"

Pilate said to them, "Should I crucify your king?"

"We have no king but Caesar!" the chief priests answered.[1053]

So then Pilate handed Jesus over to them to be crucified.[1054]

The Crucifixion

When they had mocked him, they took off the purple robe and put his own clothing on him. Then they led him out to crucify him.[1055] As they led him away[1056] out of the city,[1057] a certain man, Simon of Cyrene (the father of Alexander and Rufus), was passing by on his way in from the country.[1058] They seized Simon,[1059] placed the cross on him, and made him carry it behind Jesus.[1060] A large crowd of people was following him, including women who were mourning and wailing for him. Jesus turned to them and said, "Daughters of Jerusalem, stop weeping for me, but weep for yourselves and for your children. Be sure of this: The days are coming when they will say, 'Blessed are the childless women, the wombs that never gave birth, and the breasts that never nursed.' Then they will begin to say to the mountains, 'Fall on us!' and to the hills, 'Cover us.'[b] For if they do these things to the green wood, what will happen to the dry?"

Carrying his own cross, he went out.[1061] Two other men, who were criminals, were led away with Jesus to be executed.[1062]

They brought Jesus[1063] to a place called Golgotha, which means "The place of the skull."[1064] They offered Jesus wine to drink, mixed with[1065] myrrh[1066] gall; but when he tasted it, he would not drink it.[1067]

When they came to the place called The Skull, they crucified him there with the criminals,[1068] one on his right and one on his left.[c] [1069] Now it was the third hour[d] when they crucified him.[1070]

Jesus said, "Father, forgive them, for they do not know what they are doing."[1071]

When the soldiers crucified Jesus, they took his clothes and divided them into four parts,[1072] one part for each soldier. They also took his tunic, which was seamless, woven in one piece from top to bottom. So they said to one another, "Let's not tear it. Instead, let's cast lots to see who gets it." This was so that the Scripture might be fulfilled which says:

---

[a] The word *about* indicates an approximate time reference. Likely this was in the first part of the day, between 6 AM and 9 AM, using the time system of the Roman civil day, which began at 12 midnight. Mark 15:25 states that Jesus was crucified at 9 AM. John also seems to use Roman civil time to calculate the day in John 20:19 (because the evening is considered part of the *first day of the week*; Jewish time regarded sunset as the beginning of the next day).

[b] Hosea 10:8

[c] Some witnesses to the text include verse 28: *The Scripture was fulfilled, which says, "He was numbered with transgressors."* See Luke 22:37, where its inclusion is certain.

[d] 9 AM

> They divided my garments among them
> and cast lots for my clothing.[a]

So the soldiers did these things.[1073] Then they sat down and were keeping watch over him there.[1074]

Pilate also had a notice written and fastened on the cross[1075] above his head.[1076] The superscription stating the charge against him read,[1077] "This is[1078] Jesus[1079] the Nazarene,[1080] the King of the Jews."[1081]

Many of the Jews read this notice, because the place where Jesus was crucified was near the city, and it was written in Aramaic, Latin, and Greek.

So the chief priests of the Jews said to Pilate, "Do not write, 'The King of the Jews,' but that 'this man said, "I am the King of the Jews."'"

Pilate answered, "What I have written, I have written."[1082]

Those who passed by ridiculed him, shaking their heads and saying, "Ha![1083] You who were going to destroy the temple and rebuild it in three days, save yourself! If you are the Son of God, come down from the cross!"[1084]

In the same way the chief priests, experts in the law, and elders kept mocking him[1085] among themselves.[1086] The rulers were ridiculing him, saying, "He saved others. Let him save himself, if this is the Christ of God, the Chosen One![1087] Let the Christ, the King of Israel, come down now from the cross so that we may see and believe![1088] He trusts in God. Let God rescue him now, if he wants him, because he said, 'I am the Son of God.'" In the same way even the criminals who were crucified with him kept insulting him.[1089]

The soldiers also made fun of him.[1090] Coming up to him, they offered him sour wine, saying, "If you are the King of the Jews, save yourself!"[1091]

One of the criminals hanging there was blaspheming him, saying, "Aren't you the Christ? Save yourself and us!"

But the other criminal rebuked him. "Don't you fear God, since you are under the same condemnation? We are punished justly, for we are receiving what we deserve for what we have done, but this man has done nothing wrong." Then he said, "Jesus, remember me[b] when you come in[c] your kingdom."

Jesus said to him, "Amen I tell you: Today you will be with me in paradise."[1092]

Jesus' Compassion for His Mother

Jesus' mother, his mother's sister, Mary the wife of Clopas, and Mary Magdalene were standing near the cross.

When Jesus saw his mother and the disciple whom he loved standing nearby, he said to his mother, "Woman, here is your son!" Then he said to the disciple, "Here is your mother!" And from that time this disciple took her into his own home.[1093]

---

[a] Psalm 22:18
[b] Some witnesses to the text read *Then he said to Jesus, "Remember me, Lord...."*
[c] A few witnesses to the text read *into*.

Jesus' Death

It was now about the sixth hour,[a] and darkness came over the whole land until the ninth hour,[b] [1094] while the sun was darkened.[1095] About the ninth hour Jesus cried out with a loud voice, saying,[1096] "*Eloi, Eloi, lama sabachthani?*"[1097] which means "My God, my God, why have you forsaken me?"[c]

When some of those standing there heard this, they said,[1098] "Listen![1099] This fellow is calling for Elijah."[1100]

After this, knowing that everything had now been finished, and to fulfill the Scripture, Jesus said, "I thirst."

A jar full of sour wine was sitting there.[1101] Immediately[1102] one of them ran,[1103] took a sponge, and soaked it with sour wine. Then he put it on a[1104] hyssop branch and held it to his mouth.[1105] The rest said, "Leave him alone. Let's see if Elijah comes to save him."[1106]

When Jesus had received the sour wine, he said, "It is finished!"[1107]

Jesus cried out [1108] again [1109] with a loud voice,[1110] "Father, into your hands I commit my spirit!"[d] [1111]

Then, bowing his head,[1112] he gave up his spirit[1113] and breathed his last.[1114]

Suddenly, the temple curtain was torn in two from top to bottom.[1115] The earth shook and rocks were split. Tombs were opened, and many bodies of saints who had fallen asleep were raised to life. Those who came out of the tombs went into the holy city after Jesus' resurrection and appeared to many people. When the centurion and those who were guarding Jesus with him saw the earthquake and the things that had happened, they were terrified.[1116] The centurion [1117] who stood facing him[1118] began to glorify God, saying, "This man really was righteous,"[1119] and said, "Truly this was the Son of God."[1120]

When all the groups of people who had gathered to see this spectacle saw what had happened, they returned home beating their chests. All those who knew Jesus, and[1121] many women who had followed Jesus from Galilee and who had served him were there, watching from a distance.[1122] Among them were Mary Magdalene, Mary the mother of James the younger and of Joses[1123] (Joseph), and[1124] Salome[1125] the mother of Zebedee's sons. [1126] Many other women also came up with him to Jerusalem.[1127]

The Piercing of Jesus' Side

Since it was the Preparation Day, the Jews did not want the bodies left on the crosses over the Sabbath (because that Sabbath was a particularly important day). They asked Pilate to have the men's legs broken and the bodies taken away. So the

---

[a] Jewish time began with sunrise, so the sixth hour was about noon.
[b] 3 PM
[c] Psalm 22:1
[d] Psalm 31:5

soldiers came and broke the legs of the first man who was crucified with Jesus, and then those of the other man.

But when they came to Jesus and saw that he was already dead, they did not break his legs. Instead, one of the soldiers pierced his side with a spear. Immediately blood and water came out. The one who saw it has testified, and his testimony is true. He knows that he is telling the truth, so that you also may believe. Indeed, these things happened so that the Scripture would be fulfilled, "Not one of his bones will be broken."[a] Again another Scripture says, "They will look at the one they pierced."[b] [1128]

Jesus' Burial

Now there was a [1129] rich [1130] man named Joseph, from the Jewish town of Arimathea, who was a [1131] prominent [1132] member of the Council, a good and righteous man.[1133] He was also a disciple of Jesus,[1134] but secretly for fear of the Jews.[1135] He had not agreed with their plan and action.[1136] He was looking forward to the kingdom of God.[1137]

It was already evening, and since it was Preparation Day (that is, the day before the Sabbath),[1138] Joseph boldly went to Pilate and asked for the body of Jesus.[1139] Pilate was surprised that he was already dead. He summoned the centurion and asked him if Jesus had been dead for a long time. When he learned from the centurion that it was so,[1140] he granted the body to Joseph.[1141] Joseph bought a linen cloth.[1142] Nicodemus, who earlier had come to Jesus at night, also came bringing a mixture of myrrh and aloes, about seventy-two pounds.[c] [1143]

They took Jesus' body and bound it with linen strips[1144] along with the spices, in accord with Jewish burial customs.

There was a garden at the place where Jesus was crucified. And in the garden was a new tomb[1145]—[Joseph's] own new tomb that he had cut in the rock[1146]—where no one had yet been laid.[1147] So they laid Jesus there, because it was the Jewish Preparation Day,[1148] and the Sabbath was beginning,[1149] and the tomb was near.[1150] The women who had come with Jesus from Galilee followed after Joseph, and they observed the tomb and how his body was laid there. Then they returned and prepared spices and perfumes.[1151] [Joseph] rolled a large stone over the tomb's entrance[1152] and left.[1153] Mary Magdalene and the other Mary[1154] (the mother of Joses)[1155] were there sitting opposite the tomb,[1156] watching where the body was laid.[1157] On the Sabbath they rested according to the commandment.[1158]

---

[a] Exodus 12:46; Numbers 9:12
[b] Zechariah 12:10
[c] Literally *one hundred litras*. Greek *litra* is the Roman pound (327.45 grams or 11.55 ounces, by weight).

The Guard

On the next day,[a] which was the day after the Preparation Day, the chief priests and Pharisees gathered in the presence of Pilate and said, "Sir, we remembered what that deceiver said while he was still alive: 'After three days I will rise again.' So give a command that the tomb be made secure until the third day. Otherwise his disciples might steal his body and tell the people, 'He is risen from the dead.' And this last deception will be worse than the first."

Pilate said to them, "You have a guard. Go, make it as secure as you know how." So they went and made the tomb secure by sealing the stone and posting a guard.[1159]

---

[a] [Nisan 15, i.e. the technical first day of the 7-day Feast of Unleavened Bread, which was a high sabbath.]

Chapter XIII: He Has Risen! He Is Not Here.
The Resurrection, Appearances, and Ascension

The Resurrection

When the Sabbath[a] was past, Mary Magdalene, Mary the mother of James, and Salome bought spices so they could go and anoint Jesus.[1160] At dawn on the first day of the week,[b] [1161] very early in the morning[1162] while it was still dark,[1163] the women[c] went to the tomb,[1164] carrying the spices they had prepared.[1165] Suddenly, there was a great earthquake! For an angel of the Lord came down from heaven, and going to the tomb, he rolled away the stone and was sitting on it. His appearance was like lightning, and his clothing was as white as snow. The guards were so terrified of him that they shook and became like dead men.

[The women] were saying to each other, "Who will roll the stone away from the entrance to the tomb for us?" When they looked up, they[1166] saw that the stone, which was very large, had been rolled away [1167] from the tomb. [1168] So [Mary Magdalene] left and ran to Simon Peter and the other disciple, the one Jesus loved.[1169]

When [the women] went in, they did not find the body of the Lord Jesus. While they were wondering about this, suddenly two men stood by them in dazzling clothing. The women were terrified and bowed down with their faces to the ground.[1170] As they entered the tomb, they saw a young man dressed in a white robe sitting on the right side, and they were alarmed.[1171] The angel said to the women, "Do not be afraid! I know that you are looking for Jesus[1172] the Nazarene, who was crucified. He has risen! He is not here. See the place where they laid him.[1173] Go quickly and tell his disciples[1174] and Peter,[1175] 'He has risen from the dead! And look,[1176] he is going ahead of you into Galilee. There you will see him.'[1177] See, I have told you!"[1178]

The men said to them, "Why are you looking for the living among the dead? He is not here, but has been raised! Remember how he told you while he was still in

---

[a] [Beginning of Nisan 16, i.e. the evening just after the weekly Sabbath, since the four Gospels, and all history since that time, record the women going to the tomb early in the morning on "the first day of the week", i.e. Sunday, Nisan 16.]
[b] [Sunday, Nisan 16]
[c] Some witnesses to the text add *and some others with them*.

Galilee that the Son of Man must be delivered over to the hands of sinful men, and be crucified, and the third day rise again?" Then they remembered his words.[1179]

They went out and hurried away from the tomb, trembling and perplexed. They said nothing to anyone, because they were afraid.[1180] [Instead,] with fear and great joy, [they] ran to tell his disciples.[1181]

[Now Mary had told Simon Peter and the other disciple,] "They have taken the Lord out of the tomb, and we don't know where they put him!" So Peter and the other disciple went out, heading for the tomb. The two were running together, but the other disciple outran Peter and got to the tomb first. Bending over, he saw the linen cloths lying there, yet he did not go in.[1182]

Then Simon Peter, who was following him, arrived and went into the tomb.[1183] Bending over to look in,[1184] he saw only the strips of linen cloth,[1185] [and was] amazed at what had happened.[1186]

The cloth that had been on Jesus' head was not lying with the linen cloths, but was folded up in a separate place by itself. Then the other disciple, who arrived at the tomb first, also entered. He saw and believed. (They still did not yet understand the Scripture that he must rise from the dead.)

Then the disciples went back to their homes.[1187]

Jesus Appears to Mary Magdalene

But Mary stood outside facing the tomb, weeping. As she wept, she bent over, looking into the tomb. She saw two angels in white clothes sitting where the body of Jesus had been lying, one at the head and one at the feet. They asked her, "Woman, why are you weeping?"

She told them, "Because they have taken away my Lord, and I don't know where they have laid him."

After she said this, she turned around and saw Jesus standing there, though she did not know it was Jesus.[1188] (After Jesus had risen early on the first day of the week, he appeared first to Mary Magdalene, out of whom he had driven seven demons.)[1189]

Jesus said to her, "Woman, why are you weeping? Who are you looking for?"

Supposing he was the gardener, she replied, "Sir, if you carried him off, tell me where you laid him, and I will get him."

Jesus said to her, "Mary."

She turned and replied in Aramaic, "*Rabboni!*" (which means, "Teacher").

Jesus told her, "Do not continue to cling to me, for I have not yet ascended to my Father. But go to my brothers and tell them, 'I am ascending to my Father and your Father—to my God and your God.'"[1190]

[Now the other women were also on their way to report to the disciples what had happened.] Suddenly[a] Jesus met them and said, "Greetings!"

They approached, took hold of his feet, and worshipped him.

---

[a] Some witnesses to the text add *As they were on their way to report to the disciples, suddenly....*

Then Jesus said to them, "Do not be afraid. Go, tell my brothers that they should go to Galilee, and there they will see me."[1191]

The Guards' Report

As they were on their way, there were some members of the guard who went into the city and reported to the chief priests everything that had happened. After the chief priests had assembled with the elders and had reached a decision, they gave a large sum of money to the soldiers and said, "You are to say, 'His disciples came at night and stole him away while we were sleeping.' If the governor hears about it, we will satisfy him and keep you out of trouble." After the soldiers took the money, they did as they were instructed. And this story has been repeated among the Jews until this day.[1192]

When [the women] returned from the tomb, they[1193] went and reported[1194] all these things to the Eleven and to all the rest[1195] who had been with [Jesus], as they mourned and wept.[1196] It was Mary Magdalene, Joanna, Mary the mother of James, and the other women with them who told these things to the apostles.[1197] Mary Magdalene announced to the disciples, "I have seen the Lord!" She also told them the things he said to her.[1198]

When they heard that he was alive and had been seen by her,[1199] these words seemed to them like nonsense,[1200] and they did not believe them.[1201]

On the Way to Emmaus

Now, on that same day,[1202] after these things[1203] two of them were going to a village named Emmaus, about seven miles[a] from Jerusalem.[1204] They were talking with each other about all of these things that had happened. While they were talking and discussing this, Jesus himself approached and began to walk along with them. But their eyes were kept from recognizing him. He said to them, "What are you talking about as you walk along?" Saddened, they stopped.

One of them, named Cleopas, answered him, "Are you the only visitor in Jerusalem who does not know the things that have happened there in these days?"

"What things?" he asked them.

They replied, "The things concerning Jesus of Nazareth, a man who was a prophet, mighty in deed and word before God and all the people. The chief priests and our rulers handed him over to be condemned to death. And they crucified him. But we were hoping that he was going to redeem Israel. Not only that, but besides all this, it is now the third day since these things happened. Also some women of our group amazed us. They were at the tomb early in the morning. When they did not find his body, they came back saying that they had even seen a vision of angels, who said that he was alive. Some of those who were with us went to the tomb. They found it just as the women had said, but they did not see him."

---

[a] Sixty *stadia*; about eleven kilometers

He said to them, "How foolish you are and slow of heart to believe all that the prophets have spoken! Did not the Christ have to suffer these things and to enter his glory?" Then beginning with Moses and all the prophets, he explained to them what was said in all the Scriptures concerning himself.

As they approached the village where they were going, he acted as if he were going to travel farther. But they urged him strongly, saying, "Stay with us, since it is almost evening, and the day is almost over."[1205]

So he went in to stay with them. When he reclined at the table with them, he took the bread, blessed it, broke it, and began giving it to them. Suddenly their eyes were opened, and they recognized him. Then he vanished from their sight. They said to each other, "Were not our hearts burning within us while he was speaking to us along the road and while he was explaining the Scriptures to us?" They got up that very hour and returned to Jerusalem.[1206]

Behind Locked Doors

They found the Eleven and those who were with them assembled[1207] together[1208] behind locked doors because of their fear of the Jews.[1209]

They were saying, "The Lord really has been raised! He has appeared to Simon."[1210]

They themselves described what had happened along the road, and how they recognized him when he broke the bread.[1211] But [the disciples] did not believe them either.[1212]

Jesus Appears to the Disciples

As they were talking about these things, Jesus himself[1213] appeared to the Eleven themselves as they were reclining at the table.[1214] [He] stood among them and said to them, "Peace be with you."[1215]

But they were terrified and frightened and thought they were looking at a ghost.[1216]

After he said this, he showed them his hands and side.[1217] He said to them, "Why are you troubled? Why do doubts arise in your hearts? Look at my hands and my feet. It is I myself. Touch me and see, because a ghost does not have flesh and bones as you see that I have." When he had said this, he showed them his hands and his feet. While they still did not believe it (because of their joy), and while they were still wondering, he said to them, "Do you have anything here to eat?"

They gave him a piece of broiled fish and some honeycomb.[a] He took it and ate in front of them.[1218]

He rebuked them for their unbelief and hardness of heart, because they did not believe those who had seen him after he had risen.[1219]

---

[a] Some witnesses to the text omit *and some honeycomb*.

He said to them, "These are my words that I spoke to you while I was still with you: Everything must be fulfilled that is written about me in the Law of Moses, the Prophets, and the Psalms."

Then he opened their minds to understand the Scriptures. He said to them, "This is what is written and so it must be:[a] The Christ will suffer and rise from the dead on the third day, and repentance and forgiveness of sins will be preached in his name to all nations, beginning from Jerusalem. You are witnesses of these things. Look, I am sending you what my Father promised. But stay in the city until you are clothed with power from on high."[1220]

So the disciples rejoiced when they saw the Lord.

Jesus said to them again, "Peace be with you! Just as the Father has sent me, I am also sending you." After saying this, he breathed on them and said, "Receive the Holy Spirit. Whenever you forgive people's sins, they are forgiven. Whenever you do not forgive them, they are not forgiven."[1221]

Thomas Finally Believes

But Thomas, one of the Twelve, the one called the Twin,[b] was not with them when Jesus came. So the other disciples kept telling him, "We have seen the Lord!"

But he said to them, "Unless I see the nail marks in his hands, and put my finger into the mark of the nails, and put my hand into his side, I will never believe."

After eight days, his disciples were inside again, and Thomas was with them. Though the doors were locked, Jesus came and stood among them. "Peace be with you," he said. Then he said to Thomas, "Put your finger here and look at my hands. Take your hand and put it into my side. Do not continue to doubt, but believe."

Thomas answered him, "My Lord and my God!"

Jesus said to him, "Because you have seen me, you have believed. Blessed are those who have not seen and yet have believed."[1222]

The Purpose of John's Gospel Account

Jesus, in the presence of his disciples, did many other miraculous signs that are not written in this book. But these are written that you may believe that Jesus is the Christ, the Son of God, and that by believing you may have life in his name.[1223]

Breakfast with the Lord Jesus

After this, Jesus showed himself again to the disciples at the Sea of Tiberias. This is how he showed himself: Simon Peter, Thomas (called the Twin), Nathanael from Cana in Galilee, the sons of Zebedee, and two other disciples were together. Simon Peter said to them, "I'm going fishing."

They replied, "We'll go with you."

---

[a] Some witnesses to the text omit *and so it must be*.
[b] Greek *Didymus* is the equivalent of *Thomas* in Hebrew/Aramaic, both meaning *Twin*.

They went out and got into the boat, but that night they caught nothing. Early in the morning, Jesus was standing on the shore, but the disciples did not know it was Jesus.

Jesus called to them, "Boys, don't you have any fish?"

"No!" they answered.

He told them, "Throw your net on the right side of the boat and you will find some." So they cast the net out. Then they were not able to haul it in because of the large number of fish.

The disciple whom Jesus loved said to Peter, "It is the Lord!" When Simon Peter heard, "It is the Lord!" he tied his outer garment around him (for he had taken it off) and jumped into the sea. But the other disciples came in the little boat, dragging the net full of fish, for they were not far from shore, about one hundred yards. When they stepped out on land, they saw some bread and a charcoal fire with fish on it. Jesus said to them, "Bring some of the fish you just caught."

So Simon Peter climbed aboard and hauled the net to land, full of large fish, 153 of them. Yet even with so many, the net was not torn.

Jesus said to them, "Come, eat breakfast."

None of the disciples dared ask him, "Who are you?" because they knew it was the Lord.

Jesus came, took the bread, and gave it to them, and also the fish. This was now the third time Jesus appeared to his disciples after he was raised from the dead.[1224]

"Do You Love Me?"

When they had eaten breakfast, Jesus asked Simon Peter, "Simon, son of John, do you love[a] me more than these?"

"Yes, Lord," he said, "you know that I care about[b] you."

Jesus told him, "Feed my lambs."

A second time Jesus asked him, "Simon, son of John, do you love me?"

He said, "Yes, Lord, you know that I care about you."

Jesus told him, "Be a shepherd for my sheep."

He asked him the third time, "Simon, son of John, do you care about me?"

Peter was grieved because Jesus asked him the third time, "Do you care about me?" He answered, "Lord, you know all things. You know that I care about you."

"Feed my sheep," Jesus said. "Amen, Amen, I tell you: When you were young, you dressed yourself and went wherever you wanted. But when you are old, you will stretch out your hands, and someone else will tie you and carry you where you do not want to go."

Jesus said this to indicate the kind of death by which Peter would glorify God. After saying this, he told him, "Follow me."

---

[a] Greek *agapao*

[b] In verses 15-17, the uses of the Greek *phileo* are translated *care about* to distinguish from the uses of the Greek *agapao*, which are translated *love*.

Peter turned and saw the disciple Jesus loved following them. This was the one who had leaned back against Jesus at the supper and asked, "Lord, who is going to betray you?" When Peter saw him, he asked Jesus, "Lord, what about him?"

"If I want him to remain until I come," Jesus answered, "what is that to you? You follow me." And so it was said among the brothers that this disciple would not die. Yet Jesus did not say that he would not die, but, "If I want him to remain until I come, what is that to you?"

This is the disciple who is testifying about these things and who wrote these things. We know that his testimony is true.[1225]

"Go and Gather Disciples"

The eleven disciples went to Galilee, to the mountain where Jesus had directed them. When they saw him, they worshipped him, but some hesitated because they were uncertain.[a] Jesus approached and spoke to them saying, "All authority in heaven and on earth has been given to me. Therefore[1226] go into all the world and preach the gospel to all creation.[1227] Go and gather disciples from all nations by baptizing them in[b] the name of the Father and of the Son and of the Holy Spirit, and by teaching them to keep all the instructions I have given you.[1228] Whoever believes and is baptized will be saved, but whoever does not believe will be condemned. These signs will accompany those who believe: In my name they will drive out demons. They will speak in new languages. They will pick up snakes. And if they drink any deadly poison, it will not harm them. They will lay their hands on the sick, and they will get well.[1229] And surely I am with you always until the end of the age."[1230]

Jesus Ascends into Heaven

[Jesus] led them out as far as the vicinity of Bethany. He lifted up his hands and blessed them. And while he was blessing them, he parted from them and[1231] was taken up into heaven.[1232] Then the Lord Jesus sat down at the right hand of God.[1233]

So they worshipped him and returned to Jerusalem with great joy. They were continually in the temple courts, praising and[c] blessing God.[1234]

Those who went out preached everywhere, while the Lord worked with them and confirmed his word by the signs that accompanied it.[d] [1235]

---

[a] Or *some doubted*

[b] Or *into*

[c] A few witnesses to the text omit *praising and*.

[d] This translation includes verses 9-20 because they are included in the vast majority of Greek manuscripts that have been handed down to us. Evidence for the existence of this long ending extends back to the 2nd century. In the early centuries of the church, these verses were read in worship services on Easter and Ascension Day. However, a few early manuscripts and early translations omit verses 9-20, and a few manuscripts have a different ending.

Jesus also did many other things. If every one of them were written down, I suppose the world itself would not have room for the books that would be written.[1236]

Amen.[a] [1237]

---

[a] Some witnesses to the text omit *Amen*.

References

[1] Luke 1:1-4
[2] Mark 1:1
[3] John 1:1-18
[4] Matthew 1:1-17
[5] Luke 3:23b-38
[6] Luke 1:5-25
[7] Luke 1:26-38
[8] Luke 1:39-45
[9] Luke 1:46-56
[10] Matthew 1:18-25
[11] Luke 1:57-66
[12] Luke 1:67-80
[13] Matthew 1:18
[14] Luke 2:1-20
[15] Luke 2:21 (Compare Matthew 1:25)
[16] Luke 2:22-38
[17] Matthew 2:1-12
[18] Matthew 2:15
[19] Matthew 2:16-18
[20] Matthew 2:19-20
[21] Luke 2:39
[22] Matthew 2:21-23
[23] Luke 2:40
[24] Luke 2:41-52
[25] Luke 3:1-3
[26] Mark 1:4 (Compare Matthew 3:1; Luke 3:3)
[27] Matthew 3:2-3 (Compare Mark 1:2; Luke 3:4)
[28] Luke 3:4 (Compare Matthew 3:3; Mark 1:2)
[29] Mark 1:2
[30] Luke 3:4-6 (Compare Matthew 3:3; Mark 1:2-3)
[31] Matthew 3:5
[32] Mark 1:5-6 (Compare Matthew 3:4-6)
[33] Matthew 3:7-10 (Compare Luke 3:7-9)
[34] Luke 3:10-17 (Compare Matthew 3:11-12)
[35] Luke 3:18
[36] Luke 3:21
[37] Mark 1:9
[38] Matthew 3:13-14 (Compare Mark 1:9; Luke 3:21)
[39] Luke 3:21
[40] Mark 1:10

41 Matthew 3:15-16 (Compare Mark 1:10; Luke 3:22)
42 Mark 1:11 (Compare Matthew 3:17; Luke 3:22)
43 Luke 3:23a
44 Luke 4:1
45 Mark 1:12-13 (Compare Matthew 4:1)
46 Luke 4:2-4 (Compare Matthew 4:2-4)
47 Matthew 4:4-5 (Compare Luke 4:4)
48 Luke 4:9 (Compare Matthew 4:5)
49 Matthew 4:5
50 Luke 4:9-12 (Compare Matthew 4:5-7)
51 Matthew 4:8 (Compare Luke 4:5)
52 Luke 4:5
53 Luke 4:6 (Compare Matthew 4:9)
54 Luke 4:6
55 Matthew 4:9
56 Luke 4:6-7
57 Matthew 4:10 (Compare Luke 4:8)
58 Luke 4:13 (Compare Matthew 4:11)
59 Matthew 4:11 (Compare Mark 1:13)
60 John 1:19-28
61 John 1:29-34
62 John 1:35-51
63 John 2:1-12
64 John 2:13-25
65 John 3:1-21
66 John 3:22-36
67 Luke 3:19-20
68 Matthew 4:12 (Compare Mark 1:14)
69 John 4:1-3 (Compare Matthew 4:12; Mark 1:14)
70 John 4:4-42
71 John 4:43-44
72 Luke 4:14
73 Mark 1:14-15 (Compare Matthew 4:17)
74 John 4:45
75 Luke 4:14-15
76 John 4:46-54
77 Luke 4:16-30
78 Matthew 4:13 (Compare Luke 4:31)
79 Luke 4:31
80 Matthew 4:13 (Compare Luke 4:31)
81 Luke 4:31
82 Matthew 4:13-16
83 Mark 1:16-21 (Compare Matthew 4:18-22)
84 Mark 1:21-23 (Compare Luke 4:31-33)
85 Luke 4:33-34
86 Mark 1:24-26 (Compare Luke 4:34-35)
87 Luke 4:35
88 Mark 1:27 (Compare Luke 4:36)
89 Luke 4:36
90 Mark 1:27 (Compare Luke 4:36)
91 Luke 4:36
92 Mark 1:28 (Compare Luke 4:37)
93 Luke 4:37

References

[94] Mark 1:28
[95] Luke 4:38
[96] Mark 1:29 (Compare Luke 4:38)
[97] Mark 1:30 (Compare Luke 4:38)
[98] Luke 4:38 (Compare Mark 1:30)
[99] Mark 1:30
[100] Luke 4:38
[101] Matthew 8:14
[102] Mark 1:31 (Compare Matthew 8:15)
[103] Luke 4:39 (Compare Matthew 8:15; Mark 1:31)
[104] Mark 1:32 (Compare Matthew 8:16)
[105] Luke 4:40 (Compare Matthew 8:16)
[106] Mark 1:32-34 (Compare Matthew 8:16)
[107] Luke 4:41 (Compare Mark 1:34)
[108] Matthew 8:17
[109] Mark 1:35 (Compare Luke 4:42)
[110] Mark 1:36-37
[111] Luke 4:42
[112] Mark 1:38
[113] Luke 4:43
[114] Mark 1:38
[115] Matthew 4:23 (Compare Mark 1:39; Luke 4:44)
[116] Matthew 4:24-25
[117] Luke 5:1-11
[118] Matthew 5:1-12
[119] Matthew 5:13-16
[120] Matthew 5:17-20
[121] Matthew 5:21-26
[122] Matthew 5:27-30
[123] Matthew 5:31-32
[124] Matthew 5:33-37
[125] Matthew 5:38-48
[126] Matthew 6:1-6
[127] Matthew 6:7-15
[128] Matthew 6:16-18
[129] Matthew 6:19-24
[130] Matthew 6:25-34
[131] Matthew 7:1-5
[132] Matthew 7:6
[133] Matthew 7:7-11
[134] Matthew 7:12
[135] Matthew 7:13-14
[136] Matthew 7:15-23
[137] Matthew 7:24-29
[138] Matthew 8:1
[139] Luke 5:12
[140] Matthew 8:2
[141] Mark 1:40
[142] Matthew 8:2
[143] Luke 5:12 (Compare Matthew 8:2; Mark 1:40)
[144] Mark 1:41-44 (Compare Matthew 8:3-4; Luke 5:13-14)
[145] Mark 1:45 (Compare Luke 5:15)
[146] Luke 5:15

147 Luke 5:16 (Compare Mark 1:45)
148 Mark 1:45 (Compare Luke 5:16)
149 Mark 2:1
150 Luke 5:17
151 Mark 2:2
152 Luke 5:18
153 Mark 2:3
154 Luke 5:18-19 (Compare Matthew 9:2; Mark 2:3-4)
155 Mark 2:4
156 Luke 5:19 (Compare Mark 2:4)
157 Matthew 9:2 (Compare Mark 2:5; Luke 5:20)
158 Mark 2:6 (Compare Matthew 9:3; Luke 5:21)
159 Luke 5:21
160 Mark 2:6-7 (Compare Matthew 9:3; Luke 5:21)
161 Mark 2:7 (Compare Luke 5:21)
162 Mark 2:8 (Compare Matthew 9:4; Luke 5:22)
163 Matthew 9:4
164 Mark 2:8-11 (Compare Matthew 9:4-6; Luke 5:22-24)
165 Luke 5:25-26 (Compare Matthew 9:7-8; Mark 2:12)
166 Matthew 9:8
167 Luke 5:26
168 Mark 2:12
169 Matthew 9:9 (Compare Mark 2:13; Luke 5:27)
170 Mark 2:13
171 Mark 2:13-14 (Compare Matthew 9:9; Luke 5:27)
172 Matthew 9:9
173 Mark 2:14 (Compare Matthew 9:9; Luke 5:27)
174 Luke 5:28 (Compare Matthew 9:9; Mark 2:14)
175 Luke 5:29
176 Mark 2:15-16 (Compare Matthew 9:10-11; Luke 5:29-30)
177 Matthew 9:12-13 (Compare Mark 2:17; Luke 5:31-32)
178 Matthew 9:14-17 (Compare Mark 2:18-22; Luke 5:33-38)
179 Luke 5:39
180 Matthew 9:18
181 Mark 5:22 (Compare Matthew 9:18; Luke 8:41)
182 Luke 8:41-42
183 Matthew 9:18
184 Mark 5:23 (Compare Matthew 9:18)
185 Matthew 9:19 (Compare Mark 5:24)
186 Mark 5:24-27 (Compare Matthew 9:20; Luke 8:42-43)
187 Luke 8:44 (Compare Matthew 9:20; Mark 5:27)
188 Matthew 9:21
189 Mark 5:29-30 (Compare Luke 8:44-45)
190 Luke 8:45 (Compare Mark 5:31)
191 Mark 5:32
192 Luke 8:46-47 (Compare Mark 5:33)
193 Mark 5:33 (Compare Luke 8:47)
194 Luke 8:47 (Compare Mark 5:33)
195 Mark 5:34 (Compare Matthew 9:22; Luke 8:48)
196 Luke 8:49-51 (Compare Mark 5:35-37)
197 Mark 5:38-39 (Compare Luke 8:52)
198 Matthew 9:23
199 Mark 5:39

References

200 Matthew 9:24 (Compare Mark 5:39; Luke 8:52)
201 Luke 8:53 (Compare Matthew 9:24; Mark 5:40)
202 Mark 5:40-41 (Compare Matthew 9:25; Luke 8:54)
203 Luke 8:55 (Matthew 9:25; Mark 5:42)
204 Mark 5:42-43 (Compare Luke 8:55-56)
205 Matthew 9:26
206 Matthew 9:27-31
207 Matthew 9:32-34
208 Mark 6:1-3 (Compare Matthew 13:54-55)
209 Matthew 13:55
210 Mark 6:3-6 (Compare Matthew 13:55-58)
211 Matthew 9:35
212 John 5:1-15
213 John 5:16-47
214 Matthew 12:1 (Compare Mark 2:23; Luke 6:1)
215 Mark 2:23
216 Luke 6:1 (Compare Matthew 12:1; Mark 2:23)
217 Matthew 12:2 (Compare Mark 2:24; Luke 6:2)
218 Mark 2:25-26 (Compare Matthew 12:3-4; Luke 6:3-4)
219 Matthew 12:5-7
220 Mark 2:27-28 (Compare Matthew 12:8; Luke 6:5)
221 Matthew 12:9
222 Luke 6:6-7 (Compare Matthew 12:9-10; Mark 3:1-2)
223 Matthew 12:10 (Compare Mark 3:2; Luke 6:7)
224 Luke 6:8-9 (Compare Mark 3:3-4)
225 Mark 3:4-5
226 Matthew 12:11-12
227 Matthew 12:13 (Compare Mark 3:5; Luke 6:10)
228 Mark 3:6 (Compare Matthew 12:14; Luke 6:11)
229 Luke 6:11
230 Mark 3:6 (Compare Matthew 12:14; Luke 6:11)
231 Matthew 12:15-21
232 Matthew 9:36-38
233 Mark 3:7-12
234 Luke 6:12-13 (Compare Matthew 10:1; Mark 3:13-14)
235 Mark 3:13-15 (Compare Matthew 10:1; Luke 6:13)
236 Matthew 10:1
237 Mark 3:13-16 (Compare Matthew 10:2; Luke 6:14)
238 Matthew 10:2 (Compare Mark 3:17; Luke 6:14)
239 Mark 3:17 (Compare Luke 6:14)
240 Matthew 10:3 (Compare Mark 3:18; Luke 6:14-15)
241 Luke 6:15-16 (Compare Mark 3:18)
242 Matthew 10:3 (Compare Mark 3:18)
243 Luke 6:16 (Compare Mark 3:19)
244 Matthew 10:4 (Compare Mark 3:19; Luke 6:16)
245 Luke 6:17-19
246 Luke 6:20-26
247 Luke 6:27-36
248 Luke 6:37-42
249 Luke 6:43-49
250 Luke 7:1-3 (Compare Matthew 8:5)
251 Matthew 8:5-6
252 Luke 7:4-5

253 Matthew 8:7
254 Luke 7:6-9 (Compare Matthew 8:8-10)
255 Matthew 8:11-13
256 Luke 7:10
257 Matthew 8:13
258 Luke 7:11-17
259 Matthew 11:2
260 Luke 7:18-27 (Compare Matthew 11:2-10)
261 Matthew 11:11 (Compare Luke 7:28)
262 Matthew 11:12-15
263 Luke 7:29-30
264 Luke 7:31-35 (Compare Matthew 11:16-19)
265 Luke 7:36-50
266 Luke 8:1-3
267 Luke 11:1-4
268 Luke 11:5-13
269 Matthew 11:20-24
270 Matthew 11:25-30
271 Mark 3:20
272 Matthew 12:22 (Compare Luke 11:14)
273 Matthew 12:23
274 Mark 3:21-22
275 Matthew 12:24
276 Mark 3:22
277 Matthew 12:24 (Compare Luke 11:15)
278 Matthew 12:24-25 (Compare Mark 3:22; Luke 11:17)
279 Mark 3:23
280 Matthew 12:25-26 (Compare Luke 11:17-18)
281 Mark 3:26
282 Luke 11:18
283 Matthew 12:27-28 (Compare Luke 11:19-20)
284 Luke 11:20
285 Matthew 12:28 (Compare Luke 11:20)
286 Matthew 12:29 (Compare Mark 3:27)
287 Luke 11:21-22
288 Matthew 12:30 (Compare Luke 11:23)
289 Matthew 12:31-32 (Compare Mark 3:28-29)
290 Mark 3:30
291 Matthew 12:33-37
292 Luke 11:27-28
293 Matthew 12:38
294 Luke 11:16
295 Matthew 12:38-39
296 Luke 11:29
297 Matthew 12:39 (Compare Luke 11:29)
298 Matthew 12:39
299 Luke 11:30
300 Matthew 12:40
301 Matthew 12:41 (Compare Luke 11:32)
302 Matthew 12:42 (Compare Luke 11:31)
303 Matthew 12:43-44 (Compare Luke 11:24)
304 Luke 11:24
305 Matthew 12:44-45 (Compare Luke 11:25-26)

[306] Matthew 12:45
[307] Luke 11:33-36
[308] Mark 3:31 (Compare Matthew 12:46; Luke 8:19)
[309] Luke 8:19
[310] Mark 3:32
[311] Mark 3:31
[312] Matthew 12:47 (Compare Mark 3:32; Luke 8:20)
[313] Matthew 12:48 (Compare Mark 3:33)
[314] Mark 3:34
[315] Matthew 12:49-50 (Compare Mark 3:34-35; Luke 8:21)
[316] Luke 11:37-54
[317] Luke 12:1-3
[318] Luke 12:4-7
[319] Luke 12:8-12
[320] Luke 12:13-21
[321] Luke 12:22-34
[322] Luke 12:35-48
[323] Luke 12:49-53
[324] Luke 12:54-59
[325] Luke 13:1-5
[326] Luke 13:6-9
[327] Matthew 13:1
[328] Mark 4:1
[329] Matthew 13:2-9 (Compare Mark 4:1-7; Luke 8:4-7)
[330] Mark 4:7-9 (Compare Matthew 13:8-9; Luke 8:8)
[331] Mark 4:10
[332] Matthew 13:10
[333] Luke 8:9
[334] Matthew 13:11 (Compare Mark 4:11; Luke 8:10)
[335] Mark 4:11
[336] Matthew 13:12-13
[337] Matthew 13:14-15 (Compare Mark 4:12; Luke 8:10)
[338] Matthew 13:16-17
[339] Mark 4:13
[340] Matthew 13:18
[341] Luke 8:11 (Mark 4:14)
[342] Matthew 13:19 (Compare Mark 4:15; Luke 8:12)
[343] Luke 8:12
[344] Matthew 13:19-22 (Compare Mark 4:16-19; Luke 8:13-14)
[345] Luke 8:14
[346] Matthew 13:22 (Compare Mark 4:19; Luke 8:14)
[347] Luke 8:14-15 (Compare Matthew 13:23; Mark 4:20)
[348] Mark 4:20
[349] Mark 13:23
[350] Luke 8:15
[351] Matthew 13:23 (Compare Mark 4:20)
[352] Mark 4:21-23 (Compare Luke 8:16-17)
[353] Mark 4:24-25 (Compare Luke 8:18)
[354] Mark 4:26-29
[355] Matthew 13:24-30
[356] Matthew 13:31
[357] Mark 4:30
[358] Matthew 13:31-32 (Compare Mark 4:31-32)

359 Mark 4:32
360 Matthew 13:33
361 Mark 4:33-34 (Compare Matthew 13:34)
362 Matthew 13:35
363 Mathew 13:36-43
364 Matthew 13:44-53
365 Matthew 8:18-22
366 Mark 4:35
367 Luke 8:22 (Compare Matthew 8:23; Mark 4:35)
368 Mark 4:36
369 Matthew 8:24
370 Mark 4:37 (Compare Matthew 8:24; Luke 8:23)
371 Matthew 8:25 (Compare Luke 8:24)
372 Mark 4:38
373 Mark 4:40 (Compare Matthew 8:26; Luke 8:25)
374 Mark 4:39 (Compare Matthew 8:26; Luke 8:24)
375 Luke 8:25
376 Mark 4:41 (Compare Matthew 8:27; Luke 8:25)
377 Luke 8:26 (Compare Mark 5:1)
378 Matthew 8:28 (Mark 5:1; Luke 8:26)
379 Mark 5:2
380 Luke 8:27
381 Mark 5:2
382 Matthew 8:28-29 (Compare Mark 5:7; Luke 8:28)
383 Luke 8:27 (Compare Mark 5:3)
384 Mark 5:3
385 Luke 8:29 (Compare Mark 5:4)
386 Mark 5:4-5
387 Mark 5:6-10 (Compare Luke 8:28-31)
388 Luke 8:31
389 Mark 5:13 (Compare Luke 8:32)
390 Matthew 8:32 (Compare Mark 5:32; Luke 8:33)
391 Mark 5:13-14 (Compare Matthew 8:32-33; Luke 8:33)
392 Luke 8:35-38 (Compare Matthew 8:33-34; Mark 5:14-18)
393 Mark 5:19-20 (Compare Luke 8:38-39)
394 Matthew 9:1 (Compare Mark 5:21)
395 Luke 8:40 (Compare Mark 5:21)
396 Luke 9:1-3 (Compare Mark 6:7-8)
397 Matthew 10:5-14 (Compare Mark 6:9-11; Luke 9:3-5)
398 Mark 6:11 (Compare Luke 9:5)
399 Matthew 10:15-42
400 Matthew 11:1
401 Luke 9:6
402 Mark 6:12-13
403 Matthew 14:1 (Compare Mark 6:14; Luke 9:7)
404 Mark 6:14 (Compare Matthew 14:1)
405 Matthew 14:2 (Compare Mark 6:14; Luke 9:7)
406 Mark 6:14 (Compare Luke 9:9)
407 Matthew 14:2 (Compare Mark 6:14)
408 Luke 9:8-9 (Compare Mark 6:15)
409 Mark 6:17-18 (Compare Matthew 14:3-4)
410 Mark 6:19-20
411 Matthew 14:5

References

[412] Mark 6:20-29 (Compare Matthew 14:6-12)
[413] Matthew 14:12
[414] Matthew 14:13
[415] Luke 9:10
[416] Mark 6:30-32 (Compare Matthew 14:13; Luke 9:10)
[417] Luke 9:10
[418] John 6:1
[419] Luke 9:10
[420] John 6:2
[421] Mark 6:33-34 (Compare Matthew 14:13; Luke 9:11)
[422] John 6:3-4
[423] Luke 9:11
[424] Mark 6:34-36 (Compare Matthew 14:15; Luke 9:12)
[425] Matthew 14:16 (Compare Mark 6:37; Luke 9:13)
[426] John 6:5-7 (Compare Mark 6:37)
[427] Mark 6:38
[428] John 6:8-9 (Compare Matthew 14:17; Mark 6:38; Luke 9:13)
[429] Matthew 14:18
[430] Luke 9:14-15
[431] John 6:10
[432] Mark 6:39-41 (Compare Matthew 14:19; Luke 9:16; John 6:11)
[433] John 6:11
[434] John 6:12 (Compare Matthew 14:20; Mark 6:43; Luke 9:17)
[435] Mark 6:43
[436] John 6:13 (Compare Matthew 14:20; Mark 6:43; Luke 9:17)
[437] Matthew 14:21 (Compare Mark 6:44; Luke 9:14; John 6:10)
[438] John 6:14
[439] John 6:15
[440] Matthew 14:22 (Compare Mark 6:45)
[441] John 6:17
[442] Mark 6:45
[443] Matthew 14:22-23 (Compare Mark 6:45-47)
[444] John 6:17-18
[445] Matthew 14:24 (Compare Mark 6:47)
[446] John 6:19
[447] Mark 6:47
[448] Matthew 14:24
[449] Mark 6:48 (Compare Matthew 14:24-25)
[450] Matthew 14:26-31 (Compare Mark 6:50)
[451] John 6:21
[452] Mark 6:51 (Compare Matthew 14:32)
[453] John 6:21
[454] Mark 6:51-52
[455] Matthew 14:33
[456] Mark 6:53-56 (Compare Matthew 14:34-36)
[457] John 6:21-7:1
[458] John 7:2-10
[459] John 7:11-53
[460] John 8:1-11
[461] John 8:12-59
[462] John 9:1-41
[463] John 10:1-21
[464] Mark 7:1-13 (Compare Matthew 15:1-9)

465 Matthew 15:10-11 (Compare Mark 7:14-15)
466 Mark 7:16-17
467 Matthew 15:12-13
468 Matthew 15:15 (Compare Mark 7:17)
469 Mark 7:18-22 (Compare Matthew 15:16-19)
470 Matthew 15:19-20 (Compare Mark 7:23)
471 Mark 7:24 (Compare Matthew 15:21)
472 Matthew 15:21 (Compare Mark 7:24)
473 Mark 7:24-25 (Compare Matthew 15:21)
474 Matthew 15:22 (Compare Mark 7:25)
475 Mark 7:25-26
476 Matthew 15:22-25
477 Matthew 15:27-28 (Compare Mark 7:28-29)
478 Mark 7:29
479 Matthew 15:28
480 Mark 7:29
481 Matthew 15:28
482 Mark 7:30-31 (Compare Matthew 15:29)
483 Matthew 15:29
484 Mark 7:31
485 Matthew 15:29-31
486 Mark 7:32-37
487 Mark 8:1-5 (Compare Matthew 15:32-34)
488 Matthew 15:34-35 (Compare Mark 8:5-6)
489 Mark 8:6-8 (Compare Matthew 15:36-37)
490 Matthew 15:38 (Compare Mark 8:9)
491 Mark 8:9-10 (Compare Matthew 15:39)
492 Matthew 15:39
493 Matthew 16:1 (Compare Mark 8:11)
494 Mark 8:11-12 (Compare Matthew 16:1)
495 Matthew 16:2-4
496 Mark 8:13 (Compare Matthew 16:4)
497 Matthew 16:5 (Compare Mark 8:14)
498 Mark 8:14
499 Matthew 16:6 (Compare Mark 8:15)
500 Mark 8:15
501 Matthew 16:7-9 (Compare Mark 8:16-17)
502 Mark 8:17-21 (Compare Matthew 16:9)
503 Matthew 16:11-12
504 Mark 8:22-26
505 Mark 8:27 (Compare Matthew 16:13)
506 Luke 9:18 (Compare Matthew 16:13; Mark 8:27)
507 Matthew 16:14 (Compare Mark 8:28; Luke 9:19)
508 Luke 9:19 (Compare Matthew 16:14; Mark 8:28)
509 Matthew 16:15-20 (Compare Mark 8:29-30; Luke 9:20-21)
510 Matthew 16:21 (Compare Mark 8:31)
511 Mark 8:31
512 Matthew 16:21
513 Luke 9:22 (Compare Matthew 16:21; Mark 8:31)
514 Mark 8:32
515 Matthew 16:22 (Compare Mark 8:32)
516 Mark 8:33 (Compare Matthew 16:23)
517 Matthew 16:23 (Compare Mark 8:33)

[518] Matthew 16:24
[519] Mark 8:34 (Compare Matthew 16:24; Luke 9:23)
[520] Luke 9:23
[521] Mark 8:34-38 (Compare Matthew 16:24-27; Luke 9:23-26)
[522] Luke 9:26 (Compare Matthew 16:27; Mark 8:38)
[523] Matthew 16:27-28 (Compare Mark 8:38-9:1; Luke 9:26-27)
[524] Mark 9:2 (Compare Matthew 17:1; Luke 9:28)
[525] Matthew 17:1
[526] Mark 9:2 (Compare Matthew 17:1)
[527] Luke 9:28
[528] Mark 9:2 (Compare Matthew 17:1; Luke 9:28)
[529] Luke 9:29
[530] Matthew 17:2 (Compare Mark 9:2-3; Luke 9:29)
[531] Mark 9:3 (Compare Matthew 17:2; Luke 9:29)
[532] Matthew 17:2
[533] Luke 9:30-33 (Compare Matthew 17:3-4; Mark 9:4-5)
[534] Mark 9:6
[535] Matthew 17:5 (Compare Mark 9:7; Luke 9:34)
[536] Luke 9:34-35 (Compare Matthew 17:5; Mark 9:7)
[537] Matthew 17:6-9 (Compare Mark 9:8-9; Luke 9:36)
[538] Luke 9:36
[539] Mark 9:10-11 (Compare Matthew 17:10)
[540] Matthew 17:11-13 (Compare Mark 9:12-13)
[541] Luke 9:37
[542] Mark 9:14-16 (Compare Matthew 17:14; Luke 9:37)
[543] Luke 9:38
[544] Matthew 17:14-15
[545] Luke 9:39 (Compare Mark 9:17)
[546] Mark 9:17-18 (Compare Luke 9:39)
[547] Matthew 17:15
[548] Luke 9:39-40 (Compare Matthew 17:16; Mark 9:18)
[549] Matthew 17:16-17 (Compare Mark 9:19; Luke 9:41)
[550] Mark 9:20-27 (Compare Matthew 17:18; Luke 9:42)
[551] Luke 9:43
[552] Mark 9:28 (Compare Matthew 17:19)
[553] Matthew 17:20-21 (Compare Mark 9:29)
[554] Luke 9:43-44 (Compare Matthew
[555] Matthew 17:22-23 (Compare Mark 9:31; Luke 9:44)
[556] Luke 9:45 (Compare Mark 9:32)
[557] Matthew 17:24 (Compare Mark 9:33)
[558] Matthew 17:24-27
[559] Matthew 18:1
[560] Mark 9:33-34 (Compare Luke 9:46)
[561] Luke 9:47
[562] Mark 9:35
[563] Matthew 18:2 (Compare Mark 9:36; Luke 9:47)
[564] Luke 9:47
[565] Mark 9:36-37 (Compare Matthew 18:2; Luke 9:48)
[566] Luke 9:48
[567] Luke 9:49 (Compare Mark 9:38)
[568] Mark 9:39-41 (Compare Luke 9:50)
[569] Matthew 18:3-7 (Compare Mark 9:42)
[570] Luke 17:1 (Compare Matthew 18:7)

571 Luke 17:3
572 Mark 9:43-47 (Compare Matthew 18-8-9)
573 Matthew 18:9
574 Mark 9:47-50 (Compare Matthew 18:9)
575 Matthew 18:10-11
576 Luke 17:3-10
577 Luke 15:1-3
578 Matthew 18:12-13
579 Luke 15:5-6
580 Matthew 18:13-14
581 Luke 15:7
582 Luke 15:8-10
583 Luke 15:11-32
584 Luke 16:1-18
585 Luke 16:19-31
586 Matthew 18:15-20
587 Matthew 18:21-35
588 Matthew 19:1
589 Luke 9:51
590 Luke 17:11-19
591 Luke 17:21-22
592 Luke 17:22-37
593 Luke 18:1-8
594 Luke 18:9-14
595 Matthew 19:1 (Compare Mark 10:1)
596 Luke 9:52-56
597 Luke 9:57-62
598 Luke 10:1-24
599 Luke 10:25-37
600 Luke 10:38-42
601 John 10:22-42
602 Luke 13:18-21
603 Luke 13:22-30
604 Luke 13:31-35
605 Luke 14:1-14
606 Luke 14:15-24
607 Luke 14:25-35
608 Matthew 19:2 (Compare Mark 10:1)
609 Mark 10:1
610 Matthew 19:3 (Compare Mark 10:2)
611 Mark 10:3-11 (Compare Matthew 19:4-8)
612 Matthew 19:9-12 (Compare Mark 10:11-12)
613 Mark 10:13 (Compare Matthew 19:13; Luke 18:15)
614 Luke 18:15
615 Matthew 19:13 (Compare Mark 10:13; Luke 18:15)
616 Luke 18:15 (Compare Matthew 19:13)
617 Mark 10:14-16 (Compare Matthew 19:14; Luke 18:16-17)
618 Matthew 19:15
619 Mark 10:17
620 Luke 18:18
621 Mark 10:17
622 Matthew 19:16-22 (Compare Mark 10:17-22; Luke 18:18-23)
623 Luke 18:24

[624] Mark 10:23-28 (Compare Matthew 19:23-27; Luke 18:24-28)
[625] Matthew 19:27-30 (Compare Mark 10:28-31; Luke 18:28-30)
[626] Matthew 20:1-16
[627] John 11:1-44
[628] John 11:45-54
[629] John 11:55-57
[630] Mark 10:32 (Compare Matthew 20:17; Luke 18:31)
[631] Luke 18:31 (Compare Matthew 20:18; Luke 18:31)
[632] Matthew 20:18-19 (Compare Mark 10:33-34; Luke 18:32-33)
[633] Luke 18:34
[634] Matthew 20:20
[635] Mark 10:35
[636] Matthew 20:20-21
[637] Mark 10:35-36
[638] Matthew 20:21 (Compare Mark 10:37)
[639] Mark 10:37-40 (Compare Matthew 20:22-23)
[640] Matthew 20:23
[641] Mark 10:41-45 (Compare Matthew 20:24-28)
[642] Mark 10:46 (Compare Matthew 20:29; Luke 18:35)
[643] Matthew 20:30 (Compare Mark 10:46; Luke 18:35)
[644] Luke 18:36
[645] Mark 10:46
[646] Luke 18:36-39 (Compare Matthew 20:30-31; Mark 10:47-48)
[647] Matthew 20:31 (Compare Mark 10:48; Luke 18:39)
[648] Mark 10:49-51 (Compare Matthew 20:32-33; Luke 18:40-41)
[649] Matthew 20:33-34
[650] Luke 18:42
[651] Mark 10:52 (Compare Luke 18:42)
[652] Luke 18:43 (Compare Matthew 20:34; Mark 10:52)
[653] Luke 19:1-10
[654] Luke 19:11-27
[655] Luke 19:28 (Compare Matthew 21:1; Mark 11:1)
[656] John 12:1-11
[657] John 12:12
[658] Mark 11:1-2 (Compare Matthew 21:1-2; Luke 19:29-30)
[659] Matthew 21:2 (Compare Mark 11:2; Luke 19:30)
[660] Mark 11:3 (Compare Matthew 21:3; Luke 19:31)
[661] Matthew 21:4-5 (Compare John 12:15)
[662] John 12:16
[663] Luke 19:32 (Compare Matthew 21:6)
[664] Mark 11:4
[665] Luke 19:33 (Compare Mark 11:5)
[666] Mark 11:5-6 (Compare Luke 19:33)
[667] Luke 19:35
[668] Matthew 21:7 (Compare Mark 11:7; Luke 19:35; John 12:14)
[669] Luke 19:36
[670] Matthew 21:8 (Compare Mark 11:8; Luke 19:36)
[671] John 12:13
[672] Matthew 21:8 (Compare Mark 11:8; Luke 19:36)
[673] John 12:17-19
[674] Matthew 21:9 (Compare Mark 11:9)
[675] Mark 11:9 (Matthew 21:9)
[676] John 12:13

677 Mark 11:10 (Compare Matthew 21:9)
678 Luke 19:37-44
679 Matthew 21:10-11
680 Mark 11:11
681 Matthew 21:18
682 Mark 11:12-14 (Compare Matthew 21:18-19)
683 Mark 11:15-17 (Compare Matthew 21:12-13; Luke 19:45-46)
684 Luke 19:47-48 (Compare Mark 11:18)
685 Mark 11:18
686 Matthew 21:14-17
687 Mark 11:19
688 Mark 11:20-21 (Compare Matthew 21:19)
689 Matthew 21:20
690 Mark 11:22-26 (Compare Matthew 21:21-22)
691 Mark 11:27 (Compare Matthew 21:23; Luke 20:1)
692 Luke 20:1
693 Mark 11:27-31 (Compare Matthew 21:23-25; Luke 20:1-5)
694 Luke 20:6 (Compare Matthew 21:26; Mark 11:32)
695 Mark 11:33 (Compare Matthew 21:27; Luke 20:7-8)
696 Matthew 21:28-32
697 Matthew 21:33 (Compare Mark 12:1; Luke 20:9)
698 Mark 12:1-5 (Compare Matthew 21:33-36; Luke 20:9-12)
699 Luke 20:13-14 (Compare Matthew 21:37-38; Mark 12:6-7)
700 Mark 12:8 (Compare Matthew 21:39; Luke 20:15)
701 Matthew 21:40-46 (Compare Mark 12:9-12; Luke 20:15-19)
702 Matthew 22:1-14
703 Matthew 22:15
704 Luke 20:20
705 Matthew 22:16-17 (Compare Mark 12:13-14; Luke 20:21-22)
706 Mark 12:15
707 Matthew 22:18 (Compare Mark 12:15; Luke 20:23)
708 Mark 12:15
709 Luke 20:23
710 Matthew 22:18-19 (Compare Mark 12:15; Luke 20:24)
711 Mark 12:15 (Compare Luke 20:24)
712 Matthew 22:19-21 (Compare Mark 12:16-17; Luke 20:24-25)
713 Luke 20:26 (Compare Matthew 22:22; Mark 12:17)
714 Matthew 22:22
715 Matthew 22:23-29 (Compare Mark 12:18-24; Luke 20:27-33)
716 Luke 20:34-36 (Compare Matthew 22:30; Mark 12:25)
717 Matthew 22:30 (Compare Mark 12:25)
718 Luke 20:36
719 Matthew 22:31 (Compare Mark 12:26)
720 Mark 12:26-27 (Compare Matthew 22:31-32; Luke 20:37-38)
721 Luke 20:38
722 Mark 12:27
723 Matthew 22:33
724 Luke 20:39-40
725 Matthew 22:34-36 (Compare Mark 12:28)
726 Mark 12:29-31 (Compare Matthew 22:37-39)
727 Mark 12:32-34
728 Mark 12:35
729 Matthew 22:41-43 (Compare Mark 12:35; Luke 20:41)

[730] Luke 20:42
[731] Matthew 22:43 (Compare Mark 12:36)
[732] Matthew 22:45 (Compare Mark 12:37; Luke 20:44)
[733] Mark 12:37
[734] Matthew 22:46
[735] Matthew 23:1-7 (Compare Mark 12:38-39; Luke 20:45-46)
[736] Mark 12:40 (Compare Luke 20:47)
[737] Matthew 23:7-12
[738] Matthew 23:13-39
[739] Mark 12:41-44 (Compare Luke 21:1-4)
[740] Matthew 24:1 (Compare Mark 13:1; Luke 21:5)
[741] Luke 21:5
[742] Mark 13:1-2 (Compare Matthew 24:2)
[743] Luke 21:6
[744] Matthew 24:2
[745] Luke 21:6
[746] Mark 13:2-4 (Compare Matthew 24:2-3; Luke 21:6-7)
[747] Matthew 24:3
[748] Mark 13:4-6 (Compare Matthew 24:4-5; Luke 21:7-8)
[749] Matthew 24:5
[750] Luke 21:8
[751] Matthew 24:5 (Compare Mark 13:6)
[752] Mark 13:7 (Compare Matthew 24:6; Luke 21:9)
[753] Luke 21:9-11 (Compare Matthew 24:6-7; Mark 13:7-8)
[754] Mark 13:8 (Compare Matthew 24:8)
[755] Luke 21:11
[756] Mark 13:9
[757] Luke 21:12
[758] Matthew 24:9 (Compare Mark 13:9; Luke 21:12)
[759] Matthew 24:9
[760] Mark 13:9 (Compare Luke 21:12)
[761] Luke 21:13
[762] Mark 13:10
[763] Mark 13:11 (Compare Luke 21:14)
[764] Luke 21:14-15
[765] Mark 13:11
[766] Luke 21:16
[767] Mark 13:12 (Compare Luke 21:16)
[768] Mark 13:17 (Compare Matthew 24:9; Luke 21:17)
[769] Matthew 24:9-13
[770] Luke 21:18-19
[771] Matthew 24:14
[772] Matthew 24:15
[773] Luke 21:20
[774] Mark 13:14 (Compare Matthew 24:15)
[775] Matthew 24:15
[776] Mark 13:14
[777] Mark 13:14 (Compare Matthew 24:15-16; Luke 21:21)
[778] Luke 21:21
[779] Mark 13:15-16 (Compare Matthew 24:17-18)
[780] Luke 21:22
[781] Luke 21:23 (Compare Matthew 24:19; Mark 13:17)
[782] Matthew 24:20-21 (Compare Mark 13:18-19)

783 Matthew 24:21 (Compare Mark 13:19; Luke 21:23)
784 Luke 21:23
785 Mark 13:19 (Compare Matthew 24:21)
786 Luke 21:24
787 Mark 13:20-23 (Compare Matthew 24:22-25)
788 Matthew 24:26-28
789 Mark 13:24 (Compare Matthew 24:29)
790 Luke 21:25
791 Mark 13:24-25 (Compare Matthew 24:29)
792 Luke 21:25-26
793 Luke 21:26 (Compare Matthew 24:29; Mark 13:25)
794 Matthew 24:30
795 Mark 13:26 (Compare Matthew 24:30; Luke 21:27)
796 Mark 13:27 (Compare Matthew 24:31)
797 Luke 21:28
798 Matthew 24:32-35 (Compare Mark 13:28-31; Luke 21:29-33)
799 Matthew 24:36 (Compare Mark 13:32)
800 Mark 13:33-37
801 Matthew 24:37-51
802 Luke 21:34-36
803 Matthew 25:1-13
804 Matthew 25:14-30
805 Matthew 25:31-46
806 Matthew 26:1-2
807 Mark 14:1 (Compare Luke 22:1)
808 Matthew 26:3-4 (Compare Mark 14:1; Luke 22:2)
809 Luke 22:2
810 Matthew 26:3-5 (Compare Mark 14:1-2)
811 Luke 22:3-4 (Compare Matthew 26:14; Mark 14:10)
812 Matthew 26:15
813 Mark 14:11 (Compare Luke 22:5)
814 Matthew 26:15
815 Luke 22:6
816 Matthew 26:16
817 Luke 22:6 (Compare Matthew 26:16; Mark 14:11)
818 Luke 21:37-38
819 John 13:1
820 Luke 22:7 (Compare Matthew 26:17; Mark 14:12)
821 Mark 14:12 (Compare Matthew 26:17)
822 Luke 22:7-10 (Compare Matthew 26:17-18; Mark 14:12-14)
823 Matthew 26:18
824 Luke 22:11 (Compare Mark 14:14)
825 Matthew 26:18
826 Luke 22:11-12 (Compare Matthew 26:18; Mark 14:14-15)
827 Mark 14:16 (Compare Matthew 26:19; Luke 22:13)
828 John 12:20-50
829 Mark 14:17 (Compare Matthew 26:20)
830 John 13:2
831 Luke 22:14 (Compare Matthew 26:20)
832 Luke 22:15-18
833 John 13:3-20
834 John 13:21
835 Mark 14:18 (Compare Matthew 26:21)

[836] John 13:21 (Compare Matthew 26:21; Mark 14:18)
[837] Mark 14:18
[838] Luke 22:21
[839] John 13:22
[840] Matthew 26:22 (Compare Mark 14:19)
[841] Mark 14:20 (Compare Matthew 26:23)
[842] Mark 14:21 (Compare Matthew 26:24; Luke 22:22)
[843] Mark 14:22 (Compare Matthew 26:24)
[844] Luke 22:23
[845] Matthew 26:25
[846] John 13:23-32
[847] Matthew 26:26 (Compare Mark 14:22; Luke 22:19)
[848] Luke 22:19-20 (Compare Matthew 26:27; Mark 14:23)
[849] Matthew 26:27-28 (Compare Mark 14:23-24; Luke 22:20)
[850] Mark 14:23-25 (Compare Matthew 26:29)
[851] Matthew 26:29 (Compare Mark 14:25)
[852] Luke 22:24-30
[853] John 13:33-38
[854] Luke 22:31-34
[855] John 13:38
[856] Matthew 26:31-33 (Compare Mark 14:27-29)
[857] Luke 22:34 (Compare Matthew 26:34; Mark 14:30)
[858] Mark 14:30-31 (Compare Matthew 26:34-35; Luke 22:34)
[859] Luke 22:35-38
[860] John 14:1-31
[861] Matthew 26:30 (Compare Mark 14:26)
[862] John 15:1-27
[863] John 16:1-31
[864] John 17:1-26
[865] John 18:1
[866] Luke 22:39 (Compare Matthew 26:30; Mark 14:26)
[867] John 18:1
[868] Matthew 26:36 (Compare Mark 14:32)
[869] Luke 22:40
[870] John 18:1
[871] Mark 14:32
[872] Matthew 26:36 (Compare Mark 14:32)
[873] Luke 22:40
[874] Mark 14:33
[875] Matthew 26:37 (Compare Mark 14:33)
[876] Mark 14:33 (Compare Matthew 26:37)
[877] Matthew 26:37-38 (Compare Mark 14:33-34)
[878] Mark 14:35 (Compare Matthew 26:39)
[879] Luke 22:41
[880] Mark 14:35
[881] Matthew 26:39
[882] Mark 14:35-36 (Compare Matthew 26:39; Luke 22:41-42)
[883] Matthew 26:39
[884] Mark 14:36 (Compare Matthew 26:39; Luke 22:42)
[885] Luke 22:42
[886] Mark 14:36 (Compare Matthew 26:39; Luke 22:42)
[887] Luke 22:43
[888] Mark 14:37-38 (Compare Matthew 26:40-41)

889 Matthew 26:42 (Compare Mark 14:39)
890 Mark 14:39
891 Matthew 26:42-43 (Compare Mark 14:39)
892 Mark 14:40 (Compare Matthew 26:43)
893 Matthew 26:44
894 Luke 22:44
895 Luke 22:45 (Compare Matthew 26:45; Mark 14:41)
896 Mark 14:41
897 Luke 22:45-46 (Compare Matthew 26:45; Mark 14:41)
898 Luke 22:46
899 Mark 14:41-42 (Compare Matthew 26:45-46)
900 Mark 14:43 (Compare Matthew 26:47; Luke 22:47)
901 John 18:2
902 John 18:3 (Compare Matthew 26:47; Mark 14:43)
903 Mark 14:43 (Compare Matthew 26:47)
904 Matthew 26:47
905 John 18:3
906 Matthew 26:47 (Compare Mark 14:43)
907 Mark 14:44 (Compare Matthew 26:48)
908 Matthew 26:49 (Compare Mark 14:45; Luke 22:47)
909 Luke 22:48
910 Matthew 26:50
911 John 18:4-9
912 Luke 22:49
913 Matthew 26:50 (Compare Mark 14:46)
914 John 18:10 (Compare Matthew 26:51; Mark 14:47; Luke 22:50)
915 Luke 22:51
916 Matthew 26:52 (Compare John 18:11)
917 Matthew 26:52-54
918 John 18:11
919 Matthew 26:55 (Compare Mark 14:48)
920 Luke 22:52
921 Matthew 26:55-56 (Compare Mark 14:48-50)
922922 Luke 22:53
923 Matthew 26:55-56 (Compare Mark 14:48-50)
924 Mark 14:51-52
925 John 18:12 (Compare Luke 22:54)
926 Luke 22:54
927 John 18:12
928 Luke 22:54 (Compare Matthew 26:57; Mark 14:53)
929 John 18:13-14
930 John 18:15 (Compare Matthew 26:58; Mark 14:54; Luke 22:54)
931 Matthew 26:58 (Compare Mark 14:54; Luke 22:54)
932 John 18:15-16 (Compare Matthew 26:58; Mark 14:54)
933 Matthew 26:58
934 Mark 14:66
935 John 18:17
936 Mark 14:66
937 Luke 22:55 (Compare Matthew 26:58; Mark 14:54)
938 Matthew 26:58
939 Mark 14:54
940 Luke 22:56
941 Mark 14:67 (Compare Matthew 26:69)

References

[942] Matthew 26:69
[943] Luke 22:56
[944] John 18:17
[945] Luke 22:57
[946] Matthew 26:70 (Compare Mark 14:68; Luke 22:57)
[947] Mark 14:68 (Compare Matthew 26:70)
[948] John 18:18
[949] John 18:19-24
[950] Matthew 26:57 (Compare Mark 14:53)
[951] Luke 22:66 (Compare Matthew 26:57; Mark 14:53)
[952] Mark 14:54-61 (Compare Matthew 26:59-63)
[953] Matthew 26:63
[954] Mark 14:62 (Compare Matthew 26:64)
[955] Luke 22:67-68
[956] Luke 22:69 (Compare Matthew 26:64; Mark 14:62)
[957] Mark 14:62 (Compare Matthew 26:64)
[958] Matthew 26:65 (Compare Mark 14:63-64; Luke 22:71)
[959] Luke 22:71
[960] Matthew 26:65 (Compare Mark 14:64)
[961] Matthew 26:66-67 (Compare Mark 14:64-65)
[962] Mark 14:65 (Compare Matthew 26:67)
[963] Matthew 26:67-68 (Compare Mark 14:65)
[964] Mark 14:65
[965] Luke 22:63-65
[966] Luke 22:58
[967] Matthew 26:71
[968] Luke 22:58
[969] Mark 14:69
[970] John 18:25
[971] Matthew 26:72 (Compare Mark 14:70; Luke 22:58)
[972] Luke 22:58 (Compare John 18:25)
[973] Matthew 26:72
[974] Luke 22:59
[975] Matthew 26:73 (Compare Mark 14:70)
[976] Mark 14:70 (Compare Matthew 26:73)
[977] Mark 14:70
[978] Matthew 26:73
[979] John 18:26
[980] Matthew 26:74
[981] Luke 22:60 (Compare John 18:27)
[982] Matthew 26:74 (Compare Mark 14:71)
[983] Luke 22:60
[984] Matthew 26:74 (Compare Mark 14:71)
[985] Luke 22:60 (Compare Matthew 26:74; Mark 14:72; John 18:27)
[986] Mark 14:72
[987] Luke 22:61 (Compare Matthew 26:75; Mark 14:72)
[988] Mark 14:72
[989] Luke 22:61-62 (Compare Matthew 26:75; Mark 14:72)
[990] Mark 14:72
[991] Luke 22:62 (Compare Matthew 26:75; Mark 14:72)
[992] Mark 15:1 (Compare Matthew 27:1; John 18:28)
[993] Matthew 27:1
[994] Matthew 27:2 (Compare Mark 15:1; Luke 23:1)

995 John 18:28
996 Matthew 27:2 (Compare Mark 15:1; Luke 23:1)
997 John 18:28
998 Matthew 27:3-10
999 John 18:29-30
1000 John 18:31-32
1001 Luke 23:1-2
1002 John 18:33
1003 John 18:33 (Compare Matthew 27:11; Mark 15:2; Luke 23:3)
1004 John 18:34-37
1005 John 18:37 (Compare Matthew 27:11; Mark 15:2; Luke 23:3)
1006 John 18:37-38
1007 Luke 23:4 (Compare John 18:38)
1008 Luke 23:5
1009 Luke 23:6-16
1010 Matthew 27:12-13 (Compare Mark 15:3-4)
1011 Mark 15:4
1012 Matthew 26:13-14 (Compare Mark 15:4-5)
1013 Matthew 27:15 (Compare Mark 15:6; Luke 23:17)
1014 Matthew 27:16
1015 Luke 23:19 (Compare Mark 15:7; John 18:40)
1016 Mark 15:8
1017 Matthew 27:17
1018 John 18:39
1019 Matthew 27:17
1020 John 18:39 (Compare Mark 15:9)
1021 Matthew 27:19
1022 Matthew 27:18-20 (Compare Mark 15:10-11)
1023 John 18:40
1024 Luke 23:17
1025 Luke 23:20
1026 Matthew 27:21
1027 Matthew 27:22 (Compare Mark 15:12)
1028 Matthew 27:22
1029 Mark 15:12
1030 Matthew 27:22 (Compare Mark 15:13; Luke 23:21)
1031 Luke 23:21 (Compare Matthew 27:22; Mark 15:13)
1032 Mark 15:14 (Compare Matthew 27:23; Luke 23:22)
1033 Luke 23:22
1034 Mark 15:14 (Compare Matthew 27:23; Luke 23:22)
1035 Luke 23:22-23
1036 Matthew 27:23 (Compare Mark 15:14)
1037 Luke 23:23
1038 Matthew 27:24-25
1039 Mark 15:15
1040 Luke 23:24
1041 Matthew 27:26 (Compare Mark 15:15; Luke 23:25)
1042 Luke 23:25
1043 John 19:1 (Compare Matthew 27:26; Mark 15:15)
1044 Mark 15:16 (Compare Matthew 27:27)
1045 Matthew 27:28 (Compare Mark 15:17; John 19:2)
1046 Matthew 27:28
1047 Mark 15:17 (Compare John 19:2)

References

1048 Matthew 27:28-29 (Compare Mark 15:17; John 19:2)
1049 Mark 15:18
1050 Matthew 27:29 (Compare Mark 15:18-19; John 19:3)
1051 John 19:3
1052 Matthew 27:30 (Compare Mark 15:18-19; John 19:3)
1053 John 19:1-15
1054 John 19:16 (Compare Matthew 27:26; Mark 15:15)
1055 Mark 15:20 (Compare Matthew 27:31; John 19:16)
1056 Luke 23:26
1057 Matthew 27:32
1058 Mark 15:21
1059 Luke 23:26
1060 Luke 23:26 (Compare Matthew 27:32; Mark 15:21)
1061 John 19:17
1062 Luke 23:27-32
1063 Mark 15:22
1064 Matthew 27:33 (Compare Mark 15:22; John 19:17)
1065 Matthew 27:34 (Compare Mark 15:23)
1066 Mark 15:23
1067 Matthew 27:34 (Compare Mark 15:23)
1068 Luke 23:33 (Matthew 27:38; John 19:18)
1069 Mark 15:27 (Compare Matthew 27:38; John 19:18)
1070 Mark 15:25
1071 Luke 23:34
1072 John 19:23 (Compare Matthew 27:35; Mark 15:24; Luke 23:34)
1073 John 19:23-24
1074 Matthew 27:34
1075 John 19:19
1076 Matthew 27:37
1077 Mark 15:26 (Compare Matthew 27:37; Luke 23:38; John 19:19)
1078 Matthew 27:37
1079 Matthew 27:37 (Compare Mark 15:26; John 19:19)
1080 John 19:19
1081 Matthew 27:37 (Compare Mark 15:26; John 19:19)
1082 John 19:20-22
1083 Mark 15:29 (Compare Matthew 27:39-40)
1084 Matthew 27:40 (Compare Mark 15:29-30)
1085 Matthew 27:41 (Compare Mark 15:31)
1086 Mark 15:31
1087 Luke 23:35 (Compare Matthew 27:41-42; Mark 15:31)
1088 Mark 15:32 (Compare Matthew 27:42)
1089 Matthew 27:43-44
1090 Luke 23:36-37 (Compare Mark 15:32)
1091 Luke 23:36-37
1092 Luke 23:39-43
1093 John 19:25-27
1094 Luke 23:34 (Compare Matthew 27:45; Mark 15:33)
1095 Luke 23:45
1096 Matthew 27:46 (Compare Mark 15:34)
1097 Mark 15:34 (Compare Matthew 27:46)
1098 Matthew 27:47 (Compare Mark 15:35)
1099 Mark 15:35
1100 Matthew 27:47 (Compare Mark 15:35)

1101 John 19:28-29
1102 Matthew 27:48
1103 Matthew 27:48 (Compare Mark 15:36)
1104 Matthew 27:48 (Compare Mark 15:36; John 19:29)
1105 John 19:29 (Compare Matthew 27:48; Mark 15:36)
1106 Matthew 27:49 (Compare Mark 15:36)
1107 John 19:30
1108 Luke 23:46 (Compare Matthew 27:50; Mark 15:37)
1109 Matthew 27:50
1110 Luke 23:46 (Compare Matthew 27:50; Mark 15:37)
1111 Luke 23:46
1112 John 19:30
1113 John 19:30 (Compare Matthew 27:50)
1114 Mark 15:37 (Compare Luke 23:46)
1115 Matthew 27:51 (Compare Mark 15:38)
1116 Matthew 27:51-54
1117 Matthew 27:54 (Compare Mark 15:39; Luke 23:47)
1118 Mark 15:39
1119 Luke 23:47
1120 Matthew 27:54 (Compare Mark 15:39)
1121 Luke 23:48-49
1122 Matthew 27:55 (Compare Mark 15:40-41; Luke 23:49)
1123 Mark 15:40 (Compare Matthew 27:56)
1124 Matthew 27:56
1125 Mark 15:40
1126 Matthew 27:56
1127 Mark 15:41
1128 John 19:31-37
1129 Luke 23:50 (Compare Matthew 23:57)
1130 Matthew 23:57
1131 Luke 23:50 (Compare Matthew 23:57; Mark 15:43; John 19:38)
1132 Mark 15:43
1133 Luke 23:50 (Compare Mark 15:43)
1134 Matthew 27:57 (Compare John 19:38)
1135 John 19:38
1136 Luke 23:51
1137 Luke 23:51 (Compare Mark 15:43)
1138 Mark 15:42
1139 Mark 15:43 (Compare Matthew 27:58; Luke 23:52; John 19:38)
1140 Mark 15:44-45
1141 Mark 15:45 (Compare Matthew 27:58; Luke 23:52; John 19:38)
1142 Mark 15:46
1143 John 19:39
1144 John 19:40 (Compare Matthew 27:59; Mark 15:46; Luke 23:53)
1145 John 19:40-41
1146 Matthew 27:60 (Compare Mark 15:46; Luke 23:53)
1147 Luke 23:53 (Compare John 19:41)
1148 John 19:42 (Compare Luke 23:54)
1149 Luke 23:54
1150 John 19:42
1151 Luke 23:55-56
1152 Matthew 27:60 (Compare Mark 15:46)
1153 Matthew 27:60

1154 Matthew 27:61 (Compare Mark 15:47)
1155 Mark 15:47
1156 Matthew 27:61
1157 Mark 15:47
1158 Luke 23:56
1159 Matthew 27:62-66
1160 Mark 16:1
1161 Matthew 28:1 (Compare Mark 16:2; Luke 24:1; John 20:1)
1162 Luke 24:1 (Compare Mark 16:2; John 20:1)
1163 John 20:1
1164 Luke 24:1 (Compare Matthew 28:1; Mark 16:2; John 20:1)
1165 Luke 24:1
1166 Mark 16:3-4
1167 Mark 16:4 (Compare Luke 24:2; John 20:1)
1168 Luke 24:2 (Compare John 20:1)
1169 John 20:2
1170 Luke 24:3-5
1171 Mark 16:5
1172 Matthew 28:5 (Compare Mark 16:6)
1173 Mark 16:6 (Compare Matthew 28:5-6)
1174 Matthew 28:7 (Compare Mark 16:7)
1175 Mark 16:7
1176 Matthew 28:7
1177 Mark 16:7 (Compare Matthew 28:7)
1178 Matthew 28:7 (Compare Mark 16:7)
1179 Luke 24:5-8
1180 Mark 16:8
1181 Matthew 28:8
1182 John 20:2-5
1183 John 20:6 (Compare Luke 24:12)
1184 Luke 24:12
1185 Luke 24:12 (Compare John 20:6)
1186 Luke 24:12
1187 John 20:7-10
1188 John 20:11-14
1189 Mark 16:9
1190 John 20:15-17
1191 Matthew 28:9-10
1192 Matthew 28:11-15
1193 Luke 24:9
1194 Mark 16:10 (Compare Luke 24:9)
1195 Luke 24:9
1196 Mark 16:10
1197 Luke 24:10
1198 John 20:18
1199 Mark 16:11
1200 Luke 24:11
1201 Luke 24:11 (Compare Mark 16:11)
1202 Luke 24:13
1203 Mark 16:12
1204 Luke 24:13 (Compare Mark 16:12)
1205 Luke 24:13-29 (Compare John 20:19)
1206 Luke 24:29-33

[1207] Luke 24:33
[1208] Luke 24:33 (Compare John 20:19)
[1209] John 20:19
[1210] Luke 24:14-34 (Compare 1 Corinthians 15:5)
[1211] Luke 24:35 (Compare Mark 16:13)
[1212] Mark 16:13
[1213] Luke 24:36 (Mark 16:14)
[1214] Mark 16:14
[1215] Luke 24:36 (Compare John 20:19)
[1216] Luke 24:37
[1217] John 20:20
[1218] Luke 24:38-43
[1219] Mark 16:14
[1220] Luke 24:46-49
[1221] John 20:20-23
[1222] John 20:24-29
[1223] John 20:30-31
[1224] John 21:1-14
[1225] John 21:15-24
[1226] Matthew 28:16-19
[1227] Mark 16:15
[1228] Matthew 28:19-20
[1229] Mark 16:16-18
[1230] Matthew 28:20
[1231] Luke 24:50-51
[1232] Luke 24:50-51 (Compare Mark 16:19)
[1233] Mark 16:19
[1234] Luke 24:52-53
[1235] Mark 16:20
[1236] John 21:25
[1237] Luke 24:53

www.ingramcontent.com/pod-product-compliance
Lightning Source LLC
Chambersburg PA
CBHW072155100526
44589CB00015B/2242